OPEN DOORS

THE STORY OF LUTHERANS RESETTLING REFUGEES

RICHARD W. SOLBERG

CONCORDIA

PUBLISHING HOUSE

Pictures numbered 1, 2, 3, 4, 7, and 8 were provided courtesy the Archives of the Evangelical Lutheran Church in America, 5400 Milton Parkway, Rosemont, IL; all others by Lutheran Immigration and Refugee Service, 390 Park Avenue S., New York, NY 10016

Library of Congress Cataloging-in-Publication Data

Solberg, Richard W., 1917–
    Open doors : the story of Lutherans resetting refugees / Richard W. Solberg.
        p.   cm.
    Includes index.
    ISBN 0-570-04597-5
    1. Lutheran Immigration and Refugee Service—History. 2. Lutheran Church—Charities—History. 3. Church work with refugees—United States—History. 4. Refugees—International cooperation.
    I. Title.
    BX8074.B4S63   1992
    261.8'32—dc20   92-32164

1 2 3 4 5 6 7 8 9 10   01 00 99 98 97 96 95 94 93 92

We're all mutally associated. And in that association there seems to be room for all of us so that those who seek new lives can find them in partnership with others of good will who remember the roots from which we all came.

> — Donald H. Larsen, Executive Director of Lutheran Immigration and Refugee Service, 1986–1990, in whose memory this book is dedicated.

Contents

Foreword

This book is a history that needs telling. It records Christ's people hearing voices in pain and 50 years of response as their brother's keeper. Those who initiated this ministry could never have envisioned the far reaches of their work. History will always applaud their selfless service.

Lutheran congregations, pastors, and church leaders across our land have joined hands with others in reaching out to people escaping from violence in the wake of circumstances such as war, the loss of homeland, the fear of death or starvation. They have banded together with hearing ears, open hearts, and helping hands.

Richard Solberg has told the story well, detailing a half century of flight and displacement. His story shows how godly people welcomed and served the refugees and immigrants. Despite small beginnings and sometimes limited resources, there was ever a vision. There were temptations to apathy, inexperience in politics at home as well as inexperience in international crises. Yet their hearts were stirred. Lutheran people, as the author vividly describes, are compassionate people, those who "suffer with" others. Their compassion asks them to go where it hurts. And go they have, opening the doors of their homes and hearts and churches, offering good news for body, mind, and spirit.

At the heart of it, they have done it with the mind of Christ, who in love has given us something to do—to feed the hungry, clothe the naked, take in the stranger, accept the refugee. Even as we preach repentance and forgiveness of sins in His name to all nations, it is the same Savior who sends us out to the world with His love. By the one we are vitalized and inspired for the other. So these 50 years are really "His–story."

It is a story and an anniversary that offers also the opportunity to address the critical challenges of today and tomorrow. In continuing measure the plight of refugees and displaced persons still confronts all freedom-loving people. Particularly, for Christ's people, the millions of people in flight for their lives demonstrate the intertwining of human and religious issues. The biblical message is "I beseech you as aliens and exiles . . ." (1 Peter 2:11). That message is written for all today. Searching questions arise as God's people work out their faith. We live in a tradition of people who struggle to discern the will of God. It is God who calls us to confront seriously the need and challenge of refugees and others in need. We of Lutheran tradition have been in the forefront with interfaith colleagues in placing before the church and public the plight of refugees and displaced persons. Lutheran parishes have responded in generous measure across the years. This is what Lutheran Immigration and Refugee Service is all about.

The 50 years of history are a springboard for the future. Therein lies another great value of this book. It leads us to profound reflection, with our ears cocked to what Christ might be concocting for us who are in service to Him.

The author and the publisher of this book rightly merit our thanks for this historical recall which inspires us to build on these small beginnings. They deserve our praise also for allowing us to remember the many staff leaders across the country who have served the church so nobly.

August Bernthal

Acknowledgments

In 1989 the 50th Anniversary Committee of the Lutheran Immigration and Refugee Service commissioned the research and writing of the history of refugee resettlement by Lutherans in the United States. Members of the committee were Thomas Hurlocker, chair, August Bernthal, George Matzat, Vilis Varsbergs, Donald Larsen, Robert Lee, Benjamin Bankson, and Lily Wu.

Major research assistance was provided the author by Elisabeth Wittman, archivist, and Thomas Rick, assistant archivist of the Evangelical Lutheran Church in America. The ELCA Archives in Chicago contain the complete records of the LIRS and its predecessor organizations, including agendas, minutes, documentary materials, and publications relating to Lutheran refugee resettlement since 1939, and the records of the Miami Lutheran Refugee Service from 1961 to 1965. They also house papers of Clarence Krumbholz, Ralph Long, and Paul Empie, pioneers in Lutheran refugee work, and the unique library of interviews in the Oral History Collection, Archives of Cooperative Lutheranism. The New York offices of LIRS provided records and reports of refugee programs conducted since 1988.

Activities of the Anniversary Committee during the year of commemoration contributed additional source material for writing the history. Franklin Jensen conducted a series of oral history interviews with selected board members of LIRS, present and former staff members, field representatives, and refugees resettled by LIRS. Transcripts of these interviews were made available to the author. Persons interviewed were Betty Amstutz, August Bernthal, Ellen Erickson, John Griswold, Paul Hanson, Merill Herder, Walter Jensen, Donald Larsen, Adeline Marty, Ruth Meier, Gno Pham, Henry Ramosiner, James Smith, Uyen Trinh, Tatiana Trelin, Ly Vang, and Ingrid Walter. Benjamin Bankson also contributed the transcript of an interview with Cordelia Cox.

In preparation for the updating of the 1949 promotional film, 'Answer for Anne,' Robert Lee interviewed persons who shared recollections of the early DP program. Those interviewed were E. Theodore Bachmann, Howard Hong, Ross Hidy, and Kenneth Senft. Transcripts of these interviews and of the commemorative address delivered by Bachmann at the LIRS anniversary banquet on November 11, 1989, were made available to the author. Bachmann's address, "The Way It Was in 1939," contained material that especially enriched the opening chapter of the book.

The Pearson Library at California Lutheran University, Kenneth Pflueger, librarian, kindly offered access to its files of periodicals of the National Lutheran Council and its member churches, and of The Lutheran Church—Missouri Synod.

Additional material based on personal experiences and observations was drawn fram correspondence and conversations with Donald Anderson, Vernon Bergstrom, Neil Brenden, Ross Hidy, Walter Jensen, and Carl Pihl.

June Nelson Solberg served as research assistant and transferred the author's longhand composition to the word processor, patiently entered repeated revisions, and made valuable stylistic suggestions. She also prepared the index.

Final editing of the manuscript was done by Mary Solberg.

To all these contributors and to others who provided encouragement and support in the completion of this book, especially William Gentz and Wilbert Rosin, Theological Editor for Concordia Publishing House, I extend sincere appreciation.

Richard W. Solberg

Abbreviations

ACCGR - American Committee for Christian German Refugees
ACNS - American Council for Nationalities Service
ALC - The American Lutheran Church
CAC - Central American Concerns
CNLC - Commission for a New Lutheran Church
CWS - Church World Service
DIRS - Department of Immigrant and Refugee Services
DMM - Division of Mission and Ministry
DPs - Displaced Persons
DSPs - Direct Service Providers
ELCA - Evangelical Lutheran Church in America
ESL - English as a Second Language
FASP - Favorable Alternate Site Placement
GAO - U.S. Government Accounting Office
HEW - U.S. Department of Health, Education, and Welfare
HHS - U.S. Department of Health and Human Services
ICEM - International Committee for European Migration
INS - U.S. Immigration and Naturalization Service
IRC - International Rescue Committee
IRO - International Refugee Organization
JVAR - Joint Voluntary Agency Representatives (p. 193)
LCA - Lutheran Church in America
LCMS - Lutheran Church—Missouri Synod, The
LCUSA - Lutheran Council in the United States of America
LECNA - Lutheran Educational Conference of North America
LICS - Lutheran International Children Service
LIRS - Lutheran Immigration and Refugee Service
LIS - Lutheran Immigration Service (1960–1967)
LRS - Lutheran Resettlement Service
LSS - Lutheran Social Service
LWF - Lutheran World Federation

LWF-WS - Lutheran World Federation, Department of World Service

LWR - Lutheran World Relief

MLRS - Miami Lutheran Refugee Service

NCC - National Council of Churches

NLC - National Lutheran Council

NCWC - National Catholic Welfare Conference

ODP - Orderly Departure Program

OGA - Office of Govermental Affairs, LCUSA

OHC,ACL - Oral History Collection, Archives for Cooperative Lutheranism, LECNA

QDE - Qualified Designated Entity

RC - Regional Consultant

RRA - Refugee Relief Act, 1953

SI - Service to Immigrants

ULCA - United Lutheran Church in America

UNHCR - United Nations High Commissioner for Refugees

UNRRA - United Nations Relief and Rehabilitation Administration

USCC - United States Catholic Conference

WCC - World Council of Churches

WRY - World Refugee Year

1
They Heard a Cry

On Saturday, May 13, 1939, the Hamburg-America steamship *St. Louis* prepared to weigh anchor from its home port of Hamburg, Germany, bound for Havana, Cuba. On board was a full contingent of 937 passengers, mostly German Jewish refugees. They were among the last to receive official permission to emigrate before the Nazis implemented decrees prohibiting all Jews from leaving the country.

All passengers had purchased temporary permits from Cuban consulates to disembark in Havana, pending their eventual admission to the United States under the regular quota for German immigrants. Many of the men had been released from concentration camps on the condition that they leave Germany immediately. They were traveling alone, hoping their families could follow later. Many of the women were also alone or with their children, their husbands either still in concentration camps or waiting for them in Havana.

All passengers had paid the full round-trip fare, an arrangement that assured the shipping company of a tidy profit. Each refugee was permitted to carry out ten *Reichsmarks,* the equivalent of about four dollars. All personal property and assets left in Germany were confiscated by the Nazi government.

When the *St. Louis* arrived in Havana harbor 14 days later, Captain Gustav Schroeder was ordered to drop anchor off shore. No passengers were permitted to leave the ship. Their landing permits had been superseded by a decree issued by Cuban President Frederico Bru, barring the entry of more German refugees. While the ship remained at anchor in the harbor, friends and relatives in Havana chartered small boats and sailed out to the stranded vessel to exchange greetings across the water with their loved ones on board.

After five days of fruitless negotiations, during which tensions among the passengers approached panic proportions, President Bru personally ordered Captain Schroeder to leave the harbor. Company headquarters cabled instructions that he was to sail immediately back to Hamburg. Unwilling to return the refugees to concentration camps or death in Germany, Captain Schroeder proceeded north toward the coast of Florida while urgent requests were directed to the U.S. government, asking that the refugees be granted emergency asylum. The State Department replied that the German quota was oversubscribed; there was nothing it could do.

The *St. Louis* shifted course and headed back across the Atlantic. Two desperate attempts by younger refugees to seize control of the ship were turned aside through the intervention of a passenger committee and by assurances from the captain that he would land the refugees at any port that would allow entry.

Word finally came that the Belgian government would permit 200 refugees to come ashore in Antwerp. Queen Wilhelmina of the Netherlands offered asylum to 194. Britain accepted 350 and France 250. The passenger committee responded that their "gratitude is as immense as the ocean on which we have been traveling since May 13."

Only 240 of the 907 who returned to Europe from this "voyage of the damned" lived to tell their story.[1] Those who left the ship in Britain were the most fortunate, although the men were interned by the British government when the war began. Those who went to the Netherlands were housed in a camp that the Nazis took over following their invasion of the country in May 1940. Most of them did not survive. Many of those admitted to Belgium and France, also occupied by the Nazis the same month, managed to find their way through the underground to havens of neutrality. Some eventually reached the United States.

The U.S. government's refusal to help the refugees on the *St. Louis* was in part a reflection of the drastic change in American immigration policy that had occurred after World War I. Throughout the 19th century and until 1920, immigration was virtually unrestricted. From 1820 to 1920, more than 33,000,000 immigrants entered the United States, a number equal to the entire population of Europe in 1800.

Following World War I, however, popular disillusionment with conflict-ridden Europe fueled efforts to pass a series of laws restricting immigration. The quota system, introduced in 1921 and made permanent in 1924, especially limited entries from southern and eastern Europe and banned all immigration from Asia. In a single year only two percent of the number of persons of any given nationality in the United States in 1890 could enter the country. In 1927, for example, the total European quota was set at 150,000 persons, 60 percent of whom could come from Great Britain, but only four percent from Italy.[2]

When the clouds of totalitarianism began to thicken over Europe in the 1930s, producing thousands of refugees, the "golden door" that so long had welcomed "your tired, your poor, your huddled masses yearning to breathe free," was all but shut.

Flight from Nazism

During these same years, Adolf Hitler and the National Socialist Party came to power in Germany, the heartland of Lutheranism. In 1933 the party began a studied effort to expel Jews from public affairs and the professions. Between 1933 and 1938 thousands of Jews and Christians of Jewish admixture—defined as "non-Aryans"—left Germany. Many highly competent professionals—doctors, lawyers, scientists, musicians, and clergy—fled to other countries in western Europe, North and South America, even Asia. Some made their way to Palestine, in spite of the political tensions between the Arabs and the British, under whose mandate Palestine had been governed since World War I.

Harsh Nazi policies intended to force Jews to emigrate made life increasingly hazardous for persons of Jewish background during the thirties. On the infamous *Kristallnacht* (night of broken glass), November 9, 1938, synagogues were burned and Jewish-owned shops smashed and their proprietors beaten. From then on the Nazi government began to arrest Jews and confine them in concentration camps or forced labor camps. Exit from the country became more difficult. The voyage of the *St. Louis* became a parable of their plight.

Within Germany itself, there were some non-Jewish men and women who, at the risk of their own lives, sought to protect Jews and when possible to assist them in escaping the country. Notable among them was a Berlin pastor, Heinrich Grüber. In 1939 he established the *Büro Grüber,* through which he counseled hundreds of Jews and facilitated their flight to safety. Finally, he, too, was arrested and sent to the concentration camp at Sachsenhausen. Shot and left for dead, he miraculously survived and after the war became a prominent leader of the Evangelical Church in Berlin.[3]

Also in 1939 the nascent World Council of Churches (WCC) set up an office in London to help Christian refugees fleeing the continent. Another German pastor, Adolf Freudenberg, whose wife was from a Jewish family, managed the office. When Hitler attacked Poland on September 1 and Britain declared war on Germany, the WCC refugee office moved to Geneva in neutral Switzerland.

U.S. Protestants Respond

The U.S. government demonstrated little interest in extending a welcome to Europe's refugees. Yet within the limitations imposed by the quota system, church agencies could still assist individual refugees. In the United States the chief contact for the WCC was Henry Smith Leiper, general secretary of the American Section of the Universal Christian Conference on Life and Work. Together with the Conference on Faith and Order, Life and Work was one of the two components of the emerging World Council. In 1937 Leiper took the lead in forming a Protestant agency called The American Committee for Christian German Refugees (ACCGR).[4] Representatives of the American Section of the Lutheran World Convention (LWC) established a formal working agreement with this group on July 15, 1938. Frederick Knubel, Chairman of the American Section, and Ralph Long, a member of its Executive Committee, signed the agreement. The Lutherans agreed to open an office for "the rehabilitation and placement of Lutheran refugees," especially clergymen and theological students. The ACCGR agreed to share responsibility for other Lutheran refugees.[5]

With the establishment of a Lutheran office for refugee concerns, inquiries began to arrive from individuals and agencies seeking advice and assistance. Early in April 1938, Long had received a letter from John S. Dallmann in Chicago, himself a Jewish convert to Christianity, reporting on the work of the Hebrew Christian Alliance in assisting Jewish Christian refugees and urging organized cooperation with the Lutheran World Convention. Another letter from Dallmann in August enclosed several letters from Lutheran pastors of Jewish ancestry in Germany, seeking assistance in emigrating to the United States. Long replied that although the Lutheran World Convention could offer assistance to individual refugees, it did not yet have the means to help groups of Jewish Christians coming from Germany.[6]

An urgent letter from Otto Piper, distinguished New Testament scholar at Princeton Theological Seminary, who had left Germany in 1933 because his wife was Jewish, reminded Long that "quite a number of German ministers were living in exile in Great Britain and Holland." He especially recommended one pastor, Paul Leo, who, he felt, should be invited to come to the United States to minister to the refugee community. Leo, whose Jewish roots reached back to the composer Felix Mendelssohn, had been granted release from a concentration camp in Germany on condition that he leave the country. A widower, Leo fled to the Netherlands to join his eight-year-old daughter Anna, who had previously been evacuated on a special "children's train." With the assistance of Long's office, Leo and his daughter Anna arrived in New York in October, 1939. His service to refugees never materialized, but he served rural churches in Texas, and in time became a distinguished professor of Old Testament at Wartburg Seminary in Dubuque, Iowa.[7]

Another inquiry came to Long from General Secretary Samuel McCrea Cavert of the Federal Council of Churches. Suggesting the need for a pastor to serve refugees in the New York area, Cavert proposed a one-year appointment for Dietrich Bonhoeffer, a leading figure in the Confessing Church in Germany. Bonhoeffer was expected to arrive in New York City in June 1939 as a guest of Union Theological Seminary.[8] Shortly after his arrival, however, he elected to return to Germany. He was arrested in April 1943, imprisoned in Berlin, and executed in the Flossenburg concentration camp in April 1945, just days before it was liberated by the Allies.

Krumbholz in Command

In his 1938 annual report to the National Lutheran Council (NLC), Executive Secretary Long argued that the refugee problem, because of its international dimension, was an appropriate concern of the Lutheran World Convention. Nevertheless, he felt the Lutheran churches in America should become more directly involved. "Non-Aryan Christians who come to America as refugees," he wrote, "are for the most part members of the Lutheran church. It is in reality a tragic thing, to which we dare not close our eyes or remain indifferent. It must be translated into constructive and cooperative assistance."

To encourage such direct action by the churches, the Executive Committee of the Lutheran World Convention asked Clarence E. Krumbholz, General Secretary of the Board of Social Missions of the United Lutheran Church in America (ULCA) to take charge of the service to refugees.[9] Shortly thereafter, on June 1, 1939, when Krumbholz was appointed Executive Secretary of the new Department of Welfare of the National Lutheran Council, he brought the "Lutheran Refugee Service" under the supervision of the Council. With the exception of Krumbholz' salary, however, funding for the program remained the responsibility of the Lutheran World Convention.[10]

In the fall of 1939, when the NLC launched an emergency appeal for $500,000, its budget included the ministry to refugees. The official announcement reminded the churches that "Lutheran refugees from many lands are coming to our shores, trusting that we will help them to have a whole chance at life." In the following year's appeal—the first in which the motto "Lutheran World Action" was used—the Council earmarked $10,000 for refugee services.

Clarence Krumbholz, the man who deserves to be known as the father of Lutheran refugee services, was a pioneer in the developing field of Lutheran social ministry. He had a striking ability to inspire confidence and good will among his colleagues. Energetic but gentle in spirit and deeply committed to the church, he was characterized by a contemporary as "the personification of *diakonia,* a true servant of the Lord. His sermons and addresses . . . were factual and often forceful, as he sought . . . to elevate the real but ever indefinable 'Christian plus' in the church's ministry to those in need."[11]

Before assuming positions with the ULCA and the NLC, Krumbholz specialized in what was called "inner mission" work. He was a "city missionary" in New York, under the Lutheran Inner Mission Society in 1915–16 and returned to be the society's superintendent from 1922 to 1931. He held the same position in Pittsburgh from 1931 to 1936. Ordained in 1912, he also served two pastorates in the metropolitan New York area.[12]

Reaching Out to the Churches

Operation of a service to refugees was by no means an incidental activity of the new NLC Department of Welfare and its executive secretary. By the second year it accounted for almost half the department's work. Krumbholz viewed it as a challenge, not only to the social service agencies and institutions of the Lutheran church bodies, but also to the church as a whole—to congregations, pastors, and people. Using the columns of the church periodicals, he appealed directly to the people for the affidavits of support required by the U.S. government. In an article published in the May 17, 1939, issue of the ULCA's magazine *The Lutheran,* he asked,

> Could you find a shelter for a nine-year old boy until his father and mother can set up a home? Is there a Lutheran college that would like to engage a talented musical instructor? Can you place a Lutheran doctor as an intern until he passes his medical examinations? Day after day, week in and week out, such appeals among many others come to the Refugee Department of the Lutheran World Convention over the telephone or in letters. Affidavits are wanted for families threatened with concentration camp or prison: positions are needed for newly arrived non-Aryan men and women; pastoral care is necessary for distressed persons.[13]

Placing his finger on what would become the nerve center of later Lutheran refugee placement programs, Krumbholz wrote another article entitled "Facts About Refugees." "A congregation or parish," he said, "can be of great help in offering to resettle a refugee family in its community. It will be clear at once that these refugees cannot stay in the port of entry. Many of them do not want to. If a congregation through its Christian Service or Inner Mission Committee will set to work and find a home, suitable employment, and in some cases provide for emergency needs for one family of Lutheran refugees, the problem would not be difficult."[14]

Two staff members assisted Krumbholz: his secretary, Ann Zophs, and a retired Slovak Mission pastor, Louis Sanjek. Zophs joined the NLC staff in 1937 and continued in cooperative Lutheran work for more than 40 years, retiring in 1979. Sanjek was a native of Yugoslavia who had served as a pastor to immigrants in eastern Pennsylvania and New York since 1914. Krumbholz especially valued his fluent command of several European languages and his kindly spirit in dealing with the newly arrived Lutheran refugees.

During the early months of 1939, Sanjek averaged 25 interviews a week with Lutheran refugees, advising, counseling, and referring them to parishes in New York City and elsewhere for spiritual care. A voluminous correspondence with pastors and Lutheran welfare organizations opened placement opportunities in all parts of the country. The Lutheran Student Association of America cooperated, working to place several refugee students in Lutheran colleges. Continuing relations were maintained with the ACCGR and Church World Service (CWS), an agency of the Federal Council of Churches. The annual report of the NLC Department of Welfare for 1939 listed the names of 522 refugees, of whom 264 had been placed in self-supporting positions.[15]

With Hitler's invasion of Poland on September 1, 1939, and the start of World War II, borders were closed. Escape became even more difficult for Jews in Germany and Austria. Anguished letters pleading for refuge in the United States continued to arrive from parts of Europe not yet under Nazi control. A 26-year-old Hungarian physician, whose appointment at the University Clinic in Budapest was withdrawn because he was a Jew; a Berlin lawyer, sought by the Gestapo first in Belgium, then in France, because he had called attention to Nazi brutalities against women in the so-called race pollution trials; a young German artist and his Jewish wife who fled to the south of France after the fall of Paris; a prominent woman member of the Social Democratic Party, who had prevented Nazi confiscation of documents in party headquarters two days before the German occupation of Paris.[16]

In 1940 the number of refugees registered with the Lutheran service rose to 1128. Sanjek held over a thousand interviews during the year; telephone calls and letters averaged 15 per day. To facilitate referrals, a brochure entitled "Refugees Are People Like Us," listing names and addresses of Lutheran representatives in 24 cities across the country, was widely circulated. Another brochure spelled out in detail, "A Congregational Program for the Resettlement of a Refugee Family," suggesting step-by-step procedures and offering practical advice for welcoming the newcomers.[17] Lutheran congregations, institutions, and individuals in almost every state responded with offers of shelter and jobs. When necessary, they also provided emergency relief, and in some cases, transportation costs and grants-in-aid for students and teachers.

Homes for "People Like Us"

A children's institution in the Midwest invited a Lutheran refugee doctor to inaugurate an intensive health care program for the children. In a small town in New York State, the Lutheran church and its pastor made possible the resettlement of another refugee physician and his wife. Two Lutheran colleges provided scholarships for refugee students. Another college welcomed a refugee professor to its faculty, with a salary supplemented by the Lutheran Refugee Service. A highly trained German social worker received a year of orientation in an American school of social work before beginning her professional practice.

The Refugee Service was not always successful in placing newcomers in their specialties. Tradesmen, skilled artisans, and mechanics found ready employment. Many women accepted positions in domestic service. But a Viennese chef, a physiotherapist, a church organist, and a sculptor were among those obliged to accept more menial temporary jobs.[18]

The Lutheran Refugee Service circulated information bulletins to pastors and congregations, supplementing the articles that appeared in church periodicals. A mimeographed discussion guide entitled "The Lutheran Church and the Refugee" sought to answer frequently asked questions. Many congregations were surprised by the large number of Lutheran Christians among the Jewish refugees. The guide explained that "the largest number of recent forced immigration from the European countries are people who have some Jewish blood in their veins. Many are 'non-Aryan Christians.' That is, one or more relatives have Jewish blood—one grandparent or parent, or in the present family the husband or wife may have Jewish blood. But the family has been Christian for one, two, or three generations. They have been members of the Lutheran Church long before the world ever heard of Hitler."

Not all refugees from Germany were non-Aryan, the guide continued. Others had to leave "because they were out of sympathy with the philosophy of the Nazi government. In other words, they came to America as thousands of liberty-loving immigrants have come, because of the religious and national oppression which they cannot tolerate."[19]

As the Lutheran Refugee Service sought to find homes across the country for new arrivals, a report in the June 1941 issue of the *National Lutheran,* the NLC's official publication, emphasized that the task was far from complete. Lutheran refugees who had managed to escape from Germany continued to arrive in the United States via such temporary safe havens as Portugal and Cuba. Those who had not yet found permanent placements were reaching the end of their resources. Most of these persons tended to remain in the New York area and thus placed an added responsibility on Lutheran congregations there.

To meet their needs, the Lutheran Refugee Service joined with the New York Synod of the ULCA and the Manhattan Parish Committee to establish a special program aimed at contacting refugees in the city and introducing them to the nearest Lutheran church. This task was undertaken by Karl Burger, a refugee who had been in the United States for three years and was a former foreign correspondent. Between October 1941, and March 1942, Burger visited more than five hundred refugees and gave their names and addresses to pastors for follow-up visits. He also encouraged congregations to establish special programs for refugees. Holy Trinity in Manhattan responded with English classes that met twice each week, for both beginners and advanced students. [20]

Just before the Japanese attack on Pearl Harbor on December 7, 1941, the Lutheran Refugee Service prepared a congregational program to resettle 260 families still in Europe who were begging to be brought to America.[21] But the declaration of war with Japan and Germany brought programs of refugee resettlement in the United States virtually to a halt.

2

Europe's Displaced Persons

When the Germans surrendered unconditionally on May 7, 1945, and the war in Europe ended, the continent, from Britain and France in the west to Moscow and the Caucasus in the east, lay in shambles. London, Berlin, Rotterdam, Warsaw, and Frankfurt had been reduced to rubble. Forests were destroyed and fields burned or abandoned to weeds and underbrush.

Even more tragic than the vast physical destruction was the war's frightful human toll. Forty million persons had lost their lives during the war itself; millions of survivors faced starvation in their ruined homes and cities. Other millions filled roads and countrysides, seeking safety and survival. More than 13 million refugees streamed westward, converging on a ruined Germany, in what one observer described as, "a Tolstoyan pageant of human pathos, encompassing all the states of man from premature birth to overdue death." The countless participants in this grim parade, he wrote, "move on foot, by cart, by train, by boat; the only quiet ones are those lying for the last time where they dropped or were dropped."[1]

For most of these survivors, their most cherished hope was to find their way home and begin the reconstruction of their lives and those of whatever members of their families they could assemble. Perhaps half the survivors were able to make their way home without organized assistance.

Beginning in October 1945, steps were taken by the occupation armies and by the United Nations Relief and Rehabilitation Agency (UNRRA) to return other millions to their homelands and thus to relieve the congestion and human suffering in the hundreds of camps that sprang up all over Germany, Austria, and Italy. To distinguish them from the larger number of German refugees, who were under the jurisdiction of the Allied military forces, this group was technically known, not as refugees, but as Displaced Persons (DPs). Within three years 2,100,000 Russians, 1,500,000 French, 874,500 Poles, 704,000 Italians, and 1,400,000 nationals of Yugoslavia, Belgium, the Netherlands, and Luxembourg had been repatriated.

But in late 1945, reports began to circulate that under the provisions of the UNRRA agreement on repatriation, to which all Allies, including the USSR, were parties, some DPs were being forced against their will to return to the Soviet Union or to the Baltic states of Estonia, Latvia, and Lithuania, which the Soviets had annexed in 1940. When U.S. authorities were apprised of this, the United States protested by actively preventing Soviet officials from entering DP camps in the U.S. zone of occupation, and eventually by withdrawing its support from UNRRA. As a result of this controversy, the refugee issue fast became an aspect of the newly begun Cold War. Its political dimensions also set the course for future U.S. resettlement and immigration policies and programs. By 1947 only those persons remained in DP camps in Germany and Austria who, for political reasons, did not wish to return to their home countries.[2]

Discovering the DPs

In February 1947, the more than 700,000 DPs were placed under the special protection of the newly established International Refugee Organization (IRO), the successor to UNRRA, and after 1951, under the United Nations High Commissioner for Refugees (UNHCR). Among the DPs were approximately 185,000 Lutherans, mostly from Latvia, Estonia, and Lithuania. The first organized postwar effort at resettlement by Lutherans in the United States involved this group.

Among the DPs were also about 200,000 Jews, many of them survivors of German and Polish concentration camps, others who had managed to survive by hiding their identity. An outbreak of anti-Semitism in Poland in the spring and summer of 1946 resulted in more Jewish casualties and further stimulated the flow of Jews into Germany, where they gravitated to DP camps predominantly occupied by Jews.

The first impulse in the United States for the relief of DPs came as early as the spring of 1945 from Jewish leaders such as Rabbi Stephen Wise, founder and president of the American Jewish Congress, and U.S. Representative Emanuel Celler of New York. Based on reports of intolerable conditions among Jewish survivors in DP camps, they urged a new program for admitting refugees to the United States. This was not a popular subject at the war's end. Americans were eager to bring "our boys" home, but not Europe's problem cases. Two bills calling for the termination of immigration altogether were introduced in the 79th Congress (1945–47). A survey by the American Institute of Public Opinion on January 14, 1946, showed a majority favored either a reduction or a complete shutoff of Jewish immigration. Only five percent favored an increase.

Nevertheless, Wise and Celler persuaded President Harry Truman to send Earl Harrison, Dean of the Law School at the University of Pennsylvania and a former commissioner of the U.S. Immigration and Naturalization Service, on a mission "to inquire into the condition and needs of displaced persons in Germany who may be stateless or nonrepatriable, especially Jews." In the DP camps he visited in July 1945, Harrison found Jews dressed in the "hideous striped pajamas" they had worn in the Nazi concentration camps, existing on rations of bread and coffee, and guarded by American soldiers. He sent back a graphic report, asserting that "we appear to be treating the Jews as the Nazis treated them, except we do not exterminate them." The Harrison Report demanded significant improvements in camp conditions and immediate help for Jews to leave Germany and Austria and to emigrate to the United States and British-held Palestine.

On December 22, 1945, President Truman ordered Secretary of State James F. Byrnes to open consular offices near DP camps in the U.S. zone of occupation and to allow visa numbers to be allotted out of existing but unused annual quotas. This meant that up to 39,000 persons could be admitted from Central Europe, including 27,000 from Germany and Austria.

However, restrictionist attitudes in Congress continued to prevent the introduction of any special legislation expanding the number of DPs that could be admitted. Finally, in April 1947, lobbying by the Citizens Committee on Displaced Persons, chaired by Earl Harrison, resulted in the introduction of the first DP bill by Representative William G. Stratton of Illinois. It proposed the admission of 100,000 DPs a year as nonquota immigrants. It defined a DP as "any person in Germany, Austria, or Italy who is outside his country or former residence as a result of events subsequent to the outbreak of World War II, and is unable or unwilling to return to the country of his nationality or former residence because of fear of persecution on account of race, religion, or political opinions." Reports from DP camps in Europe had had a strong effect on U.S. public opinion, but it was still not possible immediately to pass the Stratton Bill. In June 1948, three years after the end of World War II, Congress was finally induced to approve legislation authorizing the resettlement of 205,000 DPs in the United States. Congress stipulated, however, that the number was to be charged against future immigration quotas.[3]

Bread First—Catechisms Later

German V-1 and V-2 bombs were still falling on London on February 28, 1945, when Executive Director Long of the NLC, President P.O. Bersell of the Augustana Lutheran Church, and Executive Director Lawrence B. Meyer of the Emergency Planning Council of The Lutheran Church—Missouri Synod undertook their first mission to Europe for the purpose of laying the foundations for a program of reconstruction among the Lutheran churches and reactivating the Lutheran World Convention. As a result of their visit to Geneva, Sylvester C. Michelfelder, pastor of St. Paul's Lutheran Church in Toledo, Ohio, was appointed special commissioner to Europe for the American Section of the Lutheran World Convention.[4]

Both Michelfelder and the staff of the World Council of Churches in Geneva, through whom help was to be channeled to all of Europe, knew that only governments could handle the staggering task of physically restoring a ruined continent. These church representatives were primarily concerned for the restoration of spiritual resources and the reestablishment of church ties torn asunder during six years of war.

Almost immediately, Michelfelder and other churchmen discovered that before anything else could be done, the physical needs of the people would have to be addressed. It would have to be "bread first—catechisms later!" On October 5, 1945, the international relief agencies in Geneva issued a worldwide appeal, written by Michelfelder, pleading for material relief before winter closed in. "Children by the millions," declared the appeal, "are in imminent danger of starving and freezing as winter comes to Europe, unless

26

immediate help comes from the countries which have food, clothing, vitamins, and medicines. . . . We who have seen these conditions and heard these cries for help must lay it on the consciences of all to share to the limit of their money and goods now."[5]

The first response came from the churches of Sweden. Before the end of October, 1945, the Swedes had dispatched three shiploads of food to the British occupation zone in Germany. Also in October, NLC Executive Secretary Long took the initiative to incorporate a separate agency called Lutheran World Relief (LWR) to handle emergency shipments of food and clothing gathered by Lutheran congregations in the United States. The "hard peace" policy of the U.S. government, however, prohibited shipment of food into the American occupation zone for almost a year after hostilities ceased. Only after vigorous protests by U.S. churches against the use of "starvation as an instrument of foreign policy," did President Truman lift the ban. On March 1, 1946, he issued an order opening the way for Lutheran World Relief and other private agencies registered with the Council of Relief Agencies Licensed for Operation in Germany (CRALOG) to begin relief activity in the U.S. occupation zone.[6]

Caring for Baltic Lutherans

Michelfelder's first contacts with Lutheran DPs in Germany came through a message sent by eight Latvian pastors to the World Council of Churches in March 1946. "We have been told," they wrote, "that we shall soon be sent back if our country asks our return. We have no desire to go until our country once more gains its free government and has freedom of religion." Shortly thereafter, Latvian Pastor Rudolf Krafts was able to visit Geneva to tell the full story of Baltic oppression. He urged immediate spiritual aid for other Latvians in the DP camps in Germany, where 134 Latvian Lutheran pastors were serving their people.[7]

On the strength of this plea, Michelfelder took the first steps toward opening a ministry on their behalf. After visiting the headquarters of the UNRRA, which supervised all the DP camps, and sending his new deputy, Clifford Ansgar Nelson, pastor of Gloria Dei Lutheran Church in St. Paul, Minnesota, to survey the needs of Lutherans in the camps, Michelfelder arranged for the newly named LWR representative in Munich, Carl F. Schaffnit, to assist the exiled pastors in the camps for six months, beginning late in 1946. Justine Bodensieck, whose spouse, Julius Bodensieck, was serving as commissioner to Germany for the American Section of the Lutheran World Convention, undertook similar service in Lübeck to a large group of Baltic Lutherans on behalf of the WCC.

By January 1947, the American Section of the Lutheran World Convention was ready to establish a permanent service to refugees in Germany and Austria. On Michelfelder's recommendation Howard Hong, professor of philosophy at St. Olaf College, Northfield, Minnesota, was named director, beginning in June. For six months in 1946, Hong had worked in Germany with prisoners of war under a program of the World Alliance of Young Men's Christian Associations. He accepted the appointment on condition that he could bring to Germany a small group of students from the United States to assist him. Kenneth C. Senft, a theological student from the Lutheran Theological Seminary at Gettysburg, Pennsylvania, and two St. Olaf College students, James and Elise Anderson, became the first among a large group of young volunteers who joined the Service to Refugees staff between 1947 and 1952.[8]

From June 30 to July 6, 1947, 184 delegates from 49 Lutheran churches gathered in Lund, Sweden, for the constituting convention of the Lutheran World Federation (LWF). The LWF succeeded the Lutheran World Convention, and a U.S. Committee replaced the Convention's American Section. Michelfelder was named LWF's first general secretary. Service to Refugees, recently established by the American Section, became the Refugee Department of the Lutheran World Federation.

"Like Israel confronting the ruined walls of Jerusalem," declared the Assembly delegates, "we must arise and build." Facing the fact that one of every ten Lutherans in the world was now a refugee and one of every three displaced persons in Europe was a Lutheran, they called upon their member churches to provide immediate spiritual and material help. The enabling resolution of the Assembly requested the LWF executive committee "to aid as far as possible ... in devising immigration and resettlement plans and in safeguarding the religious life of those displaced persons who belong to the household of our faith."[9]

LWF Organizes for Resettlement

When the program of spiritual conservation for the Lutheran DPs in Germany and Austria was well underway, Hong reminded the U.S. Committee that the Assembly's mandate also dealt with resettlement. Since 1946 a fleet of 36 transport ships operated by the IRO had been carrying thousands of displaced persons to Canada, Australia, and South America under government sponsored programs that promised jobs and housing in the new land. These programs often simply "dumped" the emigrants in the country of reception without provision for either spiritual or social orientation. Both Hong and the exiled church leaders felt something ought to be done to find homes for the Lutherans among these migrating members, to protect Lutheran interests, and even to channel the stream of emigration into areas where the refugees would not be lost to the church.

Early in 1948, on Michelfelder's urgent recommendation, Hong submitted a plan for a Resettlement and Emigration Division of the LWF. While the mass migration programs to Canada, Australia, and South America were in operation, the United States had no special program for the admission of displaced persons. But in May 1948, when it appeared likely that such legislation would pass Congress, the U.S. Committee of LWF asked Michelfelder and Hong to come to New York to discuss the details of Hong's plan.

According to his proposal a Resettlement and Emigration Division of LWF would operate under the direction of an executive officer, with a central office in Geneva and area offices in the countries of emigration. Offices in receiving countries would be locally managed and financed. Their task would be to develop resettlement opportunities for Lutheran immigrants and to assist them in establishing contact with local congregations. Of great significance in later resettlement operations was Hong's proposal that a revolving fund of $500,000 be established, from which overseas passage loans could be made to Lutheran migrants.

The U.S. Committee approved the proposal and appointed Stewart Herman in June as the first executive secretary of the new LWF Resettlement Division in Geneva. As pastor of the American Church in Berlin from 1936 to 1941, Herman had become well acquainted with the problems of refugees. From 1945 to 1947 he had served in Geneva as associate director of the WCC Department of Reconstruction.

Also in June 1948, the U.S. Congress passed the DP Act. In order to meet the requirements of this U.S. government program, Herman and Hong collaborated in opening 24 resettlement offices in DP camps in western Germany and Austria. In these offices DP pastors worked closely with American personnel, counseling and registering prospective candidates for resettlement in the United States.[10]

NLC Ministry to Refugees

Well before the LWF resettlement program was established, Lutheran DPs had begun to trickle into the United States under quotas released by order of President Truman on December 22, 1945. The first arrivals in early 1946 were war orphans, among them 24 Estonian children sponsored by Church World Service. Executive Secretary Krumbholz of the newly constituted NLC Division of Welfare chaired CWS's resettlement committee, as well as the American Committee for Christian Refugees. The latter had dropped "German" from its name, and in 1947 would be integrated into CWS.

Beginning in April 1946, the NLC Division of Welfare also agreed to assume direct responsibility for services to displaced persons. Krumbholz delineated six functions he expected his division to perform: assist in making resettlement plans for DPs referred by the American Christian Committeee for Refugees; work with the U.S. Committee of LWF in referring war orphans to Lutheran welfare agencies; review situations of DPs referred by relatives and pastors requesting sponsorships and determine whether such persons would qualify under President Truman's directive; assist relatives in drafting and submitting individual affidavits for sponsorships; provide information on immigration procedures; and investigate employment opportunities offered to DPs.

Krumbholz engaged Theodora Allen, who had just returned from service in Italy with the United Nations Relief and Rehabilitation Agency, to supervise the NLC program, starting in July. The Lutheran Welfare Council of New York loaned one of its social workers, Lillian Franzen, to help. She would move to Washington State in 1949 to head the Lutheran resettlement office there.[11]

The staff faced an early challenge when a group of 48 Estonians who had crossed the Atlantic in open fishing boats landed at Miami in August. These "boat people" found temporary haven in five Miami Lutheran congregations, but were promptly charged with "irregular entry" by the U.S. Immigration and Naturalization Service (INS) and interned at Ellis Island in New York harbor. The Lutheran refugee staff appealed to the INS to prevent their deportation, and the NLC executive committee passed a resolution appealing to the President of the United States "out of humanitarian considerations" to grant asylum.[12]

When neither appeal was successful, the Lutheran refugee office turned to Canadian immigration officials. Through the intervention of Lutheran World Relief of Canada, the Canadian government granted their request. Finally, in January 1948, the Estonians were escorted to their new homes in the Kitchener and Waterloo areas in Ontario. Within five days of their arrival, Canadian Lutherans provided housing and jobs.[13]

Over the course of a year and a half, the NLC in New York cared for more than 100 displaced persons. Some were members of family groups whose relatives were able to assist them upon arrival. Others were referred to pastors and church agencies who helped them find housing and jobs. Five young German Lutherans of Jewish ancestry between the ages of 18 and 25 arrived on August 31, 1946. Skilled in toolmaking, cabinet making, and lens grinding, they found employment easily.

The U.S. Committee for the Care of European Children referred a group of 21 teenage boys, most of whom were Estonians. Lutheran agencies across the country assisted in placing most of the boys in foster homes. The Lutheran Welfare Society of North Dakota placed two boys in prep school and college. The Lutheran Children's Friend Society of Nebraska accepted four boys. Lutheran Homefinding of Illinois placed two boys with an Estonian-American family. Six were placed by the Lutheran Welfare Council of New York and two by Lutheran Charities of Detroit. While Krumbholz and his staff worked out these plans, the Wartburg Orphan Farm School just north of New York City provided temporary accommodations, as well as English classes and personal counseling.[14]

Congress Passes the DP Act

While the staff of its Division of Welfare were actively serving Lutheran DPs admitted under the limited U.S. quota system, NLC

31

officials were working in concert with other religious and ethnic groups to secure special legislation for the admission of a larger number of DPs. In September, 1947, the NLC Executive Committee called for Congress to enact the Stratton Bill, introduced earlier in the year, "or some measure seeking similar objectives."[15] The Council's annual meeting the following January in Richmond, Virginia, issued another appeal, asking for "legislation which will speedily permit entrance into the United States for settlement and rehabilitation of substantial numbers of Refugees and Displaced Persons from the Continent of Europe." This resolution noted that the "prolonged presence of homeless aliens in the Displaced Persons Camps of Europe presents a tragedy in human lives and personality which weighs heavily on Christian hearts." To continue such camps, the resolution declared, is "a serious impediment to the interior peace and rehabilitation in that Continent toward which our nation labors."[16]

The persistent reluctance of Congress to authorize any new immigration was finally overcome in the Displaced Persons Act, introduced in April 1948, by Representative Frank Fellows of Maine and passed in June by both houses. The bill, a modification of the failed Stratton Bill of 1947, authorized the admission of 205,000 DPs, but contained serious limitations. Only those who could demonstrate that they had entered the western zones of Germany on or before December 22, 1945, were eligible. This restriction gave absolute preference to applicants from areas annexed by the Soviet Union during or immediately after World War II and excluded large numbers of Jews who had left Poland or the USSR after the cutoff date. The Citizens Committee on Displaced Persons and its supporters immediately charged a "pattern of discrimination and intolerance" and accused Congress of anti-Semitic bias. [17]

The new law determined the mode of operation for agencies resettling the DPs. In applying for a visa, each applicant had to have an "assurance," or promise, from an American sponsor that a job and housing would be provided. The voluntary agencies were to solicit the assurances, which in turn had to be approved by a DP Commission in Washington, D.C., before being sent to agency field staff in Europe. There the assurances were to be matched with DPs who fit the job descriptions and met other conditions. Finally, each member of the family had to meet the formidable health and political requirements of the U.S. Immigration and Naturalization Service before the visas were granted.

A guest at the 1948 annual meeting of the National Lutheran Council in Richmond, Virginia, by invitation of her pastor, was Cordelia Cox, professor at the Richmond School of Social Work. That meeting, she recalled many years later, gave her "a vision of the world interest, power, and commitment of the Lutheran Church, the LWF, the NLC, and the local church."[18]

When the doors opened for thousands of displaced persons later in the year, the NLC realized that to help these people find new homes and start their lives over again in the United States would require a greatly expanded operation. The Council drafted the social work professor from Richmond in October 1948, to organize and direct the Lutheran Resettlement Service (LRS).

3

Resettling the DPs

The NLC Accepts a Challenge

One July morning in 1948 the telephone rang in the office of Ross Hidy, a young pastor serving in the war housing ministry of the National Lutheran Council in Richmond, California. On the line was Paul Empie in New York City, recently elected Executive Secretary of the Council. "Ross," he said, "I want you to come to New York. I have a job for you. We're going to make a film about displaced persons. I want to send you over to Germany, and you've got to bring that film back on October 1."[1]

Empie's urgency characterized the style that had sparked the emergency appeals of the NLC since 1940. Lutheran congregations all across America had responded generously to the challenges of wartime ministries and postwar European relief. From 1940 to 1948 Lutheran World Action had raised more than $25 million for these special causes, including an unprecedented $10 million in 1946–47.

Empie's urgency also heralded a new dimension in the outreach ministry of the NLC. The Ten Million Dollar Appeal had been directed to the spiritual and physical reconstruction of the churches in Europe. But in 1947 the first World Assembly of the Lutheran World Federation had also called attention to the plight of millions of refugees, including tens of thousands of Lutherans. Among them were thousands of Displaced Persons who could not return to their homelands for fear of persecution. For them, resettlement was the only alternative. The National Lutheran Council prepared to commit both its energy and its resources to the challenge.

Two immediate steps were required. First, an expanded staff structure would have to be created. Second, the church constituencies, which would provide the sponsorships, would need to be informed and motivated. Empie wasted no time in setting the wheels in motion.

Between 1946 and 1948, the NLC's Division of Welfare had cared for more than 100 displaced persons, including 90 war orphans. During the early months of 1948, Mary Winston directed the Displaced Persons Project, which fielded questions from all over the church about the legislation pending in Congress and answered inquiries from people interested in adopting refugee children.[2]

During May and June 1948, the Lutheran World Federation was setting up its new Resettlement Division in Europe. Stewart Herman asked the NLC Division of Welfare to become its New York office and to assist in staffing the 24 new LWF offices in Germany and Austria for the registration and processing of visa applicants. The Division also made a special contribution to the European program by lending Henriette Lund to the LWF for a one-year term as Director of the LWF Resettlement Office in Salzburg, Austria.

In the cramped quarters of the National Lutheran Council on the fourth floor of the old Morgan Mansion at 231 Madison Avenue, purchased by the ULCA as its headquarters in 1944, the added responsibilities of the resettlement program required expansion of staff in several related areas of the Council's activity. John Scherzer returned from CRALOG in Germany to become Secretary of the European Desk and liaison with LWF in Geneva.

If thousands of refugees were to find places in Lutheran congregations in the United States, publicity would be crucial. Rollin Shaffer became Promotion Secretary, and Ross Hidy was drafted to assist in field work and in the production of a promotional film.[3]

The Lutheran Resettlement Service Takes Off

When Cordelia Cox joined the NLC Division of Welfare on July 1, 1948, as a professional field consultant, she was almost immediately drafted for resettlement work. Mary Winston continued to handle the adoptive children's program. Cox took on the rest of the service, doing, as she recalled, "everything from stapling on." In October, when the NLC officially designated the program within the Division of Welfare as the Lutheran Resettlement Service, Cox was named Acting Director.[4]

The first beneficiaries of the DP Act arrived four months after the act was signed into law on June 28, 1948. During the four-month hiatus, procedures and facilities for processing and receiving the DPs were set up. The Council's publicity office began to turn out news items and articles for church periodicals and prepared a special brochure describing procedures for sponsoring a DP family. Sequences for a promotional film, released early in 1949 as "Answer for Anne," were being shot during the summer of 1948 at the Valka DP camp, near Nürnberg in Germany. Speakers addressed church assemblies, stressing the theme, "Each congregation sponsor one Displaced Person family."[5]

There was no way that the multifaceted demands of the resettlement program could be handled by an Acting Director and one or two clerical assistants. Specialized staff was called in to handle the volumes of correspondence from churches, agencies, and individuals. The flow of multicopied documents to and from Geneva and Washington and the field offices of LRS grew. There was no longer room in the "attic" at 231 Madison. LRS moved into separate offices, which in turn also proved inadequate as the staff burgeoned to 125 persons during the peak of the DP program in mid-1949.[6]

In addition to the central staff in New York, the NLC moved to establish a network of state and area committees. Their task was to seek job and housing assurances for the 35,000 DPs judged to be the Lutheran "fair share" of the 205,000 authorized under the DP Act. Krumbholz devoted a large block of his time during these months to the organization of these committees; he was pleased to report "hearty and zealous cooperation" from Lutheran welfare agencies. Among the first agencies to accept responsibility for setting up state committees were those in Minneapolis, Toledo, Des Moines, Omaha, and Fargo. Others followed, until 33 such state or area committees were functioning throughout the country.[7]

The formal organization of the Lutheran Resettlement Service awaited the appointment of a Supervisory Committee that would represent churches who comprised the National Lutheran Council. Members of the first committee, when it assembled in New York on April 18, 1949, were Thaddeus F. Gullixson of the Evangelical Lutheran Church, F. Eppling Reinartz and Norman Finch of the United Lutheran Church in America, and Oscar Benson and S. F. Telleen of the Augustana Lutheran Church. Gullixson was elected chairman and Reinartz, secretary.

Chief among the concerns of the committee was the establishment of a vital relationship between the state and area committees and the churches and congregations that were being asked to provide sponsors for DP families. To encourage that relationship, an effort was made to select committee members representative of the church bodies of the NLC. Appointments were made by the presidents of the church bodies or of constituent synods or districts. Consultative membership was made available to Missouri Synod members in those areas where that synod was cooperating in the resettlement program.

Two patterns were approved for the operation of the program. A state committee could delegate administrative responsibility to an existing Lutheran welfare society, while maintaining responsibility for policy and program oversight. Or, in areas in which no Lutheran social service agency existed, a state committee could administer the work itself. Each state committee designated an unpaid director, often a pastor or a professional social worker. Where the size of the program required additional clerical staff, compensation was provided from New York. Whenever possible, the area resettlement offices were housed in facilities of Lutheran social service agencies. In nearly every instance the agencies provided office space without cost.[8]

Ships, Planes, and People

The first Lutheran DPs reached New York on October 30, 1948, aboard an IRO-chartered ship, the *General Black*. Forerunners of the 35,000 persons to be welcomed by the LRS reception service during the ensuing three years were met at Pier 86 on the Hudson River. "It is an unforgettable sight," Cordelia Cox recalled, "to see families coming down the gangplank, being checked off a master list by a sponsoring organization, and taken to the correct place to wait for their baggage. They come with wonder and hope and fear in their faces, holding tightly to children, walking cautiously and hesitantly, immediately responsive to the smile and welcome of a person wearing an organization arm band waiting at the end of the gangplank."

Then, continued Cox, "The Red Cross appears with coffee, cocoa and doughnuts—welcome offerings on a cold day at the pier. . . .

Then custom officials come, and after them the longshoremen to take the luggage off the pier. The families and their baggage move on to the organization desks where they receive their tickets, money, and typewritten directions for the next lap of their journey. The sponsors check the baggage, call taxis, and take travelers to stations or airports, where Travelers Aid helps them board their train or plane."[9]

Ships and planes arrived in all kinds of weather and at all times of the day or night. Commending her reception staff for their patience and faithfulness, Cox reminisced, "I never saw a place colder than a wharf in New York, or a place that is hotter. The planes seem most often to come in at night. Many times the person who was the head of our reception service would call me at 2 A.M. and say that she had put the last person on the train. When you receive one hundred or more people, and you have to get them out on trains and planes, it's no small job."[10]

Throughout the country, congregations, individuals, and Lutheran social service agencies were responding to appeals from the Lutheran Resettlement Service to provide assurances of jobs and housing. Most of these people would go directly to their sponsors. Yet on every ship there were families for whom special questions arose. A sponsor in Wyoming, for example, could not be reached by phone to tell him his family was on the way. Relatives in New York pleaded that a family destined for Oklahoma be allowed to look for work in New York, or at least to visit a while. Sponsors sometimes canceled assurances because they could not wait. In one case, a sponsor died; in another, the sponsor sold the bakery in which he had promised to employ a DP. On board ship was a DP farm family whose breadwinner died just before sailing.

By February, 1949, 166 DPs under Lutheran sponsorship had arrived in New York. Every person and family brought its own story of hardship, homelessness, and life in DP camps. Sixty-three orphans were among the earliest arrivals. Fourteen-year-old Alexander came from Stalino in Ukraine. In 1937 his mother had been deported to Siberia. His father had died in a forced labor camp in Germany. "All I want in this world," he said, "is to have a family and go to school."[11]

Eighteen-year-old Vizma Grundmanis explained that on July 14, 1941, the Soviets had deported 15,000 Latvians to Siberia. "Old people, babies, it makes no difference. They go. It's a sad day." As the Soviets advanced into Latvia in 1944, her family accompanied the retreating Germans to Saxony. At the end of the war they found their way into the DP camp at Augsburg. Through the LWF and the NLC they came to the United States. W. Gilbert Wise, Lutheran Resettlement director for Nebraska, found a home for them.

Arnolds Grikis, his wife, and their eleven-year-old daughter arrived in Lincoln, Nebraska, on January 19, 1949, to work on the George Schweers farm near Ponca, Nebraska. Grikis' first comments reflected the determination of most DPs, who for the first time in many years had the opportunity to live and work in freedom. "We are finished with running from people. Freedom is good. We hope to work, to earn food and clothing."

In the early weeks of the program, the Lutheran Service Society of Ohio sponsored 41 DPs in the area of Canton alone. Among them was Heino Trees, an M.D. from Heidelberg University. He came on an assurance of employment in a sanatorium in Canton, Ohio, and was later placed as an intern in a hospital in Cincinnati. With Trees came Mildred Ackermanis, a nurse. Two other nurses followed and were also employed by the sanatorium.[12]

The regional office in Des Moines, Iowa, reported in April 1949 that 67 DPs had already arrived in the state and 115 offers of jobs and housing had been received. Dictating up to 30 letters a day in answer to queries from Iowans, Dagmar Hamilton, director of the regional office, was certain that at least 732 assurances, Iowa's "fair share," would be forthcoming. As she observed the response of church members to the appeal for sponsorships, she commented, "I get more and more respect for the Iowa farmer as time goes on. And the Lutheran pastors are close to their parishioners. We build on that."[13]

By June 1, 1949, state and area committees had gathered 7,600 assurances and forwarded them through LRS to the Lutheran World Federation in Europe. In the same period, 2,100 Lutheran DPs had entered the United States and been placed with sponsors.

No Simple Task

A complex operation of this sort could hardly be carried off without problems and frustrations, for both the new arrivals and their hosts. "What must not be forgotten," Cordelia Cox reminded all who dealt with DPs, "is that resettlement means bringing to this country people of different nationalities and different cultures, who have faced the threat and actuality of personal and national extinction. They bring with them things that . . . will require in us a breadth of understanding that is really very great."

Besides, she continued, "We were a second choice. These are people in exile from their native land. They have taken us as second best because they cannot go home. If they were to forget home, if they were to forget the people whom they have left behind, they would be less worthy of our help than they are now."[14]

The most immediate problem for most DPs was the language. A family with five boys but without one word of English among them boarded the train to seek their fortune with a farmer in Nebraska. A Latvian family was sent to the West Coast, where a congregation had found an assurance, with job and housing in a hunting lodge. The only requirement of the Latvians' being in the lodge was that they were to care for the dogs used in hunting. They arrived in the summer; the owners of the lodge arrived in the fall, when the hunting season opened. The Latvian family fed the hunters a hearty breakfast before the hunt began. Then they discovered that the dogs wouldn't obey them. The dogs had learned to speak Latvian![15]

A more serious problem was the presence of disabled persons among the DPs. There were young men who had lost an arm or a leg in military combat. For such persons the government allowed LRS to take out bonds, guaranteeing that these people would not become public charges. Special arrangements were made for their placement. Cox remembers the Latvian who came without arms or legs and was placed in a rehabilitation hospital in New Jersey. Later he got a permanent job teaching other people how to use artificial arms and legs.[16]

Legal problems sometimes arose involving the status of one or another DP. LRS was fortunate to have the services of Michael Markel, a Washington lawyer, who had come to America many years before as a young emigrant from Romania. His interest in these new immigrants was such that he served, largely without compensation, in solving very intricate legal problems. He successfully represented LRS in a landmark case in California, where the courts ruled that a voluntary agency could not be held responsible for the care of an agency-sponsored refugee who had become mentally ill after entering the United States.[17]

One legal problem that could not be solved even by the best lawyers was the bewildering maze of procedures required by the U.S. government in approving a visa application. No fewer than 30 steps were involved from the time an assurance was given until a DP finally arrived in America. Secretaries in the LRS office complained that in those prephotocopier days, nine carbon copies were required for each document. Delays at any one of those procedural stages might postpone a family's departure for the United States and jeopardize the carefully laid plans of a sponsor or even cause him or her to cancel the sponsorship.

There were occasional failures on the part of both sponsors and those being sponsored. Some sponsors took advantage of the DPs, paying substandard wages, providing substandard housing, or reneging on promises. Sponsors complained that many DPs failed to honor the agreement to remain with the sponsor for at least a year. Quite frequently the reason for this was the painful separation from friends and family involved in an isolated rural assignment. In most of these cases the DPs who left rural areas sought out cities where more of their compatriots were.

Among the most difficult persons to place were those with specialized professions or skills. Many well-meaning sponsors thought primarily of farming or domestic service as appropriate employment opportunities for the DPs, not realizing that the training levels in the Baltic countries were very high, and that illiteracy was virtually nonexistent. A list of occupations represented among DPs, prepared by the Lutheran World Federation Emigration Service in Europe, enumerated several hundred crafts, professions, and specialized skills, ranging from actors and engineers to lawyers, doctors, bookbinders, tailors, architects, forest rangers, journalists, teachers, textile workers, and carpenters. Since the DP legislation indicated the need for agricultural workers in the United States and a disproportionate number of sponsorships offered farm-related jobs, many highly qualified professionals declared themselves to be gardeners, farmers, or unskilled workers, in order to increase their chances of being sponsored.[18]

Of the first 773 professional persons brought to the United States by LRS, only 229 eventually filled openings in their own fields.[19] Medical doctors were required to spend an internship year in a hospital before qualifying to practice their profession. Several assurances came from sparsely settled states such as North and South Dakota, where many communities were without medical services. Many colleges and universities were able to engage highly qualified professors, usually after these men and women had served an "internship" in some kind of interim employment. The faculty at Luther Theological Seminary in St. Paul, Minnesota, was enriched for many years by the services of two distinguished Latvian theologians, Janis Rozentals, a New Testament scholar, and Edmund Smits, who taught music and psychology, as well as theology. Arthur Vööbus taught students at the Lutheran School of Theology at Chicago for more than 30 years.

Students among the DPs generally found a cordial welcome. Whether they came as individuals or as members of a DP family, colleges and universities offered scholarships and employment for hundreds of them. When the DP Act was passed in 1948, the National Lutheran Council asked its Division of Student Services to serve as an adjunct resettlement committee for students. The Division contacted colleges and universities, encouraging them to grant scholarships and suggesting that campus student groups raise funds to sponsor individual students. Virtually all Lutheran colleges and many state institutions responded, not only with financial support but also with counseling as DP students adjusted to American college life.[20]

Many young men like Laimonis Akmentis, a Latvian DP, volunteered for service in the U.S. Army during the Korean War. He was wounded in action, losing his right eye. When he recovered and returned to the home of his sponsor, C.H. Schaeffer, in Waverly, New York, Schaeffer wrote to LRS, "I am proud to say I endorsed such a fine young man and fine citizen of the United States."[21]

The Church Follows Its People

Lutheran churches in the United States regarded the DP pastors, more than 100 of whom came to the United States, as a special responsibility. These pastors from the heavily Lutheran countries of Latvia and Estonia had provided spiritual care for their compatriots in the DP camps in Europe. Strong Latvian and Estonian Lutheran congregations were established in German cities like Augsburg and Lübeck. The Archbishop of the Latvian Church-in-Exile, Teodor Grünbergs, maintained an office in the city of Esslingen and exercised oversight of 110 Latvian pastors in Germany. Estonian Archbishop Köpp found refuge in Sweden, together with thousands of other Baltic exiles. DP pastors were supported in their ministry by the Lutheran World Federation Service to Refugees, and when the opportunity came, they also worked with LWF in registering their people for emigration to the United States and elsewhere.

When the DP migration to the U.S. began, the National Lutheran Council engaged two DP pastors in the United States for full-time service to the new arrivals. But the Council made clear its intention that all DPs should be integrated into the life of established congregations. In areas of larger concentration, supplemental linguistic services would be provided, but only temporarily.

The religious responses of the DPs themselves varied. Many became members of the congregations that sponsored them. Fenner Memorial Church in Louisville, Kentucky, for example, received 125 DPs as new members. Augustana Lutheran in Des Moines welcomed 123 adult members. Other DPs, according to one pastor, were so preoccupied with their efforts to gain economic independence that they had little time for the church. In the communities where larger numbers of DPs settled, Latvian and Estonian pastors gathered their compatriots into congregations in which they could worship regularly in their own language. This caused some tension within the NLC, which continued to affirm its policy of integration.[22]

At a special conference on the social adjustment of DPs in 1951, leaders of the Baltic groups met with representatives of the National Lutheran Council. The president of the American Latvian Association stated that the Council's emphasis on "assimilation" was creating a great deal of resentment among his people. He quoted Latvian Archbishop Grünbergs, who complained, "Our enemies want to destroy us; our friends want to assimilate us."[23]

While large numbers of Baltic Lutherans were assimilated into congregations of existing Lutheran bodies, both Latvian and Estonian Lutheran Churches in Exile were also organized. In 1990 the Latvian Evangelical Lutheran Church in America numbered 61 congregations. The Estonian Evangelical Lutheran Church in Exile had 24 congregations in its U.S.A. District.

The Dossier Program

In the spring of 1950, as the closing date for the entry of DPs approached, both LRS and the LWF Refugee Service became concerned for the many DPs who would not be cleared for emigration before the expiration date. Part of the problem was the preponderance of agricultural and domestic service jobs offered by sponsors in the United States, while so many of the DPs were clerks, tradespeople, or professionals, so-called white collar workers. Sixty-five percent of the first 5,000 assurances were for farmers and domestics. The difficulty of matching suitable Lutheran DPs in Germany with existing U.S. assurances increased sharply as the "more easily resettleable" DPs emigrated. Those whose age or physical handicap or family situation made them less likely to meet the stated requirements of a sponsor were in danger of becoming "hard-core" cases.

To improve the emigration prospects for the remaining DPs, the Lutheran World Federation Service to Refugees reversed its resettlement procedures in Germany. It was believed that if the Lutherans in America had a clearer picture of the type of DPs left in the camps, they would respond with appropriate assurances. With the help of the IRO and a special grant from Lutheran World Action, the LWF brought ten volunteer workers from the United States to Germany in the summer of 1950. On the basis of direct interviews with persons in DP camps, these workers prepared "dossiers" or personalized descriptions of each individual or family wishing to emigrate to the United States. At the end of the summer they sent 1759 dossiers to New York. LRS circulated them to area resettlement committees throughout the country and eventually to Lutheran congregations. A sponsor could then offer an assurance to a particular person or family, chosen on the basis of the information contained in the dossier.[24]

Members of the interview teams returned to the United States as enthusiastic publicists for the resettlement program. "It was the experience of my lifetime," said Edgar M. Waxler, pastor of Grace Church in Saginaw, Michigan, who returned eager to "get out to the state committees and make the dossiers live .... There is not one among the families I interviewed," he added, "that I could not 'sell' to my or any other congregation." Henry Daum, economics professor at St. Olaf College, was impressed with the patience, poise, and confidence displayed by DPs who might easily have become embittered by their past experiences.[25]

In addition to providing hope for the DPs still in camps, the dossier system focused attention upon the needs of a particular person or family, rather than simply finding someone qualified to fill a job. Congregations responded readily to this appeal. One pastor who interpreted the DP program to many congregations described the effect upon those who undertook such a mission of mercy. "This kind of opportunity," he wrote, "really turned the church around, from being ingrown to saying that the plight of a DP family is our opportunity to show that our faith is more than words. Congregations had to come to grips with the basic question, 'What does it mean to be the family of God in this place?' Luther put it all in one sentence, 'How do we know that the love of God dwells in us? If we take upon ourselves the need of our neighbor.' Luther wasn't in the stratosphere. He was right down where people are hurting. He said, 'If they're hurting and you're not helping, you hardly can be a Christian.' This really dug into the heart and soul of the character of the church in every community."[26]

Both before and after the dossier program went into effect, members of Lutheran congregations accepted the challenge of homeless people. A member of St. Paul's Lutheran Church in Alliance, Ohio, where the Lutheran Men's Club spearheaded the effort to resettle DP families, wrote in his assessment of the experience, "I do not believe that in the history of our church has there been such a challenge or such an opportunity." Another member of the congregation agreed. "Any of our churches which have not undertaken to bring and provide for one of these families," he said, "has deprived itself of one of the greatest and most stimulating experiences a church could have."[27]

Extending the DP Act

From the time of its passage in 1948, the DP Act came under constant fire as an inadequate solution to the problem. Chief complaints were that the two-year time limit was too short, that the number of DPs permitted to enter was too small, and that the law imposed other unnecessary restrictions. The Citizens Committee on Displaced Persons, which had led the campaign for the passage of

DP legislation, continued its efforts to liberalize the law.

As early as February 1949, the annual meeting of the National Lutheran Council had passed resolutions urging an extension of the DP Act and an increase in the number of DPs to be admitted from 205,000 to 400,000. It also called for the admission of "expellees," persons of German descent who had been driven out of their homes in communist-controlled countries in eastern Europe.[28]

The intensifying Cold War and the frenzied anti-communist crusade within the United States in 1949 and 1950 did much to arouse public and congressional support for the modification and extension of the DP Act. The Berlin blockade had begun in 1948, in the same month in which the original DP Act had been passed. The $17 billion Marshall Plan, approved earlier in 1948 to rebuild the economy of western Europe, was hailed as a counter-thrust against communism. In 1949 the NATO alliance was formed, and the Federal Republic of Germany was created. In 1950 the U.S. Congress passed the infamous McCarran Internal Security Act that violated the civil rights of U.S. citizens in its zealous efforts to root out communists. In such a highly charged climate, Congress was very sensitive to proposals for the relief of both remaining DPs and the newer crop of Jewish DPs and ethnic German "expellees" from eastern Europe, who were seen as victims of communist oppression.

On June 16, 1950, Congress passed "An Act to Amend the DP Act of 1948." It raised the number of admissible DPs from 205,000 to 341,000 and extended the period during which they could enter the U.S. by a full year, until June 30, 1951. A later amendment extended the deadline an additional six months, to December 31, 1951.[29]

The amended DP Act also granted admission to 54,733 ethnic German expellees, a tiny segment of the eight-and-a-half million who poured into Germany from east of the new German border between East and West at the Oder and Neisse Rivers. Among them were five-and-one-half million Germans expelled from their lands and homes in the German territories ceded to Poland. In addition, there were three million people of German origin, permanent residents of Romania, Hungary, Czechoslovakia, the Balkan countries, Poland, and the Soviet Union, driven out because of their German roots.

These refugees were not under the protection of the International Refugee Organization. As Germans, they were, for better or worse, regarded as a German responsibility. In most countries of the world, doors of immigration were closed to them.

According to U.S. law, the ethnic Germans admitted to the United States were required to have assurances of housing and employment, just as the DPs. However, their processing in Germany was handled quite differently. Whereas the registration of DPs was conducted in offices in the DP camps by DP pastors and LWF personnel, the German candidates for emigration registered in 18 information and counseling offices (*Beratungstellen*) of the *Evangelisches Hilfswerk,* the post-war German Protestant relief agency. The Lutheran World Federation established offices in close relationship with the *Hilfswerk,* so candidates recommended by *Hilfswerk* could be assisted in applying for U.S. visas.

Including German "Expellees"

A dossier program similar to that used in the DP program was developed to assist in placing ethnic German refugees whose entry was authorized by the amended DP Act. At the request of LWF, the *Hilfswerk* counseling offices prepared 2,000 dossiers, which were then screened by LWF and sent to New York for presentation to Lutheran congregations. Ocean travel for DPs had been assured by the International Refugee Organization since 1947; under the amended DP Act, the U.S. government accorded similar benefits to the German expellees. The government also made loans available to voluntary agencies for assisting refugees in reaching their final destinations within the United States.

LRS agreed to seek placement for 2,000 ethnic German families before the closing date of July 1, 1952. The Missouri Synod also put into operation a program to resettle 500 ethnic German families. More than 2,000 cases, representing 5,303 persons recommended by LWF in Germany, qualified for U.S. visas before the quota of 54,744 was filled in late April 1952.[30]

As December 31, 1951—the termination date of the DP program—approached, most of the DPs had been moved out of camps and resettled in countries all over the world. The United States had received the largest number, 336,000 in all.

There were, however, substantial numbers of aged and infirm

who were either unable or unwilling to move out of Germany. This "residual group," numbering about 130,000, included about 20,000 Lutherans. These people remained under the protection of the IRO and later, of the United Nations High Commissioner for Refugees. The German churches undertook the major responsibility for long-term care of the "homeless foreigners" (*heimatlose Ausländer*) through their institutional structures. The LWF continued to support the spiritual ministry among Lutheran DPs, subsidizing the salaries and travel of remaining DP pastors until the German churches assumed that responsibility, too.

As December 31 approached, an urgent effort was made to process as many DPs as possible. The resettlement staffs of LWF, IRO, and the U.S. DP Commission in Germany and Austria worked seven-day weeks. Gertrude Sovik, LWF resettlement officer, was one of those who worked at Funk Kaserne in Munich until the clock struck twelve on December 31. In retrospect, she wrote, "And so it is all over. . . . About 900 people thronged Block I, waiting as they had waited in the rain outside all day. For hours in the evening, as the clock crept closer to the new year, they stood and waited. And then the news came—no more visas." Another LWF staff member recalled that even after the announcement came many lingered in the winter rain for three more hours, unwilling to face the fact that their last hopes were gone. For them, "it was not warm in Europe."[31]

The Program in Review

In assessing this first major Lutheran resettlement program in the United States, statistics are helpful; certainly they convey something of the magnitude of the effort. At the close of the program in October 1952, Cordelia Cox reported that 16,286 families, or 30,263 DPs, and 5,303 ethnic Germans, had arrived in the United States under the sponsorship of the National Lutheran Council and its resettlement service. The largest number of families, 2,878, were placed in New York State, including 2,049 in the New York City area. California received the second largest group, numbering 2,019. Other leading states were Pennsylvania, 955; Illinois, 947; Minnesota, 827; Michigan, 747; Ohio, 730.

Among the DPs, the largest national group were Latvians, with Estonians second. At least 14 other national groups were represented, including Hungarians, Lithuanians, Poles, Russians, Czechs, Yugoslavs, Turks, Romanians, Armenians, Bulgarians, Greeks, and Ukrainians. The great majority of NLC-sponsored DPs were Lutheran, but several thousand Russian Orthodox, several hundred families of mixed marriages, and a considerable number of Jews and Catholics were also processed through the Lutheran World Federation and the National Lutheran Council. Several thousand additional Lutherans entered the United States under the sponsorship of Church World Service or the National Catholic Welfare Conference.

The total cost of the DP program can only be estimated. The United States government spent more than $100 million for the processing and ocean transport of 336,000 DPs; of that total, about $9 million was spent for 30,000 Lutherans. The National Lutheran Council spent a total of $3,427,865, contributed by Lutheran congregations through the appeals of Lutheran World Action. This amount does not include direct contributions of local congregations, communities, and individuals, or services provided through Lutheran social service agencies.

Up to September 1952, the National Lutheran Council had loaned a total of $1,340,037 to DPs and refugees, mostly for transportation to their destinations within the United States, and smaller amounts for medical care. By that same date, 85 percent of the loans had already been repaid.[32]

Of far greater significance than the statistics were the experiences of more than 4,000 Lutheran congregations throughout the United States. In opening their hearts and homes to persons from another continent—persons who spoke other languages yet professed the same faith and shared the same human emotions—they reaped unexpected benefits. Their horizons were broadened. Their understanding of the church was enlarged. The way was prepared for participation in global ministry in the decades to come.

Equally important were the individual stories of the 35,566 "delayed pilgrims" who came to the United States with Lutheran assistance between 1948 and 1952. Each one told of a release from bondage and the opening of doors to a new life and new opportunities in a new land. Bringing with them skills of both mind and hand, and strong incentives to work, these new immigrants took their place among the millions of their forerunners who came from other lands to people and build America.

4

"Who Else Shall We Welcome?"

Debating the "Open Door"

As the last of the DPs and ethnic Germans granted visas under the amended DP Act trickled into the country during the early months of 1952, the work of the Lutheran Resettlement Service appeared to be over. But the National Lutheran Council recognized a continuing responsibility for the welfare of the thousands of DPs and ethnic Germans it had brought to the country since 1948. At its annual meeting in January 1952, the Council instructed the Supervisory Committee of LRS to make plans for a program of service to resettled persons, and to study the need for a permanent immigration service. With its eye on the continuing tide of refugees flowing into West Berlin and West Germany, the Council also declared itself in favor of additional emergency immigration legislation, based on humanitarian concerns.[1]

Others, too, were concerned about the refugee problem in Europe. Several bills were introduced in Congress. The McCarran-Walter Bill, which became law on June 21 as the Immigration and Nationality Act of 1952, brought together in a single unified code all previous U.S. immigration law. It also eliminated some restrictions of long standing, such as the ban on Asiatic immigration. But in spite of strong objections raised by voluntary agencies and others, it retained the discriminatory quota system and added new grounds for the denial of entry visas and for the deportation of aliens. Critics of the bill pointed out that between 1948 and 1952, an average of 65,770 quota numbers went unused each year because they were available only to countries and persons who did not use them. The small quotas of several nations had even been "mortgaged" by the

DP Act. The number of nationals who entered the United States as DPs would be deducted from the respective national quotas "until the account is even." Fifty percent of Latvia's annual quota of 236 was "mortgaged" until the year 2274. The McCarran-Walter Act failed to correct such inequities. President Truman shared the dissatisfaction of the bill's critics and vetoed it, but Congress overrode his veto.[2]

Not long thereafter, Truman appointed a Presidential Commission on Immigration and Naturalization and charged it with developing arguments for a more generous immigration policy. The Commission was composed mostly of former supporters of the DP program. T.F. Gullixson, chairman of the LRS Supervisory Committee, represented the Lutherans. The Commission was urged to hold hearings to gather testimony from groups that had been systematically excluded from hearings on the McCarran-Walter Bill.

Paul Empie and Cordelia Cox were among the 26 witnesses who appeared during an all-day session of the first public hearings in New York City. The witnesses were unanimous in urging a change in the current immigration law and the admission of more refugees and immigrants.

In his testimony Empie declared, "The refusal to open our doors would be a staggering blow to the strength of the United States' leadership in the current ideological world struggle." Cox pointed out that the DP experience provided evidence that immigrants make good citizens and contribute to the cultural and economic wealth of the country. Moreover, she said, continuing requests from employers, relatives, and friends indicated there was both a need and a desire for more immigrants. In December 1952, just before President Truman's term of office ended, the Commission issued its report, recommending a more liberal policy. They entitled the report, "Who Else Shall We Welcome?"[3]

LRS Examines Its Mandate

Meanwhile, the Supervisory Committee of LRS pursued the request of the National Lutheran Council to examine future immigration needs and ways of meeting them. At a meeting in November 1952, the Committee noted that although movements under the DP Act had substantially ended, services to many of the DPs were continuing, especially to those with health or emotional problems and those for whom LRS had posted bonds. Increasing numbers of requests for information and assistance concerning regular immigration procedures were being received from pastors, employees, relatives, and resettled persons.

Although national staff had been reduced from 125 to 14 persons, Cox hoped LRS might retain its basic structure through 1953, with 36 area resettlement committees, in order to provide these ongoing services and to be prepared in the event of new emergency legislation. As an alternative, she recommended a permanent immigration service within the NLC Division of Welfare, an option already authorized by the NLC annual meeting in February 1952. Such an office would work toward sound legislation, offer necessary service and protection to Lutheran immigrants, and assist them in affiliating with local congregations.[4]

Early in 1953, Cordelia Cox submitted her resignation, effective April 1, and Paul Empie appointed June Anderson, head of the Services Department of LRS, as her successor. Working closely with Krumbholz, Anderson guided LRS through the transitional months to the end of 1953, preparing a closing resettlement report for LRS and initiating the new Service to Immigrants that was intended to replace LRS.[5]

Meanwhile, on the recommendation of newly inaugurated President Dwight Eisenhower, Congress had turned its attention to new legislation on behalf of refugees. The annual meeting of the National Lutheran Council passed resolutions in February 1953, urging elimination of the quota system and the admission of 300,000 refugees, "expellees," "escapees," and remaining DPs over a period of three years.[6]

Germany's Westward Movement

Since the division of Germany into two states in 1949, ethnic German expellees and fugitives from Soviet-controlled East Germany had been streaming across the borders into West Germany and West Berlin at an average rate of 15,000 a month. During these same years, economic conditions in East Germany had remained stagnant. Government policies connected with the "build-up of socialism" repressed free expression and travel. In 1952, the closing of the "green border," as the line between East and West Germany was called, caused the number of refugees to soar. This three-kilometer-wide "no man's land," bristling with barbed wire and machine guns, was established, according to the East German government, to prevent the access of subversive elements from the West. Few doubted that its actual purpose was to stop the wholesale exodus of the East German population.[7]

In the month of March 1953, 58,605 persons, an average of 2,000 per day, sought refuge in the West. Most of them were people under 25 years of age. In 12 months 335,441 people left their homes in East Germany and went west. By the end of 1955, every fifth person in West Germany was a refugee, and 300,000 people, the population of a good-sized city, had crowded into West Berlin.[8]

Relatively few of the refugees dared to attempt the dangerous crossing of the "green border." Some obtained permits for family visits and crossed legally to West Germany, but never returned. The vast majority made their escape through West Berlin. On the Wednesday after Christmas Day in 1955, the LWF representative in Berlin watched the somber procession filing into West Berlin's big reception center at Marienfelde. "They came," he recalled, "pushing baby carriages through the rain, lugging suitcases, handbags, and brief cases, and wearing all the clothing they could possibly put on. Even during these festival days, when the normal Christian . . . clings most closely to home and hearth, 1200 people registered at Marienfelde. Three days before Christmas the 150,000th refugee of 1955 arrived."[9]

No refugees were ever sent back to East Germany against their will, though those who wished to return were at liberty to do so. Temporary housing facilities had to be set up, food provided, and some opportunity offered to begin a new life. The West Berlin city government divided the refugees into three categories. Category A was reserved for refugees who could present documentary proof that their lives or personal freedom were in danger. Category B recognized those who could present proof of other urgent reasons for fleeing. Category C covered the "non-recognized," whose claim to refugee status had been rejected. Categories A and B were flown out of Berlin to West Germany, where efforts were made to place them in areas where they were most likely to find employment. Refugees of all categories were eligible for public assistance. The "unrecognized" refugees, caught between East and West, had no alternative except to remain in Berlin or to return to their homes in the East. There was, by any reasonable measure, a refugee problem of massive proportions in Germany.

A Reluctant Congress Opens the Door

Congress, however, was still not sympathetic to the refugee problem in Europe, and especially not the German refugee problem. After a bitter struggle in Congress and some pressure from President Eisenhower, a new law called the Refugee Relief Act (RRA) of 1953 finally gained approval on August 7. It authorized the granting of 209,000 nonquota visas, considerably fewer than the President had requested, over a period of two years and eight months, ending December 31, 1956.

The law prescribed several categories: nonquota visas for 55,000 German expellees from eastern European countries and for 35,000 "escapees" from East Germany. Additional quotas were designated for refugees who had found temporary asylum in Greece, Great Britain, the Netherlands, Italy, Hong Kong, and elsewhere. A large number of nonrefugee relatives of Americans were also authorized to enter the U.S. from certain designated countries.

New regulations for processing immigrants, however, seemed harsher than necessary. Contrary to what church agencies had suggested, Congress ruled that no "blanket assurances," that is, assurances given by organizations rather than individuals, would be accepted. Each applicant for a visa was required to produce evidence that an individual American citizen would provide a job and housing.[10]

Krumbholz was invited to witness the signing of the Refugee Relief Act by President Eisenhower in Washington on August 7. Immediately upon his return to New York, he and June Anderson issued a joint letter to the eight Lutheran church bodies cooperating in the National Lutheran Council and to local resettlement committees and Lutheran social service agencies, urging a renewed effort to gather job and housing assurances "as quickly as possible."

But by the time the Executive Committee of the NLC met in Chicago in October, members had had opportunity to review more closely some of the regulations attached to the law. Chagrined by what they discovered, they addressed a series of resolutions to the administrator of the Refugee Relief Act, deploring the "unduly heavy responsibilities" placed upon sponsors. Most "iron curtain" refugees faced "almost insuperable difficulties" in assembling a fully documented history covering at least the two years of their lives preceding their application for a visa. If such restrictive provisions were not modified, the NLC expressed serious doubts about its ability to participate in the program. Such regulations, the committee declared, would "likely result in the nullification of its humanitarian purpose to help freedom-loving, homeless people find a refuge and a new chance of life in the United States."[11]

Representatives of voluntary agencies took their objections directly to Washington. There they were assured by Scott McLeod, administrator of the Refugee Relief Act, that a sponsor's promise that a refugee would not become a public charge was a moral responsibility rather than a legal one. No sponsor, McLeod assured them, would ever be brought to court and forced to pay liabilities connected with such sponsorship. Both McLeod and his staff gave unqualified promises to expedite the administration of the act in a way that would assure its stated goal, the relief of refugees.[12]

The NLC Gets a Partner

On the strength of these promises, the National Lutheran Council decided at its annual meeting in Atlantic City in February 1954 to enter the program under the terms of the Refugee Relief Act. By conservative estimates 60,000 of the 209,000 eligible refugees were Lutherans. It would be unthinkable that American Lutherans could ignore the plight of so many brothers and sisters in the faith.

Once again the resettlement machinery was put in motion. Lutheran World Action called for additional contributions to finance the anticipated higher costs of the RRA program. Even before new assurance forms were available from the government, appeals went out to church bodies, congregations, and social service agencies. The dossier program, successfully employed by LWF in the DP program, was revived. In March 1954, the first eight volunteers recruited from the member churches of the NLC, arrived in Germany. The group included Frederick M. Otto, Russell W. Schilling, Henry Schumann, Herman Siefkes, Harry Wolf, Henry Daum, and Henriette

Lund.[13] Their task was to interview refugees nominated by the Lutheran World Federation and the German agency, *Evangelisches Hilfswerk,* for emigration to the United States. Their dossiers were sent back to New York and distributed to the same network of committees, agencies, and congregations that had served the DPs.[14]

The resettlement program of the National Lutheran Council took a new and unexpected turn in April 1954, when The Lutheran Church—Missouri Synod (LCMS) expressed an interest in establishing a joint operation with the NLC. While many Missouri pastors had been active in resettling displaced persons, the Synod itself had not become involved until the ethnic Germans became eligible for admission under the amended DP Act of 1950. Under that program the Synod had undertaken the placement of 500 families through its Department of Social Welfare.

The Refugee Relief Act of 1953, however, opened the possibility of entry to thousands of ethnic German expellees and other thousands of escapees from East Germany, in which more family connections with German-Americans were likely than had been the case with the DPs. The language question was also simpler, since there were more people in the U.S.—and not least in the congregations of the Missouri Synod—who spoke German. As Cordelia Cox observed, "The job of getting assurances for the ethnic Germans was somewhat of a family job, or at least, a cultural job. Getting assurances for the Estonians, Latvians, and Lithuanians was more of a mercy job."[15]

The approach by the Missouri Synod came at a most appropriate moment. Following preliminary conversations, mutual agreement was reached. The establishment of a joint operation to be called the Lutheran Refugee Service (LRS) introduced a long and rewarding relationship between the churches of the National Lutheran Council and The Lutheran Church—Missouri Synod.

A Joint Program—A New Name

The policy-making body of the LRS was to be a commission of five members, three appointed by the NLC Division of Welfare and two by the LCMS Department of Social Welfare. Initial representatives of the NLC were Francis A. Shearer, Magnus Dahlen, and Carl Reuss. Representing the Missouri Synod were Henry F. Wind and E. Buckley

Glabe. Shearer was elected chairman and Wind, secretary.[16]

Cordelia Cox agreed to return as director of the newly consti-tuted program. The national office retained the structural pattern of its predecessor, the Lutheran Resettlement Service. A Department of Assurances was headed by Elizabeth Nicholsky; Pier and Recep-tion, by Vera Cakars; Social Services, by June Anderson; and Accounts and Loans, by Mildred Meyer.

The program for 1954 followed the plan already adopted by the National Lutheran Council at its February meeting, including a re-settlement budget of $135,309, 40 percent of which the LCMS agreed to assume. A revolving loan fund similar to that operated by the Resettlement Service was to be supported on the same 60/40 formula.[17]

The Commission adopted a special set of guidelines for the field program of the Lutheran Refugee Service. Thirty-six area or state committees, called Lutheran Refugee Committees, were organized. Beginning June 1, 1954, committee members served two-year terms, on appointment by one of the nine participating church bodies. The state committees promoted the program among their congregations and other potentially interested groups. Each pastor in the area was contacted personally or by telephone or letter to explain the pro-gram and its procedures. Wherever possible, local congregational committees were formed to recruit assurances, using all possible channels for publicity, including local church publications, radio, and television. The primary tasks of the state committees were pro-motion and the direct solicitation of assurances for refugees. As immigrants began to arrive in the United States, the committees' responsibilities would shift from promotion and securing assur-ances to programs of reception and adjustment.[18]

A special document prepared by LRS contained explicit direc-tions to sponsors for filling out the official government assurance form. Six copies of this form were filled out by the sponsor, who was required to be an American citizen. Job and housing had to be assured, and the sponsor was required to guarantee that the refugee would not become a public charge. All assurances were endorsed by a Lutheran pastor and sent to LRS, where they were countersigned and sent on to the U.S. Refugee Office in Washington for approval.

In a report to the LRS Commission in August, Cordelia Cox reported that 32 area committees had been organized. Twenty staff persons paid by LRS were attached to Lutheran social service agencies in key areas of the country. Most Lutheran social service agencies contributed office facilities and secretarial support. At the same meeting Cox reported that LRS had already sent 1,298 assurances to Washington. Most of these had been provided by relatives or friends. Only 148 were responses to dossiers prepared by interviewers in Germany. By the end of 1954, however, a second team had been dispatched to Germany. Together, these teams had sent back approximately 4,000 dossiers, and the promotional program in the United States had produced 2220 assurances.[19]

The time allotted for the RRA program was nearly half over. If 15,000 Lutherans were to be resettled before December 1956, this seemed to be a slow beginning. Nevertheless, in view of the delays of the U.S. government in implementing the legislation of August 1953 and the time required to develop the structure for the joint operation of LRS, the program had made good progress in seven months.

Reorganization and Retrenchment

At the November 1954 meeting, the LCMS representatives announced that the Board of Directors of the Missouri Synod had decided to withdraw from the joint operation at the end of the year.

The LCMS had entered the joint program in April 1954 on a six-month experimental basis. Plans for 1955 called for a full-year budget of $416,475, of which LCMS was expected to supply 40 percent, or $166,590. When advised of this expectation, the LCMS Board of Directors informed the NLC that because of "a multitude of major financial commitments for educational, missionary, and welfare projects over and above the regular budget commitments in our Church during the next two years," the LCMS would not be able to continue in Lutheran Refugee Service. They were prepared, however, to appropriate $100,000 to cover all continuing commitments entailed by their participation in the program during the initial six-month trial period.[20]

Understanding this to mean that if the budget could be reduced, LCMS might still continue the joint operation, the NLC proposed a 35 percent reduction of the 1955 operating budget so that $100,000 would fulfill the LCMS share. Such a drastic cut would be accomplished by a complete reorganization of the field program of LRS. Twenty area staff, paid by LRS but responsible to state committees, would be replaced by five regional directors, responsible to the New York office. Participating church bodies would be asked to cover the expenses of their representatives on the area committees and provide any necessary staff support through the regular offices and agencies of the church bodies in each area. Church bodies would also be expected to assume full responsibility for recruiting assurances within their own membership and to accept a goal of 10,000 assurances, prorated 60/40 between NLC and LCMS bodies. Provision for the care of each resettled family after arrival would also become the responsibility of each participating church body.

The New York office would continue to receive, process, and forward new assurances, maintain government contacts, and provide for the reception of an anticipated 4,000 arrivals in 1955. They would also facilitate the movement of incoming refugees to their sponsors, advise area committees, collect loans, and interpret the program on a national level.[21]

In view of this proposal, the LCMS Board of Directors agreed to reconsider its earlier decision to withdraw. Rather than approve a single year's budget for 1955, however, the LCMS countered by proposing a total package of $1,000,000 covering the expenses of the entire RRA resettlement program from April 1, 1954 to December 31, 1957, and shared on a 60/40 ratio. With the concurrence of its constituent bodies, the NLC accepted this proposal, and immediately moved to implement the restructuring. The two parent bodies approved a formal memorandum of agreement on March 22, 1955.[22]

The restructuring of the LRS area program represented a radical experiment in joint Lutheran operations, dependent for its success upon a high degree of coordination among a very complex set of ecclesiastical structures and persons. Only to the extent that area committees, representative of cooperating church bodies, and pastors of local congregations were prepared to see the task of resettling refugees as an expression of a Gospel-mandated, collaborative outreach ministry could the program achieve its goal.

Church bodies were asked to reappoint members to 32 area committees, taking into account the expanded responsibilities. Eighteen new committees became operational in January and February, and 14 others followed. As in the 1954 program, the committees were given the option of conducting the full program themselves or enlisting the operation of a Lutheran welfare agency for administrative services, while continuing personal solicitation of assurances and promotion of the resettlement program themselves. The national office of LRS established March 15, 1955, as the date for the completion of the reorganization, and shortly thereafter scheduled a series of regional information meetings in three areas of the country.[23]

In the months that followed, one of the most useful means of informing area committee meetings concerning the progress of the program was a series of monthly letters entitled "Report to Area Committees" prepared by Cordelia Cox. These letters carried both official information and human interest stories intended to encourage congregational concern for the resettlement program.

Contending With the Government

The primary problem for the Lutheran Refugee Service in carrying out a program under the RRA was neither a financial nor an organizational one, but rather the failure of the U.S. government to fulfill its commitments to expedite the program.

Administrator Scott McLeod continued to impose stricter procedures than the Act itself required. He insisted that all job assurances be screened by the U.S. Employment Service in cooperation with local state labor offices. The formidable amount of red tape involved in this process made the system completely unworkable. Fortunately, it was dropped after one year; in the meantime, it discouraged sponsors from offering assurances and caused widespread frustration.

Late in 1954, after the Act had been in operation for a full year, the voluntary agencies discovered that McLeod's office had been setting aside assurances for refugees and giving priority to processing a backlog of regular immigration cases involving visas for family members of U.S. citizens. Whether the major reason for these delays was inefficiency or indifference to the plight of refugees, it was clear that the refugee program had been stalled. By February 1, 1955, the Lutheran Refugee Service had filed 2,409 assurances for 6,022 persons. Half of them had been submitted more than six months previously, but by February 1, only 282 visas had been issued to these applicants. Eighteen months after the RRA was passed, only 111 LRS-sponsored refugees had arrived in the United States.

Empie learned of these delaying tactics after having been assured by Scott McLeod that every effort was being made to expedite the program. Empie then delivered a strong statement to the annual meeting of the National Lutheran Council in February 1955, which was released to the press and given wide national publicity.

Not long thereafter, he and other representatives of voluntary agencies met with Secretary of State John Foster Dulles and other government officials in Washington. Scott McLeod was dispatched on a fact-finding tour to the refugee camps in Germany. Murat Williams, a high-level facilitator, was appointed to speed the processing of visa applications. The State Department also agreed to consult with an advisory committee representing the Council of Voluntary Agencies during the remainder of the RRA.[24]

With these reassurances, Empie reported back to the LRS Commission that he now looked for energetic efforts from Washington to reach the stated goal of the RRA, namely, the admission of 209,000 refugees by December 31, 1956. "It has been a long, drawn-out battle," he wrote in the *National Lutheran,* "confused by the noise and angry words and the smoke of political or administrative maneuvering. However, the air is clearing, and we must move ahead with confidence. . . . It is still possible for the Lutheran Refugee Service to bring in a minimum of 15,000 and perhaps 20,000 or more refugees before the end of 1956. The important thing is that to do this we must get the assurances as early as possible. . . . I implore every person reading these pages to take seriously the matter of giving an assurance, doing everything in his power to forward it to us before the end of 1955."[25]

Is the Emergency Over?

By the end of 1955 the RRA had finally moved into high gear, and the reorganized program of the LRS was working well. Refugees were being placed in greater numbers. Then in December 1955, the LCMS again called for a budget reduction. Instead of $1,000,000 through 1957, LCMS proposed $750,000.

Beside internal financial constraints, Lawrence Meyer, the LCMS representative, cited reports that the economic recovery of West

Germany under the stimulus of the Marshall Plan was providing employment for all who were able to work, abolishing actual physical need among the refugees. Emigration, he concluded, was no longer an emergency. He also suggested the possibility of saving funds by terminating the program before the expiration date of the RRA on December 31, 1956. Empie responded that, as far as he could see, the only way such a saving could be realized would be to reduce the number of refugees to be served below the 15,000 to which LRS had committed itself.[26]

A full-scale review of the LRS program and budget in March 1956, attended by special representatives of both LCMS and the NLC, failed to alter the LCMS decision to limit its total commitment to $300,000. At this stage of the program the NLC had little choice but to accept the reduced support from Missouri and still seek to resettle as many refugees as funds would permit.

Pastors, congregations, and agencies responded to the urgent appeals of LRS for more assurances. Visiting teams of interviewers, 26 persons in all between 1953 and 1956, continued to assemble dossiers in Germany for distribution to churches and area committees in the United States. These interviewers not only provided an important human bridge between the refugees and their sponsors in the United States. They became the promoters of the resettlement program when they returned home.

"Anyone who has listened daily for eight weeks to the plight of these people," observed Herman Siefkes, First Vice President of The American Lutheran Church, and a member of one of the teams, "knows that it is a Christian obligation to help them."[27]

Paul Empie himself, whom Cordelia Cox acknowledged as "the leading spirit in the refugee program", was one of the most passionate spokespersons for the resettlement program. According to Cox, "We did the program, but he sold it!" Few people could be indifferent to Empie's appeals. "Life would be simpler," he observed, "if the outstretched hands of our refugee brethren were not within our reach. But they are! We might at moments wish that God had arranged it otherwise, but He hasn't. As long as He has placed us in the position to be the rescuing sponsors instead of the refugees, how can we ask to be excused?"[28]

By the end of 1955 the newly reorganized LRS system had assembled 3946 assurances, very close to the year's goal of 4000, set in March. More than 3200 of them had been secured since the new program had begun in June. Visiting teams in Germany and Austria had brought back 4000 additional dossiers. During the year a total of 3828 LRS-sponsored refugees had arrived in the United States, far short of the eventual LRS goal of 15,000 by the end of 1956, but still an encouraging contrast to the 111 arrivals of 1954.[29]

Most of the refugees were either East Germans or ethnic German expellees from one of nine different countries of eastern Europe. Some were DPs who had not been able to emigrate under the DP Act of 1948. A few others were refugees from places as widely separated as Greece and Hong Kong.

Forty percent of the 1955 arrivals had come as passengers aboard the *General Langfitt,* a ship chartered by the International Committee for European Migration (ICEM), which crossed the ocean seven times during that one year. About a third had arrived on chartered planes. The rest came on 80 different crossings by commercial ships bearing the U.S. flag. Members of the LRS Pier Service Department met them all and sent them on their way to 45 states.

Reports from Europe early in 1956 seemed to contradict the theory that the refugee emergency had passed. Eugene Ries, LWF Supervisor of U.S. Immigration in Germany, reported that new registrations had doubled since December 1 and were averaging 250 to 300 families per month. In Austria Gertrude Sovik reported a similar increase.[30]

Even the burgeoning economy of West Germany was unable to keep up with the continuing procession of refugees crowding into West Berlin at the rate of 500 per day. Cordelia Cox described a family of recent refugees from the East Zone who registered for emigration to the United States. A carpenter and his family under both economic and political stress in the East had fled to West Germany, using as an excuse that they wanted to attend a relative's funeral. Not recognized as a political refugee by the Bonn government, the man had great difficulty finding employment and shelter. For the sake of survival, he took a temporary laboring job, while his wife found work as a waitress. They were forced to place their children in an institution until the family could be reunited. Not only did they face a serious economic problem, but in order to be considered for emigration to the United States, they would have to reconstruct their history for two years prior to immigration to prove they were not communists.

Still another family who had come to America five years earlier had left behind a mother and a teenage brother who had a spot on his lung. The mother later died and the brother was left alone in Germany. If he tried again, he might pass the U.S. health exams. Even at the risk of further disappointment, it was worth a try![31]

While preparing dossiers in Frankfurt, Germany, Henriette Lund concluded that "families are actually worse off now than earlier. It is no longer only a matter of physical need, which is tangible and can be met, but also an emotional and spiritual need, which is harder to get at. People seem so much more distressed of soul than I have known them to be earlier. Now it is a conviction that they must get into a new land and get a new start."[32]

In spite of hardships, disappointments, and delays on both sides of the Atlantic, refugees arrived in the United States in increasing numbers during 1956. Congregations and pastors who understood their mission to be resettling lives rather than filling jobs responded with assurances at the astonishing rate of 750 per month. During the year a total of 11,000 assurances were processed by LRS in New York. Each month over an average of 1,000 LRS-sponsored refugees arrived in the United States by plane and ship. They were welcomed at airports and seaports by LRS personnel and volunteers who assisted them to trains, planes, or buses to reach their destinations in almost every state.

Reports from the Resettled

These new Americans experienced elation, fear, and loneliness, just as the DPs before them had experienced—or as any number of the millions of immigrants to American shores. Letters to LRS from resettled refugees recounted a wide variety of experiences. One man complained that his sponsor had fired him because he answered an ad in a German paper about a job. A skilled mechanic who had been promised a specific wage was paid only half the promised amount "because you are a foreigner who doesn't know my kind of work." One man sponsored by his own relatives was threatened with deportation if he left owing them money.

But more letters expressed satisfaction with both jobs and sponsors and sincere appreciation for help, especially for the travel loans provided through LRS. One young man wrote, "I am happy that you have made it possible for me to find a new home in this country. I have a good job and am very satisfied with it. Only the language makes it a little difficult. However, I study English every day, and this difficulty will soon be overcome."

The president of a large machine company in New York State wrote in reply to a letter from LRS. "We are sorry to learn that your refugee program is necessarily coming to a conclusion. We have been very glad to cooperate with you in placing some of your people. . . . We find without exception that the men you have referred to us have been good employees in every sense of the word. The same good things can be said of your services. You have given us complete information about the applicants, and, from the quality of the people you have been helping, it would seem to us that your entire organization has been doing a good job."[33]

The report Cordelia Cox sent to the LRS area committees on December 8, 1956, indicated that by Christmas Day at least 13,000 refugees would be resettled through the LRS program. Cox gave credit to the local congregations, pastors, sponsors, and Lutheran social service agencies through whose personal conviction and generous effort the task had been completed. The most significant statistic of all was the item, "Dossiers still to be covered by assurances." There was a zero beside it. All the families LRS had accepted for resettlement had received offers of jobs and housing.

When the remaining applicants still in Germany or Austria reached the U.S. in the early months of 1957, the LRS total reached 16,006. The projected goal had been achieved.[34]

Revolution in Hungary

On October 23, 1956, students and factory workers of Budapest rose against the Soviet-imposed communist regime. In six days of fighting in the streets, they forced government troops to withdraw from the city. For four days the brief vision of freedom persisted. Then, on November 4, Soviet tanks stormed back into the city. Heavy artillery blasted buildings. Regrouped Soviet troops crushed the revolution and for seven days wreaked vengeance on the city.

A letter from Budapest described the battle for the city. "Day and night the thunder of cannons, tanks, and shells could be heard. . . . great ruins, death, and devastation from fires. . . . Boy and girl students, full of life, fought with guns, shells, bottles of gas, and even with their hands alone, and died. . . . Young university students went out on open lorries with the Red Cross flag in their outstretched hands to gather in the wounded and dying. . . . What will come now . . . who knows?"[35]

Most of the world remembers the closing radio broadcast out of Budapest. "Civilized people of the world, in the name of liberty and solidarity, we are asking you to help. Our ship is sinking. The light vanishes. . . . Listen to our cry. . . People of the world, save us. S–O–S! Help! Help! Help! God be with you and with us!"[36]

Then the radio went silent.

As the resistance weakened, surviving fighters and other victims of the struggle fled toward the Austrian border. By November 21, ten days after the resistance in Budapest had ended, more than 50,000 Hungarians had fled the reprisals. Other thousands followed.

Although no help was sent to the "freedom fighters" during their struggle, countries all over the world were ready to receive them as refugees. Great Britain took in 21,000; West Germany, 15,000; France, 13,000; other European countries, several thousand; Australia, 16,000; Canada 37,000; and Israel, 2,000. The United States, whose broadcasts from Radio Free Europe had encouraged the resistance forces in Hungary, but whose substantive help at the moment of greatest need failed to materialize, took 21,500 Hungarian refugees.

Indeed, while the resistance was still active in Hungary, President Eisenhower announced that 5,000 visas under the Refugee Relief Act would be made available for the Hungarians. The rest were admitted through a special procedure, a loophole in the immigration law that allowed the Attorney General to "parole" aliens into the United States "for emergency reasons or for reasons deemed strictly in the public interest." Congress understood that this loophole was being expanded, but out of sympathy for the Hungarians took no immediate steps to reassert its own authority to regulate immigration. The new refugees, concluded one observer, were "easily the most popular group of refugees in U.S. history because of their battle with communism."[37]

The special treatment extended to their processing for immigration. Rigid procedures employed for DPs and ethnic Germans were set aside. Under the DP Act, the U.S. Immigration and Naturalization Service had sent its officials to Europe to be sure entry permits, visas, and clearances of all kinds were in order before the refugees were allowed to enter the U.S. As the Hungarian refugees poured into hurriedly established centers in Austria, they simply registered with voluntary agencies such as the Lutheran World Federation and indicated their intended destination. Those who chose America were placed aboard planes and flown directly to the United States. The INS established offices at Camp Kilmer, a military base in New Brunswick, New Jersey, for processing the refugees and issuing visas. The Army arranged for housing and food and provided hospital facilities for any who were ill. The first planeload arrived at nearby McGuire Army Airfield on November 23, during the Thanksgiving weekend.

President Eisenhower appointed Tracy Voorhees as special coordinator for the Hungarian program. To facilitate the interviewing process and to move the refugees on as quickly as possible to relatives or other sponsors, the government invited voluntary agencies to set up special offices at Camp Kilmer. The six accredited agencies included Lutheran Refugee Service, National Catholic Welfare Conference, Church World Service, Tolstoy Foundation, International Rescue Committee, and Hebrew Immigrant Aid Society. Estimating the number of Lutherans in Hungary to be about five percent of the total population, LRS expected to receive 500 to 1,000 refugees as its share.

Cordelia Cox immediately moved the LRS office and staff from New York to Camp Kilmer and sent out an emergency call for sponsors to 30 area resettlement committees. According to the Refugee Relief Act, under which the initial 5,000 visas were authorized, assurances of jobs and housing had to be provided. Cox and her staff made personal calls to Lutheran social service agencies and congregations requesting, whenever possible, "covering" or "un-nominated" assurances, expressing willingness to sponsor any qualified refugee recommended by LRS.[38]

Response was enthusiastic. Offers of assistance flowed in from congregations and pastors, from Hungarians, including relatives who had settled in the United States, and from the general public. Within two weeks of the Hungarians' arrival, LRS had received and processed 75 refugees at Camp Kilmer. Processing time was cut short because the next planeload was soon to arrive. Most of the LRS people were on their way within three days to sponsors in ten different states. Many were sent to Cleveland, Ohio, which had a large Hungarian population and several Hungarian Lutheran congregations.

By the end of December, as military transport ships with greater capacity were called into service, 13,400 of the 21,500 Hungarian refugees due to arrive in the United States had entered the country. Nearly 7,000 had already passed through Camp Kilmer. Of the 700 refugees assigned to LRS, 484 had found found homes and employment in local communities.

The makeup of the Hungarian refugee group differed markedly from the DPs and ethnic Germans. There were fewer families, and even fewer single women. Most of the refugees were young single men who had fled in fear of imprisonment or even death.

Many highly trained professional persons were among the refugees, particularly doctors, engineers, and persons skilled in the physical sciences, like the research scientist who was placed with International Business Machines in Poughkeepsie, New York. There were virtually no farmers or domestic workers.

Cox noted that because of the rush and urgency of the process, many Hungarians did not stay long with their sponsors. "These were people," she said, who "had their own ideas as to where they wanted to live and what they wanted to do. It was hard for sponsors to understand that what these people were fighting for was a place to stand where they could be free and independent and find their own way. Therefore, when they came and accepted these jobs, they didn't always stay."[39]

More than 1300 persons assisted by LRS entered the United States as "parolees." Through the National Lutheran Council, LRS urged Congress to pass legislation granting them permanent residential status, eventually opening the way for them to apply for U.S. citizenship.[40] In 1958, Congress authorized the full legalization of parolees after a two-year residence in the country. At the same time, additional refugees were admitted as parolees, including Hungarians who had fled across the border from Hungary into Yugoslavia.

Coming suddenly and unexpectedly as it did, the Hungarian program laid a special burden upon government offices, voluntary agencies, and the American public. Agencies were still trying to complete the resettlement of ethnic German refugees under the RRA program before it closed on December 31, 1956. Although the Hungarian program was in every respect a U.S. government-sponsored initiative and the government paid all transporation costs, no financial support was offered to the voluntary agencies. Nevertheless, the six private agencies, including LRS, devoted unstinting efforts to the completion of the program in only 90 days.

On March 14, 1957, Cordelia Cox announced both the completion of the Hungarian refugee program and her resignation as director of LRS, effective July 1. Having led LRS for nine years filled by three successive programs that resettled 57,000 refugees, Cox left LRS to accept a position as director of the Lutheran Welfare Council of New York. "I left because I didn't want to be a part of just a sustaining program," she reminisced thirty years later. "I left thinking the program was practically over." But, she added, "It didn't get over, and it won't ever get over!"[41]

Actually, however, the decade of post-World War II refugee resettlement in the United States had come to an end. There would be a caretaking role for LRS during the next few years, assisting some refugees in meeting personal or legal problems, and a few hundred more refugees each year would need a helping hand. But another decade would pass before a Lutheran agency again became involved in a major resettlement program.

Lutherans in Transit

One of the great benefits to the church from the postwar refugee programs was a renewed awareness of the movement of people from one country to another. If any denominational group in America should have been sensitive to such a phenomenon, it was the Lutheran church, whose growth in the late 19th and 20th centuries was almost entirely the product of immigration and large families. If the Lutheran churches in both Europe and America had followed their migrating members, the Lutheran church in America today would probably number 30 million instead of nine million.

Services to Immigrants

The idea of a permanent service to Lutheran immigrants had been proposed in 1952 when the DP program was ending. Then new refugee legislation in 1953 rekindled energies for the resettlement of ethnic German refugees. In 1957, as the Hungarian program tapered off, the call for a comprehensive program to serve all Lutherans moving from one country to another was raised again. Just before the World Assembly of Lutherans in Minneapolis in August 1957, Carl Lund-Quist, Executive Secretary of the Lutheran World Federation, wrote to Cordelia Cox, asking for her views. In response she wrote of the need for a program to "follow all Lutheran immigrants as they move from one country to another, in ways that will insure that the immigrants will have the opportunity to relate themselves to the Church in whatever country they settle."

"Looking into the future," she continued, "I would wish that LWF and its national counterparts would begin to define a long-range, worldwide program for immigrants; that in so doing it would realistically and practically explore who among Lutherans is immigrating, how these people can be reached before immigration and after immigration, how many of them need and wish the good offices of the Church as they transplant themselves, and how responsive local pastors might be to a regular flow of information about incoming immigrants."[1]

At the LWF Assembly in Minneapolis, Paul Empie called upon member churches of the LWF to consider "the inauguration of a joint service to Lutherans migrating to other countries, by which immigrants would be assisted and guided into spiritual contacts in the new homelands."[2]

On January 1, 1958, responding to these appeals, the National Lutheran Council established a new office in its Division of Welfare called Service to Immigrants (SI). Members of its supervisory board were George Whetstone, chairman, Magnus Dahlen, and Albert H. Lueders. Although SI functioned out of the same office and with the same staff as the Lutheran Refugee Service, the National Lutheran Council made a clear distinction between the two services. The purpose of SI was "to coordinate existing services and develop further services to nonrefugee immigrants coming to the United States." Its primary intent, however, was to mediate a spiritual ministry through an international referral of the names of Lutheran immigrants to pastors in the communities in which the immigrants would reside.[3] The NLC appointed Vernon E. Bergstrom, an attorney from St. Paul, Minnesota, as director of the new agency.[4]

In accord with action taken at its World Assembly in Minneapolis, the LWF took steps to enlist the cooperation of Lutheran churches in all other countries of major Lutheran emigration and immigration, especially Germany, Norway, Sweden, Denmark, Finland, Canada, and Australia. An estimated 20,000 Lutherans migrated from these countries to the United States each year. In the first few months of its operation, Bergstrom's office referred the names of 2,552 persons to Lutheran pastors in the United States.[5]

With the resignation of Cordelia Cox in April of 1957, the Lutheran Refugee Service had had to seek new leadership. It chose David R. Salmon, a social work consultant in New York City, but health problems limited his service to a few months. The commissioners then turned to Vernon Bergstrom, the newly appointed director of the Service to Immigrants, and asked him also to serve LRS on a part-time basis. Anticipating the continuing decline and eventual phasing out of LRS, Henry Whiting, the new chairman of the LRS Commission, invited Bergstrom in January 1958 to become full-time director of both LRS and Service to Immigrants.[6]

Although the activities of LRS were significantly curtailed in 1958, some additional attention to refugee services was required by the enactment of amendments in September, 1957, to the McCarran-Walter Immigration and Nationality Act of 1952. Known as Public Law 85–316, the amendments liberalized certain sections of the 1952 Act. Refugees previously denied admission because of present or past tubercular conditions could be granted visas under personal affidavits from relatives who secured statements from TB sanitoriums guaranteeing hospital care in case of necessity. Restrictions on the admission of children, especially orphans, were relaxed. Mortgages imposed on the quotas of certain countries affected by the DP Act were lifted. In addition, about 18,000 nonquota visas authorized under the RRA but unused when the Act expired on December 31, 1956, were made available to bona fide refugees who had fled their countries to avoid persecution on account of race, religion, or political opinion.[7]

Of a total of 838 refugees resettled by LRS during 1958, almost all had arrived from Germany and Austria, even though among them were persons born in 19 different countries. In 1959 LRS resettled 807 refugees, mostly hardship cases, including 48 persons with TB records, sponsored by relatives who submitted personal affidavits. Others were sponsored by relatives or entered under agency affidavits, according to which LRS agreed to find sponsors who would assure jobs and housing.[8]

During the closing months of 1959, LRS also had opportunity to review the results of the loan program that had assisted more than 59,000 refugees since 1948. Most of the loans had been granted for ocean transportation or inland travel in the United States. Mildred Meyer, Supervisor of Accounts for LRS, who had managed loan funds during the entire eleven-year period, reported that a total of $4,440,936 had been loaned. More than 84 percent of all loans had been collected by December 1959, and a balance of $650,255 was being reduced at the rate of $26,000 per month.[9]

The decline in the number of refugees served by LRS during 1958 and 1959 should not be understood as a flagging of either interest or concern for the refugee issue. The admission of immigrants, whether refugees or nonrefugees, is a prerogative of government. Only insofar as governmental action authorizes special programs for the admission of refugees is it possible for voluntary agencies to engage in extensive resettlement efforts. With the termination of the Refugee Relief Act (RRA) on December 31, 1956, there was no further legislation in effect authorizing the admission of significant numbers of refugees to the United States. This is why the NLC shifted its emphasis from resettlement to immigration and services to immigrants.

Moreover, all experience since 1945 had demonstrated that the general climate of the country and of the Congress was not favorable to immigration into the United States, even for refugees. The passage of the DP Act of 1948 and the RRA of 1952 had been achieved only against persistent resistance. Even the admission of the Hungarian "freedom fighters" was authorized by presidential order rather than congressional legislation.

World Refugee Year

Leaders of the NLC were therefore greatly encouraged by an announcement on December 5, 1958, from the General Assembly of the United Nations, declaring the period from July 1, 1959, to July 1, 1960, as World Refugee Year (WRY). The U.N. resolution called upon member governments to "focus attention on the refugee problem and encourage additional financial contributions from governments, voluntary agencies, and the general public for its solution."

At its annual meeting in February 1959, the National Lutheran Council strongly endorsed the idea and declared its readiness to cooperate toward the attainment of its goals. The Lutheran World Federation urged its members to contribute an additional $1 million toward a series of special refugee-oriented projects.[10]

Forty nations responded by setting up special committees to coordinate WRY activities. President Eisenhower proclaimed a World Refugee Year in the United States. He invited all citizens "to support generously, either through the voluntary welfare agencies or the United States Committee for Refugees, the programs developed in furtherance of that Year for the assistance of refugees." The U.S. State Department earmarked $4,000,000 for grants to assist the integration of refugees, clear refugee camps, and provide housing, food and supplies. Congress authorized the President to spend $10 million for refugee aid.

By early 1960, however, only a small portion of these government funds had been utilized. Several bills calling for the admittance of more refugees into the United States had been introduced in connection with World Refugee Year, but Congress took only limited action, extending earlier provisions caring for orphans and other special cases.

Vernon Bergstrom, director of LRS, called upon Lutherans in the U.S. to write to their Congressional representatives and to the President, urging the admission of more refugees. In an address delivered at the annual meeting of the NLC in Atlantic City in February 1960, Bergstrom sounded a prophetic note for Lutheran resettlement when he reminded the Council that Asia, Africa, and the Middle East were now the scene of the world's greatest refugee problems.

"Throughout these years", Bergstrom said, "Lutherans in the United States have successfully resettled fellow Lutherans, to the extent that the 'Lutheran family' is now pretty well in order. We ought now to examine our responsibility to resettle non-Lutherans in need of such assistance. Just as we have championed the cause of the Europeans of the Lutheran faith, should we not now champion the cause of a Chinese in a hovel in Hong Kong in his attempts to rejoin his family or friends in the United States? Should the excellent and efficient resettlement system developed through our congregations and agencies be left to 'wither on the vine,' or should it be placed at the disposal of the uprooted from strange, far-off, non-Lutheran lands, who have very compelling reasons to resettle here? Should we now seek to mobilize Lutheran opinion throughout our land and bring it to bear upon Congress, urging that that body enact refugee legislation which permits the entry of such groups as Chinese, Arabs, and others? Should we now make our collective influence felt in seeking to direct our country's eyes away from a rebuilt and flourishing Europe to Asia, Africa, and the Middle East, where the real migration problems exist?"[11]

The World Refugee Year provided an appropriate background for Bergstrom's call for expanded advocacy on behalf of refugees throughout the world. The NLC itself had for many years spoken for member churches, directing resolutions to Congress, to the President, and to the general public on behalf of refugees and immigration legislation. Cox, Whiting, and Empie had often appeared before congressional committees, and more recently, Bergstrom had also filed testimony with the Senate Subcommittee on Immigration.

The apparent lethargy of both Congress and the President in fulfilling their stated intent to give tangible support to the World Refugee Year led the National Lutheran Council to issue a sharply worded critique. "In recent years," stated the Council, "the phrase 'matching words with deeds' has appeared frequently, as our government challenges the good intentions of Communist countries. It is clear that in this instance the United States has not matched words with deeds." The resolutions attached to this statement were sent to the White House and released to the press. The NLC challenged the government to use all the funds appropriated for U.S. participation in the World Refugee Year and to authorize up to 20,000 nonquota visas for refugees and escapees. Such action, declared the Council, would be "in line with moral and humanitarian considerations, as well as other factors furthering the national interest."[12]

Lutheran thinking on immigration policy had come a long way since the late 1920s, when the National Lutheran Council objected to immigration laws because they did not have larger quotas for predominantly Lutheran countries.[13]

Morality and the National Interest

The paper presented by Paul Empie during the NLC annual meeting in 1960, entitled "Immigration Policy: Moral Issues and the National Interest," reflected the more inclusive Lutheran vision. A nation's immigration laws, Empie began, reflect its basic attitudes toward other nations and races. They also expose for all to see its concept of justice, its view of human rights, and the quality of its moral principles. He contended that many thoughtful Americans who had been examining U.S. immigration policies in this perspective had been disturbed by what they had found. The arbitrariness of the quota system and the discriminatory character of its national origins base appeared to be in sharp contradiction to American claims to champion the equality and dignity of all people, and to be concerned about wholesome international relations. Such disparities, he warned, carried the risk of serious consequences for the United States in years to come.

While Empie acknowledged the validity of "national interest" as a basis for a nation's policies and actions, he insisted that the exercise of moral judgment was an essential element in the concept of national interest. So also was human compassion, as opposed to selfish privilege. An immigration policy thus motivated would not eliminate all controls nor permit an unrestricted flood of immigrants. But a policy that within an overall limitation of numbers afforded all people an equitable and nondiscriminatory opportunity would not only strengthen the nation's moral sense, but would remove many barriers to international understanding and world peace.

Empie made no effort to spell out patterns of operation. But he recommended a series of five objectives for U.S. immigration laws:

1. To supply our permanent population with a steady proportion of newcomers who have chosen the United States as their new homeland and who can impart to their American neighbors an understanding of the cultures, attitudes, and interests of other races and peoples of the world.
2. To assume the United States' proper share of international responsibilities for resettlement of refugees and of other persons urgently in need of the compassionate haven of a new homeland.
3. To facilitate the reuniting of families.
4. To facilitate the entry of persons posessing special skills or other capacities needed by the American economy and culture.
5. To admit annually a reasonable number of the persons described above on an objective basis of selection which, while discriminating, will not be discriminatory with respect to race, national origin, color, or religion, testifying thereby to the United States' recognition of the interlocking and mutual interests of all nations with regard to the migration of peoples, the interaction of cultures, and respect of universal human rights.

The National Lutheran Council adopted Empie's statement as a policy document and voted to advocate the appointment by the President or Congress of a National Commission on U.S. Immigration. Such a commission should include in its study all aspects of world population pressure and U.S. responsibility. On the threshold of the sixties, with their passionate and often stormy advocacy of human rights and universal justice, the Council and its Service to Immigrants had established a sound basis upon which to apply these principles to U.S. immigration law.[14]

Renewal of a Partnership

The shift in primary focus from the resettlement of refugees to the social and spiritual care of immigrants resulted in a change in the existing pattern of inter-Lutheran cooperation. Both the NLC and the LCMS regarded resettlement of refugees as an emergency program, established to deal with a temporary crisis. On this basis the member churches of the NLC had given their approval to the original agreement with the LCMS, and it had therefore been possible to renew the joint operation of LRS on a year-to-year basis since 1954.

In September 1958, the LCMS proposed expanding the cooperative agreement with the NLC to include the Service to Immigrants, which the NLC had established eight months earlier. The Service to Immigrants, however, and especially the system of referring members of Lutheran congregations abroad to Lutheran congregations in the United States, was viewed by the NLC as part of the church's permanent ministry, rather than an emergency action. Consequently, the separate approval of the eight member churches of the NLC was required to authorize a cooperative agreement with the LCMS.[15]

Pending this approval, an interim arrangement was worked out for 1959, involving the purchase of services by LCMS. Representatives of the NLC and the LCMS then began to develop plans for 1960. By November 1959 final ratifications were secured for the establishment of the Lutheran Immigration Service (LIS). This new association was charged with the task of carrying out the functions of both the LRS and SI, beginning January 1, 1960.

The content of the agreement reflected the shift in focus. Its preamble defined the intent of the partners to fulfill "residual services" to refugees resettled under previous programs, while eight of the nine major services projected for the agency dealt with immigration concerns. LIS expected to

a. represent the position of Lutheran churches on immigration to governmental and voluntary agencies;
b. work with the LWF on matters of joint interest on behalf of im-

migration of individuals, families, and groups of people;

c. plan for port reception services for incoming immigrants;

d. plan for referral of immigrants to local congregations;

e. plan and coordinate services by churches and Lutheran welfare agencies for protection, guidance, and counsel of immigrants;

f. coordinate a Lutheran service for unattended immigrant children with Lutheran child placement agencies;

g. give information and counsel on immigration procedures;

h. complete the residual work of previous resettlement programs; and

i. study and interpret immigration issues for the churches.[16]

LIS was to be administered by a joint supervisory committee called the Lutheran Immigration Service Committee, five of whose seven members were to be appointed by the Division of Welfare of the NLC and two by the Department of Social Welfare of the LCMS. George Whetstone, an NLC pastor, was elected chairman; William H. Kohn and Leslie F. Weber, both LCMS, were elected vice-chairman and secretary, respectively. Other NLC members were Albert H. Lueders, Theodore E. Matson, Gjermund S. Thompson, and Harry Wolf. Henry Whiting, NLC, and Henry F. Wind, LCMS, acted as advisers.[17]

Program at the local level was carried out with the assistance of Lutheran social service agencies affiliated with LCMS or with member churches of the NLC. The annual budget, supported on a 70/30 ratio by the NLC and the LCMS, was projected on a three-year cycle, but approved annually.

Since the work of its two predecessor agencies had been combined in a single office and carried out by the same staff, the LIS began its operations on January 1, 1960, without any staff changes. Vernon Bergstrom continued as director; Raymond Kissam as supervisor of social services and referrals; Mildred Meyer, accounts; and Ingrid Walter, reception services.

A Lutheran Referral System

The referral system depended on close cooperation and communication between Lutheran churches and agencies in Europe and the United States. Its greatest problem lay in the differing concepts of church membership in Europe and America. In both Scandinavian countries and Germany the state church tradition prevailed. Churches were supported by the state or through taxes collected by the state. A person became a member of the church by birth.

In the American tradition both church membership and church support were voluntary. Lutheran immigrants from Germany or Scandinavia became members of the Lutheran church in the United States only if they took initiative to join. Unaccustomed to this pattern, newcomers might remain fully unchurched, or they might join a non-Lutheran church that had a vigorous outreach program. In either case they would be lost to the Lutheran community.

In following the mandate of the World Assembly of 1957 in Minneapolis, the LWF encouraged member churches in Europe to identify those members emigrating to the United States or to other countries in which there were Lutheran churches. Bruno Muetzelfeldt, Director of the LWF Department of World Service, carried responsibility for this program and organized special consultations among Lutheran church leaders to promote a worldwide referral network. Pastors were urged to forward to Geneva, through their church offices, the names and destinations of their members who were emigrating. The Department of World Service in turn sent the names to cooperating Lutheran church offices in the countries of destination.

Muetzelfeldt reported that the average pastor in Europe knew only five percent of his own members, because of the large numbers of people who were nominally members of his parish. He estimated that a pastor would forward only one or two percent of his known membership who migrated.[18]

Because of this, the LWF sought to develop other ways of securing names and addresses from secular sources such as travel agencies, shipping agencies, and consulates. The U.S. consulates in Scandinavia agreed to distribute a brochure produced by the churches to emigrants when they received their visas. The *Innere Mission* and the *Hilfswerk* in Germany prepared a similar brochure for distribution to emigrants. Ship chaplaincies were set up on certain ships from Germany. Chaplains gathered emigrants' names and addresses and sent them to LIS for referral to Lutheran parishes. In the summer of 1960 LIS received 117 names and addresses from the chaplain aboard the SS *Bremen*.

LIS sent the names to parish pastors or to Lutheran social service agencies, which contacted the nearest Lutheran pastor. A letter from LIS requested the designated pastor to visit the immigrant family and invite them to his congregation. LIS also requested a report on the pastor's home visit.[19]

A special booklet was prepared for immigrants, explaining the American voluntary church structure and the nature of services available through a local congregation and also through LIS and the Lutheran social service agencies. A series of conferences during 1960 and 1961 interpreted the referral program and encouraged congregations and pastors to participate as an expression of the mission outreach of the church.

Over a six-year period from 1958 to 1964 a total of 4,747 families, mostly from Germany, were referred to LIS from overseas churches. More than 2,800 of the names were referred from travel and shipping agencies; only 233 from churches. LIS itself gathered 1,047 names from incoming refugees or immigrants. Of the 4,747 families referred by LIS to pastors and congregations, LIS received 2,620 responses. Replies indicated that 900 families had affiliated with NLC churches, 466 with Missouri churches, 51 with other Lutheran churches, and 331 with non-Lutheran churches. Referrals were distributed to all 50 states, with the largest numbers to New York, New Jersey, Illinois, and California.[20]

The immigration and refugee program underwent another change in leadership when its director, Vernon Bergstrom, submitted his resignation effective January 1, 1962. Bergstrom was eager to resume the practice of law in his home state of Minnesota, but he also cited the erection of the Berlin Wall in August, 1961, as a factor in his decision to leave the LIS. Since more than 90 percent of the Lutheran referrals came from Germany, he felt the blocking of the exodus of East Germans into West Berlin would reduce to a minimum the number of potential referrals for which LIS had been established.[21]

The volume of Lutheran referrals did, in fact, decline significantly in 1962 and the years immediately following. But the need for social and legal services to immigrants already in the country remained, and a limited number of Lutheran refugees continued to seek resettlement in the United States, mostly under national quotas. Many of these were sponsored by relatives. For others, LIS provided agency affidavits, based on the expressed willingness of individual congregations to assure jobs and housing.

The task of meeting the new challenges of the 1960s was given to Donald E. Anderson, a layman of The American Lutheran Church, who took office as Vernon Bergstrom's successor on March 1, 1962. At the age of 33, Anderson had already performed significant service in international refugee and relief work. In 1954 he had been a resettlement officer in Hamburg, Germany, for the World Council of Churches. From 1957 to 1960 he had served as Secretary for Resettlement and Material Relief for the LWF Department of World Service in Geneva, work for which he received a special citation from the Standing Conference of Voluntary Agencies.[22]

6

From Hong Kong
to Havana

Shortly after the inauguration of President John F. Kennedy in January 1961, the influx of refugees from mainland China into the British colony of Hong Kong accelerated to alarming proportions. Within the limits of an already overcrowded city, somewhere between 350,000 and 500,000 refugees lived under intolerable conditions, in hovels built of scrap metal or packing boxes. The less fortunate found shelter under bridges, on rooftops, or in the alleys or gutters.

Since 1954 the Lutheran World Federation had maintained a relief program for these refugees under the direction of Karl Ludwig Stumpf, a German national. Supported by Lutheran churches throughout the world, Stumpf's office distributed food and clothing and maintained medical and dental facilities, a vocational training program, and a program for the rehabilitation of handicapped and tubercular cases. It also aided in developing small handcraft industries and designed a student aid program to assist refugees to become self-supporting. LWF also carried out a limited resettlement program jointly with the World Council of Churches.

Moved by the appalling conditions in Hong Kong and conscious of the fact that the U.S. immigration quota virtually excluded Chinese nationals, President Kennedy issued an executive order in March 1962, authorizing the admission of 5,000 to 7,000 Chinese refugees to the United States as parolees.[1]

LIS Director Anderson expressed gratification over the President's announcement. "In view of the heavy commitments of the Lutheran churches in relief programs within the Colony," he said, "LIS is planning to cooperate in the resettlement of these refugees within the United States." At its meeting in June 1962, the LIS Committee confirmed its willingness to assist up to 300 Chinese families in their movement from Hong Kong to the United States.[2]

Ingrid Walter, an Estonian refugee who first joined the Lutheran Refugee Service in 1950, was placed in charge of the Chinese refugee program. LIS agreed to use the services of the Lutheran World Federation and the World Council of Churches already existing in Hong Kong to identify and recommend candidates for immigration to the United States and to handle the necessary processing for visas. Cases brought to the attention of LIS by pastors and sponsors in the United States were referred to the Hong Kong office for investigation. If approved, LIS provided agency sponsorships, or, in case of family sponsorships, assisted in arranging for necessary affidavits. For those who needed travel assistance, LWF made available its revolving loan fund.[3]

The first three Chinese families sponsored by LIS arrived in San Francisco in early October 1962. Chan Chi Tien, his wife and their four children went to relatives in the Oakland, California, area. Chu Sang Woo, with his wife and their two children, remained with relatives in San Francisco. Leung Chu, his wife and their seven children, were sponsored by family friends in Fresno, California. Their eighth child, 15-year-old Yan Kit, was suffering from tuberculosis and was temporarily delayed while special travel arrangements were being made for her. When she arrived later in October, she became a patient at the City of Hope Medical Center in Duarte, California. Lutheran Welfare Society of Los Angeles made arrangements for her care without cost to the family. Mr. Leung found employment as a garage mechanic in Fresno, while Mr. Chan went to work in an aircraft factory in Oakland, and Mr. Chu in an office in San Francisco. The Leung and Chan families were Lutheran; the Chu family were members of the Chinese Christian and Missionary Alliance.[4]

During the nine months of the special Chinese program initiated by President Kennedy, LIS approved loans in the amount of $40,795 for the movement of 133 persons to the United States. In January 1963, U.S. Immigration officials in Hong Kong discontinued accepting new applications from Chinese refugees desiring to emigrate to the United States.[5]

Flight from Castro's Cuba

In 1959 the people of Cuba, under the leadership of a young army officer named Fidel Castro, overthrew the government of the

U.S.-supported dictator Fulgencio Batista. As Castro consolidated his control, supporters of Batista, mostly people of wealth and political influence, sought refuge outside Cuba, many of them in the United States. In this early migration, members of the well-educated professional classes comprised 31 percent of the total, compared with nine percent of the general Cuban population in 1953. The United States government imposed no limitations on this "golden exodus."

As economic embargoes and quarantines were imposed on Cuba by the United States government, Castro's policies also hardened, and he turned to the Soviet Union for support. By the end of the Eisenhower administration, a clandestine plan for the invasion of Cuba was being readied for action by the CIA. When John F. Kennedy became president in January 1961, he authorized an assault on the Bay of Pigs that prepared the way for the missile crisis of 1962 and the confrontation with the Soviet Union that brought the world to the brink of nuclear war.

Throughout these events the flow of refugees from Cuba to the United States continued without interruption. By the end of 1960, despite Castro's attempt to prevent their exit, more than 100,000 Cubans had arrived in the United States. During the ensuing decade an average of 50,000 persons entered the United States each year. Until the Cuban "invasion," the United States had been a country of second asylum, free to decide how many refugees it was willing to accept from other countries, or whether it would accept any at all. The influx of Cuban refugees changed this, and the United States began to experience the special problems of a country of first asylum.[6]

Shortly before he left office, President Eisenhower had opened the Cuban Refugee Center in Miami. In January 1961, President Kennedy directed his Secretary for Health, Education, and Welfare, Abraham Ribicoff, to assess the Cuban refugee situation. As a result, Congress passed the Migration and Refugee Assistance Act of 1962, providing authorization for a Cuban refugee program. For the first time the federal government provided reimbursement through the Department of Health, Education, and Welfare to state and local agencies for cash assistance, medical aid, social services, and educational assistance to Cuban refugees.[7]

Although Cuba's population was largely Roman Catholic, several Lutheran congregations in Cuba were affiliated with The Lutheran

Church—Missouri Synod. About 50 members of these congregations made their way to Miami as refugees during 1960 and 1961. Eugene Gruell, formerly an LCMS missionary in Cuba, enlisted the assistance of Missouri congregations in Miami on their behalf. With the encouragement of William von Spreckelsen, Executive Secretary of the LCMS Florida-Georgia District, and Werner Kuntz, Executive Director of the Synod's Board of World Relief, Gruell opened a Lutheran Emergency Center in April 1961, in St. Matthew Lutheran Church in Miami.[8]

Refugee families who registered with the U.S. government's Refugee Center in Miami were eligible for a monthly rental allowance of $100, and the Public Welfare Department of the State of Florida granted a biweekly food ration. The Lutheran Emergency Center distributed food to about 200 families per week and supplied clothing and blankets donated by Lutheran congregations. Some help was given on job procurement, but jobs were scarce. By December 1962, the Center had also resettled 11 Lutheran families from Cuba in Lutheran congregations from Paramus, New Jersey, to Kansas City, Missouri. About 100 non-Lutheran families were referred for resettlement to Church World Service, the resettlement agency of the National Council of Churches (NCC).[9]

In January 1962, James MacCracken, director of the Church World Service (CWS) immigration department, met with the LIS Committee in New York to urge direct participation by LIS in the resettlement of Cuban refugees. He asked for support and possible LIS participation in a "Freedom Flight" being planned by CWS, through which local councils of churches would solicit enough assurances in their communities to fill a plane with refugee families. In view of the fact that there were very few Lutherans among the Cuban refugees, the LIS Committee concluded that participation in this program should be decided by local Lutheran congregations, in cooperation with local councils and committees. About 31 Lutheran congregations responded to this suggestion during 1962.

At the same time the LIS committee assured CWS that LIS would find sponsors for the few Lutherans who might request resettlement, but it asked CWS to provide for their processing under its government contract, thereby avoiding the necessity of a separate agreement between LIS and the government. CWS agreed to this arrangement.[10]

In April, shortly after Donald Anderson took office as LIS director, he received letters from both MacCracken and Gruell, again urging direct participation by LIS in the general resettlement program. Since about 95 percent of the Cuban refugees were at least nominally Roman Catholics, Anderson responded by reaffirming the policy that had been followed by each of the predecessor agencies of LIS with regard to the confessional relationships of refugees and migrants. If LIS were to engage in resettling Catholic refugees, he wrote to MacCracken, it would do so only with the concurrence of the National Catholic Welfare Conference (NCWC). Anderson added that in conversations with James Norris, director of NCWC, he and Paul Empie had been assured that NCWC was both prepared and willing to resettle all those who normally belonged on the NCWC caseload.[11]

Both MacCracken and Gruell disagreed sharply with the LIS decision, pointing out that NCWC was resettling only 500 of the 2000 refugees arriving each week. They asserted that the NCWC seemed comfortable with the increasing number of Catholics in Florida, in spite of the insistent expressions from U.S., state, and local officials, urging the moving of the refugee population out of the congested Miami area.

Social Ministry in Miami

With respect to additional programs of social welfare and material relief in Miami, LIS took a different position. At its meeting in June 1962, the Committee indicated its willingness to consider requests for the support of assistance projects in areas like Miami, where there were no Lutheran welfare agencies. The Committee authorized the LIS director to meet with pastors in Miami, where the LCMS had already initiated a relief program.

By November 5, following a consultation in Miami, local pastors proposed a project of two years' duration entitled "Miami Lutheran Refugee Service Program," that would expand the relief effort initiated by the LCMS. Both the Executive Committee of the National Lutheran Council and the LCMS Board of World Relief approved the proposal and appropriated $40,000 and $30,000, respectively, toward the first annual budget of the refugee program. An additional $10,000 was earmarked from unexpended LIS 1962 budget funds.

On January 8, 1963, 14 Lutheran pastors and lay people of the Miami area met at St. Matthew Church to organize the Miami Lutheran Refugee Service (MLRS). Werner Kuntz represented the LCMS and Donald Anderson the LIS. Oliver Grotefend of the National Council of Churches was present as a consultant. Eugene Gruell attended as Acting Director.[12]

Plans were laid for the election of a 15-member supervisory committee, with five representatives each from the Missouri Synod and five each from the recently constituted Lutheran Church in America and The American Lutheran Church, nominated in consultation with synod or district welfare committees. In an election in February, Oliver Grotefend was chosen as director of MLRS. In accord with its statement of purpose, the supervisory committee agreed to develop and administer a relief and social service program for Cuban refugees in the Miami area; to coordinate its program with other Protestant agencies, especially the NCC; to assist students to continue their education; to assist local congregations and pastors to relate to the needs of Cuban refugees; to assist refugees to reestablish themselves and their families in cooperation with resettlement agencies and within the policies of LIS. About half of the projected budget was to be used for personnel and administration, and half for direct relief.[13]

During its first year of operation under Grotefend's direction, the MLRS carried on its program through four main departments: social services, material assistance, medical, and resettlement. A paid staff of nine persons included four in the social service department, three in the medical clinic, one in material aid, and one part-time custodian. Ten additional volunteers supplemented the paid staffs in the medical and social service departments. During 1963 the Center assisted 3,565 families, representing more than 10,000 persons. Eighty percent of these families required only temporary assistance and were able to reestablish themselves in the Miami community.

In addition to the distribution of emergency food and clothing, especially to new arrivals, medical services made up a major portion of the Center's caseload. In a single month the Cuban staff doctor reported seeing 523 patients, and the pharmacist distributed 1,030 medications. The social workers attempted to make home visits to families who reported special needs. More than 50 families, assisted by the resettlement counselor during 1963, were referred to CWS or NCWC for resettlement elsewhere.[14]

In June 1964 Grotefend resigned as director, and Gruell, taking a leave of absence from his Spanish-speaking Lutheran congregation, returned to the refugee center.

One of the creative ventures of the Miami Lutheran Refugee Service was the Sharing English Plan, initiated in 1964. Intended to supplement the formal language instruction available through government assistance, this program provided the Cuban refugees with the opportunity to spend an hour a week in conversations with sympathetic and helpful local people. Matilde O'Reilly, a local church member, coordinated the program, matching the Cubans with competent volunteers from Lutheran congregations. Fifteen groups were meeting regularly by the end of the year.[15]

Another project to which Pastor Gruell gave special attention was the Free Fishermen's Association. Among the Cuban refugees were many independent fishermen who owned their own small boats and had made the 90-mile voyage to Florida at great hazard, bringing their families with them. Sixty-four-year-old Luis Rioseco, his wife, and their two sons, had fled Cuba in 1961. They were rescued from their small boat after drifting for six days. Julio Medina, 50, escaped in 1964 with his wife and their three sons. Fearful of trying to purchase a compass and map in Cuba lest his plans be suspected, he trusted to luck for two nights and a day before being rescued by a U.S. Coast Guard cutter.

A group of 50 such independent fishermen, eager to reestablish themselves in their profession, organized the Free Fishermen's Association. Lutheran Immigration Service and Church World Service gave the association start-up grants of $1500 and $1000. The MLRS provided small loans to enable them to repair their boats and secure needed equipment. Unfortunately, the Association encountered opposition from the Florida Fishermen's Association, who felt the competition hazarded their own livelihood.[16]

Gruell's appointment officially expired on December 31, 1964. However, in view of its decision to phase out the services of the Miami Center during 1965, the LIS Committee asked him to continue throughout the year on a part-time basis. In explaining the LIS decision, Donald Anderson said the Committee had concluded "that the total Cuban refugee problem in the Miami area would be reduced to a point—by the end of 1965—where the type of assistance given through the MLRS program would no longer serve a primary need."[17]

Of the 170,000 Cuban refugees registered with the U.S. government office, 85,000 to 90,000 had been resettled throughout the country. Most of the 80,000 remaining persons had become established in the Miami community. Approximately 12,000 "hard core" cases, which required specialized programs, were to be handled as a public responsibility.

In his year-end report in December 1964 Gruell reviewed the achievements of the previous two years. In the earliest stages of the program, he observed, the main task had been to stave off hunger and panic. But as the number of persons requiring emergency aid had declined, MLRS had developed social services to help refugees become self-supporting.

By the end of 1964, the center was able to close its food and clothing warehouse. By March 31, 1965, all registration of new cases was terminated. By October 31, all remaining medical cases were transferred to other programs. As the Center concluded its three years of service, it had offered assistance to almost 12,000 refugees, distributing 41,245 pounds of clothing and 14,084 packets of food. Medical assistance had been given to 4,427 refugee patients, and $18,820 in contributed medicines had been distributed. In three years the total Lutheran contribution to Cuban refugee aid was $249,114.

While church, community, and government agencies had conducted separate programs during the crisis of 1959–65, they maintained close cooperative relationships. Gruell was a member of an ad hoc committee of the Dade County Welfare Planning Council that included representatives of several of these agencies. The National Council of Churches had been represented by Oliver Grotefend, Executive Secretary of the Protestant Latin American Emergency Committee. In July 1965, William J. Black arrived in Miami as Executive Director of the Commission on Cuban Refugees of the Greater Miami Council of Churches.

On September 30, 1965, Fidel Castro announced that all Cubans who wished to live in the United States were free to leave Cuba. The result was a new influx of Cuban refugees into Florida at the rate of 1,000 per week. To meet this challenge the churches of Miami, supported by the National Council of Churches, agreed to establish a unified program of health and welfare services. With Eugene Gruell as chairman of a provisional board of directors, the Christian Community Service of Dade County began formal operations on January 1, 1966. Joan Gross, former Executive Director of the Episcopal Church Agency for Cuban Refugees, was chosen Executive Secretary. The National Lutheran Council and The Lutheran Church—Missouri Synod authorized LIS participation and approved a grant of $35,000, divided on a 70/30 ratio between the NLC and the LCMS. Lutheran social ministry to Cuban refugees was continued on an ecumenical basis.[18]

Call for Immigration Reform

In his annual report to the LIS Committee in 1964, Donald Anderson acknowledged that since the conclusion of the Hungarian program, most of the refugee services of LIS had been directed to the social or legal problems of refugees already resettled in the United States. Since 1960, most of the new refugees had come from Cuba and were at least nominally Roman Catholics. In keeping with its established principle to avoid any appearance of proselytizing, LIS had not actively engaged in the resettlement of Cuban refugees. But Anderson, like his predecessor Vernon Bergstrom, had continued to urge a more liberal policy on the part of the U.S. government for both refugees and immigrants.

The introduction of a bill by Senator Philip Hart of Michigan in March 1962, cosponsored by 13 other senators, provided LIS and other voluntary agencies the opportunity to launch an energetic advocacy effort for the removal of the national origins quota system. While Hart's bill stopped short of eliminating the national origins system, it modified many of its discriminating features.

It proposed an increase in the number of quota visas to 250,000 per year, 50,000 of which would be available to refugees without regard to quota areas. Of the remaining 200,000, 80,000 would be divided among countries in proportion to their population. One hundred twenty thousand visas would be allocated proportionately, based on the average of the total immigration of each country during the preceding 15 years. Preferences would be given to reuniting families and to admitting persons possessing special skills needed in the United States.

In introducing the bill, Senator Hart called attention to the 1960 platforms of both political parties, which were sharply critical of the national origins quota system as contradictory to the founding principles of the nation, and "inconsistent with our belief in the rights of man." In an address to the President and members of Congress, Senator Hart asked that the names of 50 voluntary agencies that had endorsed his bill be inserted in the *Congressional Record*.[19]

After analyzing the bill in relation to the five objectives listed in Empie's 1960 paper, "Moral Issues and the National Interest," which the NLC had adopted as a policy guideline, the LIS Committee added its own endorsement. It described the proposed legislation as "a step forward in the development of a nondiscriminatory national immigration policy," and commended it to churches and members of Congress for their support.[20]

On July 23, 1963, before the Hart bill was brought to a final vote, President Kennedy proposed new legislation to eliminate the national origins quota over a period of five years. The LIS welcomed Kennedy's proposal as a further step toward "a nondiscriminatory and more compassionate immigration law." At the same time it registered a reservation concerning the "unusually broad discretionary powers" vested in the Executive Branch.[21]

Three months after delivering his immigration message to Congress, President Kennedy was assassinated in Dallas, Texas. The following January, his successor, Lyndon Johnson, met with members of Congress, labor leaders, and officials of voluntary agencies, including the Executive Director of the NLC and the Director of LIS, and reaffirmed his support for the immigration reforms originally submitted to Congress by President Kennedy.

Throughout 1964, an election year, as the Kennedy proposal was being debated in Congress, the LIS continued its advocacy for immigration reform. On August 10, Donald Anderson appeared before the House Judiciary Committee's Subcommittee on Immigration, Refugees, and International Law, and presented the LIS and NLC positions, submitting for the record the complete 1960 statement on "Moral Issues and the National Interest." Later in August, he addressed the Democratic Platform Committee at its meeting in Atlantic City, New Jersey, on behalf of the 47 member agencies of the American Immigration and Citizenship Conference.[22]

The End of National Quotas

On January 13, 1965, strengthened by the mandate of a successful election in November, 1964, President Johnson submitted to Congress his own proposal for immigration reform. When the NLC convened for its annual meeting in Los Angeles on February 8, it adopted a resolution endorsing Johnson's bill as a significant contribution to "the fulfillment of the basic hopes and objectives" of the NLC for immigration reform. Walter F. Wolbrecht, Executive Secretary of the LCMS, authorized Empie to state in a letter transmitting the resolution to government officials and members of Congress that the LCMS also endorsed the NLC resolution. The LIS Committee followed suit at its meeting on March 12.[23]

Advocacy efforts continued throughout 1965. In late March, Anderson testified before the Senate Subcommittee on Immigration and Naturalization, speaking on behalf of LIS and 21 other member agencies of the American Council of Voluntary Agencies for Foreign Service. A signed statement from these agencies declared their belief "that the basic provisions in the proposed legislation will not only eliminate the discriminatory national origins quota system, but will constructively change our immigration laws so that they serve the common good of our people and reflect what is best for the interests of the United States, both domestically and internationally."

In explaining the unanimity of diverse groups on an issue as complex as immigration law, Anderson reminded the subcommittee that the basis of discrimation inherent in the national origins quota system "is not too dissimilar from that which ended in tragedy and death for millions in Europe within our lifetime."[24]

Joining Anderson in presenting the LIS testimony were William H. Kohn, President of the Southeastern District of the LCMS and since 1964, chairman of the LIS Committee; Wayne K. Hill of the legal firm Markel and Hill, counsel for LIS; and Robert Van Deusen, secretary of the NLC Division of Public Relations in Washington, D.C.

On August 25, the same day the House of Representatives approved its version of the immigration reform bill, a full-page advertisement appeared in the *Washington Post,* urging passage of the bill. Signed by about 300 persons, it was sponsored by the National

Committee for Immigration Reform, a citizens' group that included several Lutheran church leaders.

On October 3, 1965, President Johnson signed Public Law 89–236, an Act to Revise the Immigration and Nationality Act of 1952. As he signed the new law on Liberty Island, in the shadow of the Statue of Liberty, the President described it as "one of the most important acts of this Congress and this Administration. It repairs a deep and painful flaw in the fabric of American justice," he declared. "It corrects a cruel and enduring wrong in the conduct of the American nation. It will make us truer to ourselves as a country and as a people. It will strengthen us in a hundred unseen ways."

The new bill was by no means a general relaxation of all restrictions on immigration to the United States. The President reminded the world that "the days of unlimited immigration are past. But those who come," he said, "will come because of what they are—not because of the land from which they sprung."[25]

Under the basic provisions of the new law, a total of 390,000 visas were made available to immigrants each year. For the first time an overall limit of 120,000 immigrants from Western Hemisphere countries was imposed, a provision that the President feared might damage U.S. relations with our close neighbors. For the Eastern Hemisphere, covering Europe, Asia, Africa, Australia, and Micronesia, 170,000 visas were made available, with a ceiling of 20,000 from any one country. The 170,000 visas were to be allocated on the basis of categories giving preference to family relationships, persons with professions or skills of special value to the United States. The "seventh preference" provided for refugees from communist-dominated countries.[26]

Three days before the President signed the new law, Fidel Castro had announced that any Cubans who wished to leave Cuba for the United States were free to do so. President Johnson issued a declaration addressed to the people of Cuba that, "those who seek refuge here will find it. . . . Our traditions as an asylum for the oppressed will be upheld." In keeping with the new law, the President promised first concern for the reunification of the families of refugees already in the United States. By December 1, under an agreement with Castro mediated by the Swiss government, daily chartered flights were bringing 1,000 Cuban refugees to the United States each week.

Learning to Live in LCUSA

For American Lutheranism, January 1, 1967, was a landmark date. It marked the launching of a cooperative interchurch venture called the Lutheran Council in the United States of America (LCUSA), bringing together 95 percent of all Lutherans in the United States.

During 1960 and 1962, members of the National Lutheran Council had entered into mergers that reduced the number of member church bodies from eight to two, namely, The American Lutheran Church and the Lutheran Church in America. While this major movement was in process, Paul Empie, Executive Director of the NLC, sensed that the time might also be appropriate for broadening inter-Lutheran cooperation. He therefore proposed a conference of NLC member churches "to examine present cooperative activities in American Lutheranism and the possibility of the extension of such activities," and suggested that non-Council Lutherans be invited to participate as observers.[1]

Although they were in the midst of discussing their own proposed mergers, the member churches accepted the invitation and, after some hesitation, The Lutheran Church—Missouri Synod also agreed to take part in the discussion. During 1960 and 1961 three separate consultations were held. Enough consensus emerged among the church bodies to project a new cooperative agency to replace the National Lutheran Council and to include the LCMS. By 1964 a constitution was prepared and submitted to the churches. Between 1964 and 1966 it was formally approved by all three church bodies, and the Lutheran Council in the USA began operation on January 1, 1967.

According to its new constitution, LCUSA was to carry out its work through five distinct divisions, each of which would be governed by a committee of ten members. The LIS became the Department of Immigrant and Refugee Services (DIRS) in the LCUSA Division of Welfare Services. The Department, in turn, had its own

Standing Committee of six members on which the participating church bodies were equally represented. Committee members officially elected at the LCUSA Constituting Convention in Cleveland, Ohio, on November 16–18, 1966, were Richard Fenske and John Groettum of The American Lutheran Church; William Kohn and Adolf Meyer of the LCMS; and Henry Whiting and Albert H. Lueders of the Lutheran Church in America. The Committee elected Kohn chairman and Whiting secretary.[2]

The staff of the new Department of Immigrant and Refugee Services remained unchanged. Donald Anderson was reappointed to head the department. Ingrid Walter, Tatiana Trelin, and Ruth Dieck continued as assistants. Programs, too, remained essentially unchanged.

At its first official meeting in February 1967, the DIRS Standing Committee affirmed its cooperative relation with the Lutheran World Federation Department of World Service and with congregations and agencies in the United States. About 40 Lutheran social service agencies and pastors were designated as official contacts. Steps were taken to restudy the document on immigration policy previously adopted by LIS, with a view to recommending its official adoption by LCUSA.[3]

Operational reports submitted to the semiannual meetings of the Standing Committee, beginning in August 1967, indicated a declining caseload in the resettlement of refugees. The continued gradual reduction of the number of persons requesting these services reflected improved economic conditions in Europe. Moreover, the legislation of 1965 changed the pattern of U.S. immigration, placing major emphasis on family reunification. In 1968, for example, 74 percent of all immigration visas were issued to persons with close family relationships in the United States. In the same year, the LCUSA Department of Immigrant and Refugee Services resettled only 18 families in the United States, ten of whom were sponsored by local Lutheran congregations.[4]

Nevertheless, the new department continued to dispense a variety of services both to new refugees and immigrants and to those in the process of adjusting to their new homes in the United States. Many of these services involved "preprocessing" of refugees or potential immigrants overseas in cooperation with the LWF Department of World Service. Congregational sponsorships were arranged for a limited number of refugees. The DIRS reception service continued to welcome and assist arrivals at piers and airports. Other families were assisted with personal or legal postimmigration problems in the United States. Between 1967 and 1971 the DIRS ministered to the needs of about a thousand persons each year. It was also concerned over the continued improvement of immigration laws and the maintenance of nondiscriminatory government policies. For the first time the Department undertook a study of Mexican immigrants entering the United States illegally in search of employment.[5]

Climate of International Unrest

Although neither the U.S. government nor the voluntary agencies mounted any new programs of refugee resettlement during these years, two world events in 1967 and 1968 reminded them that a climate of crisis still persisted. In June 1967, the Six Day War erupted between Israel, Syria, Jordan, and Egypt, creating in its wake thousands of Arab refugees or potential refugees in Jerusalem, Gaza, and the West Bank. The DIRS declared its willingness to cooperate with other voluntary agencies to resettle up to 10,000 Arab refugees in the United States and to seek supporting congressional legislation. The director of DIRS discussed the proposal with the United States government and with other voluntary agencies between August 1967 and September 1968. He found little encouragement for the proposal, but also little evidence that Arabs were interested in moving out of occupied territories.[6]

In 1968 the Soviet army invaded Czechoslovakia and crushed the movement for democratic reform known as the "Prague Spring." Remembering the sudden emergency program that followed the Hungarian Revolution in 1956, DIRS anticipated a similar exodus of refugees from Czechoslovakia. But Czech asylum seekers found refuge instead in neighboring European countries. Some individual Czech citizens who were in the United States at the time of the Soviet occupation registered for resettlement with the National Catholic Welfare Conference or with an ethnically oriented organization, the American Fund for Czechoslovak Refugees.[7]

The Uganda Program

The next identifiable refugee program sponsored by the U.S. government dealt with expellees from the East African republic of Uganda. Following a military coup led by General Idi Amin in January 1971, ousting President Milton Obote, General Amin issued an order in August 1972 that all persons of Indian origin leave the country within ninety days.[8]

The order affected about 75,000 Asian Indians. Many Indians had come to Uganda in the 19th century while Uganda was a British protectorate. When the railroad system they had come to build was completed, many remained and others joined them; many became successful business people, professionals, and farmers. Most of them retained British passports, but after three or four generations of residence, many became citizens of their adopted country.[9]

Amin's expulsion decree made no distinctions between Ugandan and British citizens. All were ordered to leave. Those who held Commonwealth passports were legally able to take refuge in Britain or one of its dependencies. An estimated 12,000 Asian Ugandans, deprived of their citizenship, became stateless.

The United Kingdom appealed to the Intergovernmental Committee for European Migration (ICEM) to help with the resettlement of about 50,000 refugees in Britain or another Commonwealth nation. It also appealed to other countries for help in resettling those who were stateless. In a conversation with the British Home Secretary, President Nixon agreed to admit 2,000 stateless Ugandan refugees to the United States as parolees. Half of these were to be persons whose assets outside Uganda would assure that they would not become public charges. On the basis of a special consultation between the State Department and executives of resettlement agencies in the United States, the second thousand would be admitted under "blanket assurances" provided by seven accredited voluntary agencies. Each of the agencies agreed to accept a share of the refugees. The DIRS accepted a quota of 75 families.

The State Department undertook elaborate plans for the rapid movement of these stateless people. The U.S. consulate in Kampala, Uganda's capital city, selected the thousand refugees, gathered the necessary data, and arranged with ICEM for their transfer out of Uganda to some temporary intermediate point. The State Department paid their airfare on chartered flights to the United States. In a precedent-setting gesture, the U.S. government made a grant of $300 to the voluntary agencies for each person processed and resettled.[10]

From the standpoint of the voluntary agencies, and especially of the DIRS, the proposal to resettle Ugandans introduced still other unusual features. While the DIRS and its predecessors had never confined their efforts to serving only Lutherans, the majority of their clients had come from countries with large Lutheran populations. The Ugandans were divided between Moslems and Hindus, and represented cultures quite different from the European-based culture familiar to most American Lutheran congregations.

Because of the time pressure imposed by General Amin's deadline for evacuation, there was little time to prepare DIRS governing boards, staff, or field structure for the Ugandan venture. With the emergency approval of the Standing Committee, Donald Anderson implemented a program to settle the Ugandans in clusters, so the families could be mutually supportive. After consulting with a group of pastors and social welfare executives from selected areas of the country, he decided to concentrate efforts in designated areas in Iowa, Florida, Pennsylvania, Minnesota, and Texas. Through specially called area meetings, pastors and congregations were invited to offer sponsorships and to assist in welcoming the refugees. By November 8, two weeks after the first requests for sponsorships had been made, 261 congregations had made firm commitments for the resettlement of 1,300 persons. Orientation brochures were prepared for both sponsors and refugees. An advisory committee of East African Asians already living in the United States provided information on diet, skills, and education of the expellees.[11]

Each member of the five-person DIRS staff in New York was called upon for a variety of services. Staff members of other LCUSA units volunteered their services for special assignments, such as airport reception. Tatiana Trelin recalled coming to the office one morning in October and noting that her colleague, Ingrid Walter, was absent, asked where she was. Walter, she was told, had left for Europe because the refugees were about to arrive in a processing center in Rome.[12]

Most of the Ugandans were taken by ICEM first to Italy; others were placed in refugee camps in Austria, Belgium, Malta, and Spain.

Walter went to all these places, meeting people assigned to DIRS and advising them on the resettlement process. She visited camps in England and Wales, where wives and children who had British passports were given shelter until they could rejoin their stateless husbands and fathers who had been moved to the United States.[13]

The first group of 82 refugees to be resettled through DIRS arrived at Kennedy Airport in New York on November 2, 1972. Thirteen of these were en route to Harrisburg, Pennsylvania, where five Lutheran congregations in the area had agreed to find housing and jobs for them. This group included a family of eight, in which father and one son were electrical engineers and another son was a radio engineer. Among the others were an auto mechanic, a teacher, another engineer, and a 54-year-old shop owner who had left behind his radio repair business and personal possessions worth $50,000. He had operated his own firm for 35 years.[14]

These early arrivals in Harrisburg were the first of about 100 Ugandans eventually resettled by congregations in central Pennsylvania. Sister Betty Amstutz was a social worker on the staff of Tressler Services, a Lutheran social service agency in Pennsylvania that served as a bridge between the DIRS and congregations in securing sponsorships. She recalled the initial orientation meeting of 20 pastors, selected because she thought they "might be open to experimenting with something they didn't know anything about." At that meeting, nine pastors had responded positively. Their spirit was transmitted to their congregations, which eventually found jobs and housing for 100 Ugandans, including both Moslems and Hindus.[15]

Another cluster centered in Des Moines, Iowa. Arthur Marck, Executive Director of Lutheran Social Services of Iowa, had accepted Anderson's invitation to meet in New York with other area leaders to set up the cluster system. Eleven congregations in the Des Moines area responded with sponsorships. Eleven families, numbering 52 individuals, eventually were reunited with the help of these congregations, after being scattered around the globe in England, Pakistan, Canada, Egypt, India, and Malta, following their expulsion from Uganda. Seven of the families were Moslem, two were Hindu, and one family was Christian. Housing was supplied for each family; cupboards were fully stocked with groceries. Jobs were provided for the head of each household, and the children were enrolled in local schools.[16]

A plane on its way to Minnesota carried a nervous family of six—a widowed mother and her three grown sons, a daughter-in-law, and a two-week-old grandchild born in Italy. The mother had been reluctant to come to the United States because she had heard Vietnam rumors and feared for her three sons of military age. The oldest son had secured visas for the family at the American embassy in Kampala. "I will gladly die for the United States," he told his mother, "but not for General Amin."

As the plane landed in Minneapolis on a cold winter morning, the mother looked apprehensively out at the snow-covered airport and to her horror saw a large group of people carrying placards and moving toward the plane. "You see," she said to her son, "they have come to picket us already."

With trepidation the family deplaned and were suddenly greeted with a loud cheer. The crowds were members and friends of their sponsoring congregations. Their raised placards spelled out the refugee family's surname, and underneath in large letters, was the word, "WELCOME!"[17]

After the first group of Ugandans arrived in Minneapolis on November 21, similar receptions greeted refugees sponsored by Lutheran congregations in the Twin Cities area. Coordinated by Luthard Gjerde, Executive Secretary of Lutheran Social Service of Minnesota, and Morris Wee, a retired Lutheran pastor who volunteered his services, more than a dozen churches and colleges arranged apartments, jobs, and job interviews for more than 60 refugees. Einar Oberg, pastor of Gustavus Adolphus Lutheran Church, marveled at the response in his parish. "We collected bedroom furniture, pots and pans, and enough money for two months' rent," he said, "just by standing the ushers by the door on Sunday." Kenneth Born, a realtor and member of Mount Olivet Lutheran Church, arranged for Mohammed Ahmed and his family of nine to move into a home in St. Louis Park. Central Lutheran Church paid the rent for three months, and a member of the congregation agreed to pay up to $100 a month for utilities.[18]

Another pastor, Harlan Robbins, learning that Abu Ahmed Bachelani's wife spoke no English, found women who spoke Swahili to take her shopping. The pastor observed that this was an example of the extensive resources of a large church. When the DIRS office in New York requested that Twin City congregations sponsor 20 more families, Oberg announced it in church the same day. The head of the congregation's Committee on Social Ministry said it was the first time she did not have to ask anyone to help. She just answered the phone![19]

As the first phase of the Ugandan resettlement program neared completion in December 1972, the DIRS had assisted in the placement of 344 Ugandan Asians, almost 40 percent of the total allocated to voluntary agencies. This number included 155 parolees assigned to the DIRS by the State Department and an additional 189 persons comprising mainly large families, transferred by other agencies to DIRS while in refugee centers in Italy and upon arrival in New York. In addition to these placements, the DIRS had received "firm indications" from 354 additional congregations ready to help in the resettlement of up to 1770 persons.[20]

When the Attorney General of the United States authorized the admission of an additional 500 Ugandans from holding centers in Europe in April 1973, the DIRS was prepared to resettle its proportionate share. When the program was finally terminated, DIRS had placed a total of 600 Asian Ugandans.[21]

In a gesture of appreciation, the Ismailia Community of the United States, a Moslem association, arranged a special event honoring the leaders of LCUSA and the DIRS on December 16, 1972. Abdul S. Dewji, leader of the Community, gave eloquent expression of the thanks of his people. He acknowledged that assistance had been given to the refugees "without any strings attached or expecting anything in return." Quoting from a booklet on the life of Christ, Dewji continued, "On earth, in the time of Tiberius, He was the man who was hungering for bread and love, who was like a stranger in His own country, not recognized by His own brothers, who stripped Himself to clothe those shaking with cold, who was sick with sorrow and suffering, and no one comforted Him. He has gone on living under the appearance of the poor and the pilgrim, of the sick and persecuted, of wanderers and slaves. And on the last day He pays His debts. Mercy shown to those 'least' was shown to Him, and He will reward that mercy." This, said Dewji, represented the spirit in which the DIRS and its associated Lutheran congregations had served the Ismaili refugees.[22]

Testing the LCUSA Structure

As the Ugandan program concluded in early 1973, the Lutheran Council had just completed a review and revision of its internal structure. Since 1967, when the Council was formed, Immigrant and Refugee Services had been a department within the LCUSA Division of Welfare Services. According to the new format, a Division of Mission and Ministry (DMM) was formed, incorporating immigrant and refugee services and several other functional areas of the Council, such as institutional chaplaincies, clinical pastoral education, volunteer services, and the housing coalition. Harold Haas became the Executive Director of the new DMM.[23]

During 1973, following the LCUSA reorganization, a special subcommittee of the DIRS, headed by the newly elected chairman of the DIRS Standing Committee, Bernard Spong, conducted an extensive study of the role and function of the DIRS within the reorganized Council. It reported that in the new LCUSA structure there was no clear conduit from the DIRS to the Lutheran World Federation. DIRS programs, loan funds, and operating agreements were related to the Department of World Service in LWF. But in LCUSA the DIRS was placed in the Division for Mission and Ministry, which had only a tangential relation with the Lutheran World Federation.

In fact, since the LCMS was a member of LCUSA, but not a member of the Federation, there could be no direct organizational channel between LCUSA as such and the LWF. The LCA and the ALC related directly to the LWF as the USA National Committee of the Federation.

The subcommittee therefore suggested that the DIRS be transferred administratively to operate under a new Committee on World Service of the USA National Committee, and become known as "Lutheran Immigration and Refugee Service, an agency of the USA National Committee and The Lutheran Church—Missouri Synod." Anderson prepared a document embodying this proposal, which would have given the DIRS essentially the same relationship to the LCA and the ALC, former members of the National Lutheran Council, and to The Lutheran Church—Missouri Synod, that pertained before the formation of LCUSA.[24]

As discussions continued into 1974, a second option was offered by the Standing Committee that would allow the DIRS to remain within the structure of the Council. Anderson proposed that the DIRS become a specialized department, responsible to the LCUSA General Secretariat, until LCUSA should create a Division of World Service to coordinate DIRS programs with the corresponding department of the LWF.[25]

It seems probable that even during the Ugandan program Anderson sensed the potential problems posed by LCUSA's intricate organizational structure in administering complex resettlement programs. Such problems did not occur during the Uganda program, however, because it had been launched by the U.S. government with virtually no advance notice and little opportunity for internal consultation by the participating agencies. Under Anderson's personal direction the program was implemented by existing DIRS staff as an emergency program, and was nearly completed before the new administrative structure of LCUSA had become fully functional.

The introduction of direct federal funding of voluntary agencies involved in resettlement added to Anderson's concern about the future management of DIRS. He viewed the granting of financial support by the government as an important acknowledgment of a partnership between public and private agencies and as a major contribution of the Ugandan program toward the continuity of refugee assistance programs. He felt it gave official public recognition to the value of the resettlement work of congregations, churches, and related agencies. For the first time it was possible to foresee the kind of funding and cooperation between church and state that would assure sound programs to aid refugees. He was concerned that decisive action on future government programs would be inhibited by the LCUSA hierarchy of departmental, divisional, and agency committees.[26]

The climate within LCUSA, however, was not receptive to either of the proposals by Anderson and the DIRS Standing Committee. Both the new General Secretary of LCUSA, George Harkins, and the new Executive Director of the DMM, Harold Haas, felt the revised structure should be tested in actual operation before further changes were introduced. There would be ample opportunity in the ensuing months to test both staff and structure under the impact of the largest refugee influx of the century, from Southeast Asia.

8

Legacy of a Lost War

When the last helicopter lifted off from the U.S. Embassy roof in Saigon in South Vietnam on April 29, 1975, the official presence of the United States in Vietnam came to an end. For ten years, under four presidents, the United States had become more and more deeply involved in an ill-starred effort to hold back the advance of communism in Southeast Asia. More than 2,500,000 American troops had been committed. Fifty-eight thousand American lives had been sacrificed, and the American people had experienced years of divisive internal controversy over the most unpopular war in the nation's history.

Finally, in 1973, U.S. military forces were withdrawn, and the defense of South Vietnam left in the hands of its own army. By the spring of 1975 North Vietnamese forces were within striking distance of Saigon, and the collapse of the capital was imminent.

The Evacuation of Saigon

As the North Vietnamese army bombarded the city and prepared for the final assault, hundreds of thousands of South Vietnamese whom the U.S. government had promised to protect feared for their lives. Thousands swarmed over the Saigon airport, and on the last day hundreds scaled the walls of the U.S. Embassy to board the helicopters carrying American and Vietnamese personnel from the embassy rooftop to the safety of U.S. ships in the South China Sea.[1]

In spite of the deteriorating military situation of its allies in Southeast Asia in early 1975, the U.S. government had done little to prepare for the evacuation of Saigon, or of the Cambodian capital of Phnom Penh, which was also under siege. The Ford administration continued to press an unwilling Congress for supplemental military aid to shore up these crumbling pro-American governments. Even after the Cambodian capital fell on April 12, the U.S.

Embassy in Saigon took no preparatory action, fearing a public announcement of Vietnamese evacuation plans would cause the government of President Thieu to collapse. Only on April 17, when Saigon was surrounded by North Vietnamese troops, less than two weeks before the surrender, did President Ford finally appoint an Interagency Task Force to coordinate evacuation planning.

Time pressure and regional opposition to granting long-term asylum ruled out the initial plan to resettle Vietnamese refugees in neighboring Southeast Asian countries. Senior members of the Task Force solicited asylum offers from European nations, but, except for France, to no avail. International agencies such as the UNHCR and ICEM viewed the Indochina crisis as a U.S. problem, and the Vietnamese evacuees as U.S. allies rather than bona fide refugees. There seemed to be no other option except to employ the parole authority of the President and bring them to the United States.

The U.S. Opens Its Doors

On April 22, the Justice Department announced that at least 150,000 Indochinese would be admitted to the United States under special parole. Under White House orders, each branch of the U.S. Armed Forces—Army, Navy, and Air Force—was invited to "volunteer" an installation in the United States to serve as a temporary processing center. Ships were positioned offshore in the South China Sea and the Gulf of Thailand to receive evacuees. Civil and military authorities on Guam were instructed to prepare short-term hospitality for an estimated 50,000 refugees en route to the United States.

U.S. officials intended to give first preference to the 17,600 Vietnamese who were U.S. government employees. Such was the disorder in the final days, however, that many with less valid fears of possible reprisals managed to board departing planes. Between April 21 and 29, helicopters shuttled a steady stream of evacuees to U.S. ships, and American transport planes rolled off runways day and night at the rate of almost two each hour, bound for Clark Air Base in the Philippines. The United States provided the means for about 65,000 Vietnamese to leave the country by air and by boat.

Another 65,000 arranged their own transportation. Many had access to planes or ships. Vietnamese Air Force pilots loaded their planes with family and friends and flew to U.S. bases in Thailand. Vessels of the Vietnamese Navy evacuated crew members and their families and headed for Subic Bay in the Philippines. Others fled by sea in small boats, barges, and rafts, and were picked up by friendly ships. Still others fled overland, through Cambodia to Thailand.

Preparations by the U.S. government for the resettlement of Vietnamese were as inadequate as the plans for their evacuation— which was seen primarily as a rescue operation rather than a resettlement program. This probably explains why the voluntary agencies, with their long experience in resettling refugees, were not consulted by the Task Force as it made its plans.[2]

Enlisting the Voluntary Agencies

The first involvement of voluntary agencies with Indochinese refugees came in response to a request from the State Department to assist in resettling a group of Cambodians. When the communist Khmer Rouge captured the Cambodian capital of Phnom Penh on April 12, 1975, the U.S. ambassador arranged for the evacuation of the entire embassy staff, including 800 Cambodian employees, by helicopter to Bangkok, Thailand. When the Thai government, faced with a mass invasion of Cambodians fleeing the Khmer Rouge, refused to grant asylum, the U.S. government agreed to resettle these embassy employees and their families in the United States.

The State Department contacted the voluntary agencies to request their assistance in placing the refugees. Nine selected agencies, including LIRS,* were assigned lists of Cambodians to be resettled, and were advised that they would be arriving within a week or two. LIRS immediately began to mobilize its network of social service agencies and congregations to request sponsorships. It also assembled a committee of Southeast Asians in the United States to prepare orientation brochures for both sponsors and refugees.[3]

No Cambodians had yet arrived when LIRS suddenly heard news of the first Vietnamese evacuees. While working in the New York

---

* (LIRS was the same as DIRS. Since the designations were used interchangeably, LIRS, Lutheran Immigration and Refugee Service, will be used hereafter.)

office at 7 o'clock in the evening of April 28, Donald Anderson received a phone call from John Schauer, an officer of the American Council of Voluntary Agencies. Schauer had just received word from Washington that the first transports of Vietnamese refugees were arriving from Guam at Camp Pendleton in California, Schauer intended to leave immediately. Anderson turned to Ingrid Walter, who was with him in the office, and said, "You must go along!"

This was the introduction of LIRS to the program for resettling Vietnamese refugees in the United States, and it forecast the frantic pace at which the program would move during the coming months. The next morning Walter and Schauer boarded a plane for Los Angeles.[4] The LIRS Standing Committee was summoned to New York on two days' notice to give its blessing to LIRS participation and to request the Executive Committee of LCUSA to approve an emergency allocation of $50,000 from LIRS reserve funds.[5]

LIRS Emergency Response

Ingrid Walter and John Schauer arrived at Camp Pendleton, near San Clemente, 50 miles south of Los Angeles, two hours before the first transports landed. U.S. Marines were feverishly engaged in setting up tents, mess halls, and sanitary facilities for 20,000 refugees. The camp commander wasn't sure what the role of civilian resettlement officers might be, and several hours passed before their status was clarified and they were assigned tents for their offices. U.S. government staff representing President Ford's Special Task Force, personnel from the Immigration and Naturalization Service, the Department of Health, Education, and Welfare, and the American Red Cross were all arriving at the same time, trying to get settled.

Finding staff to conduct the registration and processing of the refugees was as important as locating facilities in which to work. The day after her arrival, Walter contacted Joel Schlachtenhaufen of LCUSA's World Brotherhood Exchange, who happened to be in California at that time. While Walter arranged for equipment and office facilities, Schlachtenhaufen canvassed Lutheran leaders and pastors in the area for volunteers. Within days, a working staff of 28 persons was assembled.[6]

Clarence Lund, pastor of Our Savior's Lutheran Church in San Clemente, visited the camp and was asked by an LIRS staff member to "stick around and get involved." Lund, his wife, and other members of their congregation became active volunteers.[7] Neil Brenden, a social worker from Berkeley who had worked in Vietnam in the sixties, extended a one-day visit to a weekend, then to a week, and finally resigned his job in Berkeley and joined the expanding LIRS central staff in New York.[8]

During the first weekend in May, Donald Anderson, Ruth Dieck, and Tatiana Trelin arrived; for the moment, the entire permanent LIRS staff from New York was present to plan strategy and activities. Ingrid Walter remained temporarily as LIRS camp director with Ruth Dieck as her associate. Trelin went on to represent LIRS at Camp Chaffee in Arkansas, the second of the four refugee camps to be established for Indochinese refugees. Donald Anderson returned to New York to meet with the Executive Committee of LCUSA and to brief them on the breathtaking developments of the week.[9]

As the government opened additional camps, the scenarios enacted at Camp Pendleton were repeated. Camp Chaffee, near Fort Smith, Arkansas, with a capacity of 24,000 refugees, opened on May 5. LIRS was represented by Tatiana Trelin of the New York staff; two days later, Robert Eledge, an LCMS pastor from Florida, arrived to direct LIRS operations, and Gertrude Sovik from St. Olaf College, a veteran refugee worker who had served with LWF in Austria in 1951, joined the team as chief interviewer. Volunteer interviewers, receptionists, and typists raised the staff total to 26.

A third tent city was set up in mid-May at Eglin Air Force Base in Florida, with accommodations for 5,000 refugees. Abner Batalden, a professor from Augsburg College in Minneapolis, directed LIRS operations there until he moved to Indiantown Gap in eastern Pennsylvania, where the government established its fourth refugee camp later in May to accommodate 15,000 persons. LIRS operations in both of these camps were also liberally supported with volunteer staff.[10]

In New York Anderson had immediately taken steps to reactivate the network of Lutheran congregations that had provided sponsorships for more than 50,000 refugees in resettlement programs since 1948. With thousands of refugees already pouring into the country, the conventional pattern of a carefully prepared appeal for sponsorships through church papers and congregational announcements was out of the question. Instead, Anderson turned directly to the presidents of the major Lutheran bodies: Robert Marshall of the Lutheran Church in America, David Preus of The American Lutheran Church, and J. A. O. Preus of The Lutheran Church—Missouri Synod. He proposed that a mailgram be sent to every Lutheran pastor, requesting that an emergency appeal be read from every Lutheran pulpit in the United States on Sunday, May 4. The presidents agreed. Congregations were reminded of the words of Jesus, commending the exercise of hospitality, "I was a stranger and you took me in," and were urged to sponsor an Indochinese refugee family.[11]

Anticipating a prompt and generous response, Anderson began immediately to assemble a volunteer staff to receive and record assurances of sponsorships from congregations. Drawing upon his ties with St. Olaf College, where he had served as alumni director before joining LIRS, he persuaded a number of students and faculty to contribute their summer vacations to handle telephones and correspondence for LIRS.

The LIRS staff was transformed within a few weeks from a director and three associates in New York to more than one hundred locally recruited field staff at the four resettlement centers and a central staff of more than 20 full-time workers. During the early summer the limited office space at 315 Park Avenue South was crowded beyond capacity with eager volunteers.[12]

Working at top speed, as the shape of the government's requests and expectations of the voluntary agencies emerged, Anderson drew up detailed organizational and procedural plans for LIRS. Several additional staff members, some from the New York area, were recruited to supervise major programmatic units: sponsorship procurement, camp operations, and social services. Each person was advised that these were emergency appointments, short-term in character, and subject to immediate change.

Sponsorship procurement was initially supervised by Ralph F. Baumbach, and subsequently by Arnold J. Athey, both pastors of The American Lutheran Church, whose congregations granted them temporary leaves of absence. Abner Batalden was in charge of Field Operations, administering LIRS personnel and programs at the four refugee camps. He came to New York after brief stints at Camp Chaffee in Arkansas, and Indiantown Gap, Pennsylvania. Neil Brenden moved to New York to head the unit on social services.

Associate Director Ingrid Walter was responsible for matters relating to national immigration policy and law; she also served as liaison with the U.S. Immigration and Naturalization Service. Karl Fritch maintained the financial records for LIRS.[13]

The Search for Sponsors

Sponsorship procurement was the major programmatic activity of the central office in New York. The U.S. government still required assurances that refugees would not become public charges, but the procedures used in the Vietnam program were greatly relaxed. In previous programs a sponsor had been required to present a lengthy affidavit of support before an agency could begin to process a refugee's request for a visa. Under new regulations the INS simply accepted a two-line affirmation by a voluntary agency: "The above-named refugees are approved to be moved for resettlement to (a specified destination) under the auspices of the Lutheran Immigration and Refugee Service, LCUSA." On such assurance the INS formally released the refugee family from the camp and provided them with transportation to their destination. LIRS was required to submit a 45-day report confirming that the sponsorship had been fulfilled. Additional quarterly reports were expected throughout the balance of the year.[14]

On May 22 Congress approved the Indochina Migration and Refugee Assistance Act, authorizing a massive federal role in refugee reception and resettlement for a period of two years. Following a precedent established during the Uganda program, the government authorized a $500 grant to voluntary agencies to cover processing costs for each refugee resettled. No conditions were attached to the use of these funds, except that they were to be expended within the program for which they were granted, and that the government would conduct periodic audits.

To affirm the principle that refugee resettlement was an international concern and not a narrowly construed national responsibility, LIRS insisted that its contract with the U.S. government be signed by the Lutheran World Federation, Department of World Service, in Geneva. Authorizations for payment were approved by the U.S. Mission in Geneva on the basis of certified lists of resettled refugees provided by LIRS. Payments were made by the U.S. government directly to LIRS in New York. The contract signed on May

31, 1975, authorized an eventual total payment of $5,150,000 to LIRS.[15]

As these financial resources became available, LIRS established a separate resettlement account from which salaries for both field staff and the expanded central office staff could be paid. Desirable as this development was, the necessity of setting salary levels and employment conditions for erstwhile volunteers and emergency appointees created some internal problems of morale and tended to dim the spontaneity that had characterized the volunteer program.

It also created administrative problems within the Lutheran Council, since the size of the grant placed at the disposal of a subunit of the Council was several times larger than the annual budget of the entire Council. Moreover, the rapid growth of the LIRS staff created a physical imbalance that not only imposed on the limited office space in the LCUSA headquarters, but seemed to some to minimize the role of other programs in the Council.[16]

The Sponsorship Procurement Unit, headed by Baumbach in New York, worked closely with 37 state coordinators, usually parish pastors or Lutheran social service agency staff, who served as field representatives for LIRS. It was their task to organize and promote the program of sponsorship procurement in their state. They divided their territories into subareas, headed by area coordinators who, in turn, promoted sponsorships through "clusters" of congregations and pastors. Since LIRS viewed the resettlement program as a ministry of the church, it sought to develop sponsorships by congregations rather than by individuals. When responding to offers from individuals, LIRS referred them to the nearest Lutheran pastor for verification. This was done both to protect the refugee and because LIRS would eventually be required by the U.S. government to report on the fulfillment of the sponsorship.

State coordinators channeled instructions and information from LIRS to their local networks and supplied the public media with news items and feature stories prepared by the LCUSA communications office in New York. They distributed brochures explaining the process of sponsorship, describing the cultural background and characteristics of the Vietnamese and Cambodian people, and offering suggestions for welcoming refugee families.

LIRS established an initial national goal of 2,400 sponsorships and assigned to each state or area a proportionate quota. Arthur

Marck, state coordinator for Iowa, reported the appointment of ten area coordinators throughout his state, each working with several local clusters of congregations. Richard Rhyne, coordinator for North Carolina, held meetings with 210 pastors in a single week. Luthard Gjerde reported that some congregations in Minnesota were forming joint sponsorships. He anticipated resettling 80 families in the Twin Cities area alone.[17]

The task of placing Vietnamese and Cambodian families was not an easy one. Public sentiment, never enthusiastic toward the admission of more foreigners to the country, associated the Vietnamese and Cambodians with a war most Americans were eager to forget. A Gallup poll indicated that 54 percent of the American public was opposed to receiving any refugees. Moreover, the Asian refugees represented a culture and spoke a language quite different from those familiar to the majority of U.S. citizens.

In mid-1975 the country was experiencing an economic recession. High unemployment figures for many areas underscored the traditional fear that the new immigrants might take away jobs from Americans.[18] Carl Thomas, director of Lutheran Social Services of Michigan, reported 15 percent unemployment in his state. James Smith, Lutheran Social Services of Central Ohio, recalled that in the early stages of the program he developed a "red book" containing 12 pages of the kind of excuses he heard from congregations, explaining why they could not sponsor a refugee family.[19]

In spite of these hazards, the Lutheran congregations of the country responded to the appeal to welcome strangers into their communities and to assist them in beginning a new life. By September 1975, sponsorship agreements for 2,126 families, 88 percent of the initial goal, had been secured.[20]

Working the Camps

The Director of Field Operations, Abner Batalden, supervised the unit that lay closest to the heart of the program. It was in the camps themselves that LIRS met the people for whom the resettlement effort was being conducted. From the first introduction and interview in the quonset or trailer that served as the LIRS office to the farewell at the bus depot or airport, staff workers knew that they were involved in a life-changing drama.

Each of the camps was headed by a director hired by LIRS in New York, who supervised staff personnel in two subunits. The Dossier and Orientation subunit interviewed the refugee families, prepared a family profile containing the necessary information for "matching" or placement with a sponsoring congregation. Members of this subunit interpreted the LIRS program to the family through orientation sessions with the help of a brochure prepared in the Vietnamese or Cambodian language. The subunit included a supervisor who approved each family registered for the LIRS program, receptionists, interviewers, and typists who completed the necessary documents. All the camps made liberal use of volunteers from among the refugees themselves, many of whom were fluent in English and able to serve as receptionists and interpreters.

The other important subunit in the camp team was the Transportation and Movement Coordination group. When the documentation of a family was completed and matched with an assured congregational or individual sponsorship, the refugee family received official clearance from the U.S. Immigration and Naturalization Service in the camp and tickets for transportation to their destination. The LIRS Transportation subunit was responsible for coordinating departure and arrival dates with the pastor of the sponsoring congregation and the LIRS state coordinator and accompanying the family to the airport or other point of departure. Each person was sent on his or her way with an LIRS button pinned to shirt or coat for easy identification en route and upon arrival.[21]

The same organizational pattern was used by LIRS at each of the four camps, but the size of the staff varied with the size of the camp. Beginning with Camp Pendleton in California, which opened first, on April 29, the other camps opened during the month of May. Pendleton closed on November 1. Indiantown Gap in Pennsylvania, the last to open and also the last to close, shut its doors in late December. Over a period of six months, more than 130,000 Vietnamese and Cambodian refugees were processed and placed with sponsors throughout the country. LIRS processed 3,937 family units and 851 individuals, or a total of 15,897 persons. More than 4,000 Lutheran congregations provided sponsorships.[22]

The refugees who entered the United States under this program came from predominantly urban areas in Vietnam and Cambodia; they were well-educated and from relatively favorable economic circumstances. A survey of 10,000 heads of households, based on a sample of 53,000 records, indicated that 31 percent had been engaged in professional, technical, or managerial activities. Many of these persons had been employed by the U.S. or Vietnamese government or military. Twenty-five percent had held clerical, sales, or service positions. Only ten percent had been engaged in farming or fishing, and five percent in trades and construction. Knowledge of English was common among heads of families, but less so among dependents.

Meet the Refugees

The Tho and Nguyen families from Saigon were the first two families processed by LIRS at Camp Pendleton in May, 1975. Ton Phat Tho had practiced dentistry in the Vietnamese military for 17 years. Hiep Tri Nguyen had been a member of the military police. Together with their pregnant wives and small children, they fled Saigon by helicopter the day the capital fell, and were transferred at sea to a U.S. naval vessel that brought them to Guam. Upon arrival at Camp Pendleton both families were sponsored by Grace Lutheran Church in Winter Haven, Florida, served by August Bernthal. A large contingent of the congregation welcomed the families at the airport and assisted them in settling into homes arranged by the congregation. The former military policeman began work as assistant jailer at the city jail but later established his own business in Winter Haven. Ton Phat Tho was employed at Cypress Gardens as a painter. He and his family later moved to California where, with the partial assistance of an LIRS loan, he entered dental school. Dr. Tho now has a large practice in San Jose, California.[23]

During the summer of 1975 Samuel and Marilyn Michaelson, a faculty couple from Wartburg College in Waverly, Iowa, served as LIRS volunteers at Indiantown Gap, Pennsylvania. When they discovered that it was especially difficult to secure sponsors for young single men, Michaelson called Wartburg College and asked the admissions office if the college would be willing to sponsor six young men as students. The college agreed, and the six young men became the first Indochinese refugees to be accepted by an American college. With the assistance of special courses in written and spoken English, taught by Michaelson himself and tutored by other Wartburg students, all six graduated, one magna cum laude and two cum laude. All went on to good jobs in engineering, teaching, and other fields. Since then Wartburg College has sponsored more than sixty refugees, mostly Vietnamese.[24]

David Kim was an airplane mechanic for the South Vietnamese Air Force. He and his wife Mai and their small daughter fled Saigon in a tugboat on April 30, 1975, two hours before the city fell. They were taken on board a commercial ship with 4,500 other refugees. They first reached Singapore, then the Philippines, and finally Guam, where their second daughter was born. At Camp Pendleton the Kims were matched with an LIRS sponsorship from Peace Lutheran Church in Tifton, Georgia. Eighteen months later they moved to Vienna, Virginia, near Washington, D.C., where Kim got a job as a janitor at the *Washington Post.* Employed by Xerox Corporation in 1978, he was subsequently advanced to Senior Customer Service Representative.[25]

Cheng Heng, former president of the Cambodian National Assembly and member of the three-man Supreme State Council under Lon Nol in 1973–74, was in Paris seeking to negotiate peace when Cambodian resistance to the Khmer Rouge collapsed on April 12, 1975. Twelve members of his extended family fled Cambodia with only their personal baggage and joined Cheng in Paris. In cooperation with the Lutheran World Federation in Geneva, LIRS brought the entire family to Brookfield, Wisconsin, where they were supplied temporary housing with four families of Calvary Lutheran Church. Cheng, who described himself as an administrator, was offered a management position in a Milwaukee manufacturing plant.[26]

James Smith, a Lutheran Social Services staff member in Columbus, Ohio, told the story of the Kong family with six children, who arrived in Columbus in 1975. One 24-year-old son had studied for one year in a Saigon college before 1975. Over a period of eight years, all six children graduated from Ohio State University. Two boys who had entered with virtually no knowledge of English graduated with averages of 3.9 and 4.0, respectively. One of the boys became a medical doctor; one a computer expert with IBM in France; two boys were employed by the U.S. government as accountants. While the Kongs were a very unusual family, Smith also reported that in the Columbus school system at least three of the 14 or 15 high schools had refugees as valedictorians.[27]

The Need for Social Services

For most of these persons the major problems were not physical deprivation, disease, or starvation, so often associated with refugees. All of them, and especially families with children, had suffered the psychological shock of being suddenly uprooted, torn away from home, jobs, friends, and community. Some had been forced to leave members of their family behind. All were subjected to the often demeaning experience of camp life, loss of privacy in sharing a tent with twenty other people, and the uncertainties and fears about the places and people who would sponsor them. Above all, there were apprehensions about life in a strange land with strange customs and a strange language. Such assaults on the human spirit could often be as debilitating as physical hunger or illness.

It was to meet and help to heal such spiritual wounds and to offer a helping hand to these uprooted families that the LIRS system of congregational sponsorship was designed. The chairman of the LIRS Standing Committee, August Bernthal, described sponsorship as "a response to the ministry our Lord gave. It afforded opportunity for the most thorough method of resettlement—to sponsor a family with dozens, sometimes hundreds of individuals in a congregation behind the sponsorship. It makes the essential tasks of community orientation, finding housing and jobs, and offering training in English, not only the responsibility but the privilege of many people."[28]

To support such congregational efforts Donald Anderson established a special unit in the New York office. The need for such supporting services was first suggested by calls from congregations experiencing crosscultural adjustment problems in dealing with Vietnamese and Cambodian families. Neil Brenden, who had had experience as a social worker in Vietnam, was able to recruit a Vietnamese refugee, Nguyen Van Ninh, formerly the program director of the Vietnam Christian Service in Saigon, and a Cambodian, Hav Benheang, who had been a member of his country's delegation to the United Nations. Both these men were able to perform valuable services as "troubleshooters" for congregations and refugees.[29]

Further evidence of the need for such advice and counsel appeared when the 45-day reports required by the United States government began to come in from the sponsoring congregations. Most reports reflected encouraging progress in the adjustment of refugees to a totally new life style and culture. Certain common problems, however, were apparent. While most heads of families were employed, many expressed frustration because their jobs were not commensurate with their skills and education. Language proficiency was seen as the most significant barrier to advancement. Feelings of loneliness and apprehension about the future were common, especially among the women.[30]

During its monthly meetings in the summer of 1975 the Standing Committee of LIRS discussed the possible role of Lutheran social service agencies in assisting special problem cases. Betty Amstutz, a Lutheran deaconess and social worker, and herself a member of the Standing Committee, encouraged a closer relationship between the social service agencies and LIRS. Without usurping the role of congregations and pastors, she reminded her colleagues on the committee, the professional skills of social workers in counseling and family services and referrals to health care facilities would be an important supplementary resource. Moreover, the Lutheran social service agencies also regarded their work as an integral ministry of the church.[31]

Although these agencies had worked closely with LIRS in previous resettlement programs, especially in developing sponsorships, the LIRS director and several members of the Standing Committee expressed strong reservations concerning an expanded role for the agencies. They feared that the concept of refugee resettlement as a ministry of the church, centered in its congregations, might be subordinated to what they saw as a more secular social service orientation.[32]

The issue was further complicated by the internal structure of LCUSA. Strong support for an expanded role for social service agencies came from the Division of Mission and Ministry, which coordinated the work of Lutheran social service agencies for LCUSA. At the same time, it exercised administrative oversight of LIRS, as a department within the Division of Mission and Ministry. Consequently, support for an expanded role for social service agencies was added to the already existing administrative tensions over the scope of responsibility in decision making and staffing in LIRS and the management of the government resettlement grants.[33]

Under the overwhelming pressure of the Indochina program itself, members of the Standing Committee of the Division of Mission and Ministry and the officers and Executive Committee of LCUSA also felt it necessary to seek ways in which responsibilities concentrated in the central office of LIRS could be more broadly shared. The organization and implementation of an emergency program that resettled nearly 16,000 refugees in eight months was little short of a miracle, but the tensions over control of the operation weighed heavily on the physical stamina and the morale of staff.

The report of an outside consultant confirmed the seriousness of the situation, but laid much of the responsibility on the clumsy and inflexible structure of LCUSA, which tended to encourage conflict rather than facilitate action. Major policy decisions concerning the handling and use of government funds and other decisions affecting program and personnel had to be cleared through three levels of committees: the Standing Committee of LIRS, the Standing Committee of the Division of Mission and Ministry, and finally, the Executive Committee of LCUSA itself. Staffing and fiscal procedures of the Council, geared to more leisurely time schedules, were not prepared to handle the explosive expansion of LIRS staff and program. The frequent emergency decisions demanded by the refugee operation produced growing tensions, especially between the director of LIRS and his administrative superiors.[34]

Matters came to a head in September 1975, when Anderson presented an elaborate chart of organization encompassing both central and field operations for LIRS to the Standing Committee and asked for immediate confirmation of both structure and personnel. Alarmed by the implications of such a sweeping decision, the Committee moved to postpone action pending the appointment of an ad hoc committee on Finance and Personnel Policies to review the organizational structure, position descriptions, financial procedures, and working budgets.[35]

In making the decision to establish the ad hoc committee, the Standing Committee took note that while LIRS had already resettled nearly 15,000 persons, several thousand refugees were still waiting in camps to be placed before the end of the year. The program was not over, and the administrative tensions were continuing to drain the energy and morale of the staff. In order to bring the program to a successful conclusion, the Committee concluded that LIRS personnel policies and accounting procedures would have to be more closely coordinated within the administrative structures of the Lutheran Council.

Donald Anderson's knowledge and expertise in immigration and refugee affairs were highly respected both in professional and government circles and within the Council. His commitment to the church and his understanding of congregational sponsorship of refugees as a vital spiritual ministry was beyond reproach. His driven style of management, however, coupled with an exhausting, self-imposed work schedule undermined his physical health. Shortly after the September meetings, he suffered a physical collapse and was forced to take an extended leave of absence, and eventually to relinquish the directorship of LIRS.

1. Cordelia Cox, Director, Lutheran Resettlement Service, 1948-57; Paul C. Empie, Executive Director, National Lutheran Council, 1948-66; Clarence E. Krumbholz, founder and first director, Lutheran Refugee Service, 1939-47.

2. Walter E. Freed, pastor of St. Paul's Lutheran Church, Wilmington, NC, conducts service of Holy Communion on board ship, August 19, 1948, for 15 Estonian refugees who crossed the Atlantic in a 37-foot sloop.

3. Henry Kleckley, pastor of the Lutheran Church of the Redeemer, Macon, GA, with Latvian and German refugees who joined this church after resettlement.

4. Edgar Witte, Lutheran Charities of Chicago, and George Schoberg, professor, Concordia College, Moorehead, MN, members of an LRS "dossier team", interview candidate for resettlement, Stuttgart, Germany, October 1955.

5. Group of German refugees leaving Munich for resettlement in the U.S., 1955.

6. Ingrid Walter (left) and Tatiana Trelin (right), Estonian refugees, joined the LRS staff in 1950 and 1954, respectively. Walter served as Director of LIRS, 1977-85.

7. Eleven-year old Andrejs Suritis (center) arrives from Latvia to rejoin two brothers, Janis, 9, (left) and Dainis, 7, (right) in Kalamazoo, MI, May 1960.

8. Donald Anderson, Director, LIRS, 1967-75, (center), and his wife, welcome a 3-generational family of Ugandan refugees in November 1972.

9. Southeast Asian boy learning English in a special class in Grace Lutheran Church, Winter Haven, FL.

10. Members of LIRS Standing Committee and LCUSA staff, 1976; l. to r. (standing): Adolf Meyer, Gustav Bernthal, Walter Jensen, Harold Haas, Donald Larsen, Merill Herder; l. to r. (seated): Ruth Haas, Betty Amstutz, Margaret Horst, George Harkins.

11. Vietnamese farmer, Lam Tuan Duc, and family, welcomed by Le Thi Tu, social worker and translator with LSS of Minnesota, January, 1980.

12. David Kim and family escaped from Saigon 2 hours before the fall of the city, April 30, 1975.

13. Kao Lor, 100,000th refugee resettled by LIRS since World War II, with family and tutor. He was sponsored by the Refugee Task Force, Augustana College, Sioux Falls, SD.

14. Refugees lined up for processing in Southeast Asian refugee camp.

15. Kurdish family, among more than 100 Iraqi refugees resettled by LIRS, mainly in North Dakota, 1976.

16. Carol Smalley, LIRS Specialist in English as a Second Language, leading a teacher training class, 1980.

17. A young Amerasian father and his child prepare to leave Vietnam for U.S. resettlement. LIRS has placed more than 7,742 Amerasians and their family members into the U.S.

18. "Boat people", Southeast Asian refugees who escaped from their homelands in small boats, often without fixed destinations.

19. Haitian refugees held in detention centers in Florida, awaiting hearings before immigration courts.

20. Vietnamese family featured in LIRS film, "Room for a Stranger," celebrating achievement of two sons who have become Eagle Scouts.

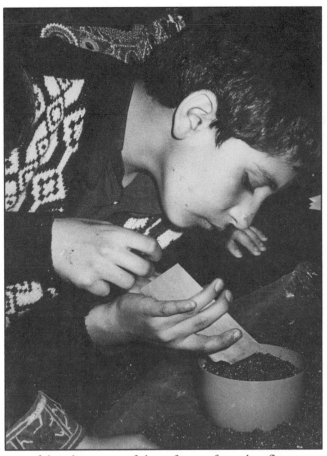

21. Afghan boy, one of the refugees forced to flee to Pakistan during Soviet occupation and civil war in Afghanistan during the 1980s.

22. The Tran family, reunited in the U.S. in 1986, after two sons escaped from Vietnam in a fishing boat in 1979.

23. Hmong refugees from Laos, planting tomatoes on a Farmers' Cooperative in Minnesota.

24. Montagnards from Southeast Asia being welcomed by Grace Lutheran Church, Raleigh, NC, in 1986. LIRS was selected by the U.S. State Department as the sole voluntary agency to resettle 220 Montagnards into North Carolina.

25. Russian Pentecostal pastor, Adam Bondurak, and his family welcomed by Richard Miesel, pastor of the Lutheran Church of Our Savior, South Hadley, MA.

26. Executive Director Donald Larson unveils banner commemorating the 50th Anniversary of LIRS in Washington, D.C., Nov. 1989.

Support for New Arrivals

The major concern facing Ingrid Walter, who was asked to serve as Acting Director of LIRS during Donald Anderson's leave of absence, was to develop plans for the follow-up phases of the Indochina program. Anderson had proposed a plan in early September to establish an LIRS presence at approximately ten locations thoughout the United States, mostly in selected LSS offices. By mutual agreements LIRS staff would be placed in these Lutheran social service offices as special consultants to congregations, agencies and sponsors for refugee concerns. They would be directly responsible to LIRS through a new office for Resettlement Services and Congregational Relationships.[1]

His plan, however, was set aside in favor of a program developed by Neil Brenden, in which Lutheran social service agencies played a more prominent role. According to this plan, the Standing Committee of LIRS designated 23 Lutheran social service agencies, regionally distributed throughout the United States, to assist Lutheran congregations and sponsors in the process of integrating Indochinese refugees into their communities.[2]

Indochina, Phase II

The goal of this second phase of the Indochinese program was the attainment of self-sufficiency by Indochina refugees through a partnership between congregations, agencies, and LIRS. The congregation would continue to be the first resource, but when additional expertise or information was needed, Lutheran social service agencies would provide added support. If its resources were not adequate, the Lutheran social service agency would contact LIRS in New York. Expert personnel services were to be backed by a supplementary program of grants and loans drawn from the resettlement funds.

During the placement of Indochina refugees, it had been LIRS policy that any part of the $500 per capita grant from the U.S. government not expended for the actual processing of refugees was to be segregated in a special "Resettlement Fund" and used in support of refugees' integration into their new communities or for emergency situations. While some other voluntary agencies had made cash payments of $200–300 directly to individual refugees, LIRS had simply provided $10 in pocket money for use in travel from camp to destination. The balance, after processing costs had been paid, was deposited in the Resettlement Fund for follow-up services to refugees.[3]

Under the Phase II resettlement plan, beginning January 1, 1976, a budget of $1.5 million from the Resettlement Fund was allocated to 23 regions, based on proposals they submitted to LIRS. In addition to basic service allocations to the agencies, congregations and individual sponsors were encouraged to submit project requests for job training, scholarships, language programs, cultural activities, congregational and community programs, or emergency situations. Regional consultants and other Lutheran social service professional staff advised pastors and sponsors in preparing requests.[4]

An educational project called "New Life" was developed by LIRS to introduce Christianity to Vietnamese resettling in the United States. About 75 percent of the refugees settled by LIRS were Buddhists, 10 percent Roman Catholics, and five percent Protestants. The intent of the project was informative, promoting discussion and understanding of basic Christian beliefs.

The 45-day reports from refugees indicated a strong desire for personal contacts, and expressed gratitude for community-sponsored events bringing them together with other Indochinese. Many of these events took place in the context of congregations, and questions concerning the church and the faith of hosts and sponsors arose quite naturally. For this reason a bilingual informational booklet was produced, organized for eight weekly discussion sessions. As a result, many Vietnamese families accepted the Christian faith and became members of their sponsoring congregations.[5]

Learning the Language

Among the new programs emerging from the federally funded Vietnam resettlement program was the ESL (English as a Second

Language) Project. Almost every refugee could testify that fluency in communication was the most crucial tool for a successful transition into American society. LIRS in New York began its program of social services by employing Vietnamese and Laotian staff members to assist and answer questions from distressed newcomers in their own languages when they phoned or came to the office. Most of their problems were related to failures in communication.

Classes in English were offered by volunteer teachers in many congregations that sponsored refugees, but they frequently needed advice and professional assistance in setting up such programs. At the suggestion of Betty Amstutz, LIRS staff submitted a proposal to the U.S. Department of Health, Education, and Welfare.[6] Under the terms of a contract with HEW, LIRS was able to engage an ESL Specialist, Ann Lomperis. During her first year, Lomperis handled telephone inquiries and correspondence in the New York office, organized local and regional language teaching programs, and advised teachers and congregations. She also developed a handbook called *Learning English: An Introductory Guide for Sponsors of Indochinese Refugees.*

LIRS regional consultants in Nebraska and South Dakota requested her services and scheduled meetings for her to encourage ESL training programs. She conducted training workshops for sponsors volunteering as ESL teachers and met with adult education and community college administrators, advising them on the availability of U.S. government funding opportunities. In South Dakota, LIRS regional consultant Ellen Erickson arranged ESL workshops with refugee committees of congregations in Sioux Falls and Brookings.[7]

In 1979 a second ESL specialist joined the LIRS staff in New York, eventually replacing Anne Lomperis. Carol Smalley, the daughter of missionaries, had spent her early years in Southeast Asia. With a master's degree in sociolinguistics, she had taught in the Tokyo Women's Christian University and in adult education programs in the U.S.[8]

In addition to local casework with sponsors and others, Smalley directed workshops and institutes for LIRS in several states. In New York she conducted a summer institute for Cambodians living in the Bronx, where three separate classes met twice each week. At Brooklyn College she advised fifteen students who were tutoring 75 Cambodians and five Ethiopians.

At Luther College in Decorah, Iowa, she conducted a four-day workshop as part of a winter interim course for students preparing to train other students and community volunteers to teach English to Vietnamese refugees. Luther College submitted a proposal to the Exxon Foundation to fund tutoring services for 15 Indochinese students to be admitted to the college each year for four years. LIRS contributed $5000 for student aid. The college also sponsored a summer conference bringing together representatives of other colleges, universities, and vocational schools from a five-state area to share program and curricular ideas.[9]

In 1980 LIRS was invited to join with the American Council for Nationalities Service (ACNS) in a major overseas English language training program in Southeast Asia. Sponsored by the United Nations High Commissioner for Refugees (UNHCR) and financed by the U.S. State Department, the program was conducted in refugee camps and holding centers in Thailand, Hong Kong, Indonesia, and the Philippines. LIRS agreed to participate in the Hong Kong project, and Carol Smalley helped to write the program and engaged staff for the joint operation.[10]

About 1,800 refugees, mostly Vietnamese, registered in the Hong Kong camp for a 12-week course, with 600 starting each month. Together with English language instruction, teachers explained American cultural concepts and practices in Vietnamese. Only one member of a family, the one likely to be the chief breadwinner, was assured a place in the school. As Franklin Jensen, Associate Director of LIRS, observed after visiting the camp, "So enthusiastic and diligent are the students that of the 1,800 studying during a single month, only eight had any absences at all."[11]

Saving and Serving the Children

Another special program that emerged from the Vietnamese refugee migration was the care and placement of unaccompanied minor children. The need for such a program first came to light when a large group of children was identified by LIRS at Camp Chaffee during the height of the resettlement effort in 1975. At that time LCUSA was able to arrange a contract with the Department of Health, Education and Welfare through which Lutheran social service agencies placed the children in foster homes.[12] With the encouragement of Betty Amstutz and Neil Brenden, LIRS developed a network of Lutheran social service agencies willing to assist in placing unaccompanied minors who continued to appear in the stream of incoming refugees. These agencies contracted with state governments to receive reimbursement for their services, both for placement and for subsequent supervision by agency caseworkers. States, in turn, were reimbursed by the federal government under refugee legislation. The agencies in cooperation with LIRS in New York selected the foster homes. LIRS was reimbursed for national staff costs by the U.S. Office of Refugee Resettlement.[13]

Marta Brenden, who became director for social services for LIRS in 1976, developed the agency's program for refugee children into one of the most influential foster care programs in the country. LIRS and the United States Catholic Conference (USCC) were the only two voluntary agencies authorized to conduct programs for the placement of unaccompanied minors.

Under Brenden's direction LIRS developed a network of 24 Lutheran social service agencies licensed to provide child placement. By 1988, with the cooperation of these agencies, LIRS had provided foster homes for more than 4,000 children, most of them teenagers separated from their families.[14]

Brenden was active in the professional field of child welfare as a leader and contributor to conferences both on the national and international levels. She visited Thailand in 1982 to facilitate the processing of unaccompanied Cambodian children as admissible refugees. In that same year she played a significant role in the shaping of congressional legislation to admit Amerasian children—fathered by American GIs, born to Asian mothers—from Vietnam, Thailand, and Korea. Amerasian children in Vietnam were able to emigrate with their families under the U.S. government's Orderly Departure Program.[15]

In December 1987, Congress passed the Amerasian Homecoming Act, allowing for the admission of as many as 10,000 children and accompanying family members during a two-year period. Under this legislation, because their fathers were Americans, the children were admitted as immigrants, rather than as refugees, but were nevertheless accorded the social benefits and services otherwise reserved for refugees.

These young people had suffered discrimination and injustice in Vietnam because they were considered Americans. In America, the country of their fathers, they also faced identity problems and rejections. As one 19-year-old resettled Amerasian said, "In Vietnam they called me an American, and here they don't know who I am."[16]

LIRS made careful plans for resettling its share of Amerasians. After selecting prospective sites in Utica, New York; Philadelphia; Washington, D.C.; Greensboro, North Carolina; and Portland, Oregon, LIRS arranged a conference in Utica. Utica was chosen because the LIRS affiliate, the Mohawk Valley Resource Center for Refugees, had resettled 360 Amerasians since 1983, more than any other site in the United States. The LIRS conference brought together 40 LIRS staff from seven affiliates for a three-day meeting in August 1988. The Vietnam Veterans of America sent one of its officers to the conference as a participant and adviser. Topics discussed included developing church sponsors for Amerasians, employment strategies, and special adjustment problems. During the two-year life of the Homecoming Act, LIRS was able to place several hundred Amerasian youth.[17]

Over the course of 15 years, the LIRS children's program was able to reunite many families, long separated by the accidents and misfortunes of refugee life. Phat and Loi Tran, aged 15 and 13, recalled how their father, a small grocery store owner in Saigon, had saved his money for four years to buy places on a fishing boat for them to escape in 1979. Two of their older brothers had been sent out similarly the previous month and had drowned when their boat was lost on the high seas. Phat and Loi were more fortunate. Although they were robbed of all their valuables by pirates, the boatload of 74 young men with whom they escaped finally reached the Pula Besar refugee camp in Malaysia.

There they were put in touch with the LIRS program for unaccompanied minors and eventually landed in Denver, Colorado, together with seven other Vietnamese boys. Phat and Loi were placed in the home of Ronald and Joanne Gadde and their two teenage children in Arvada, Colorado. Ronald Gadde was pastor of St. Andrew's Lutheran Church, and Joanne was employed in the resettlement office of Lutheran Social Services of Colorado.

Adjustments for the boys were not easy, but both entered school, learned English, and looked forward to the day they might bring their parents to America. Seven years later, in 1986, the day came.

Through the Orderly Departure Program, a special arrangement between the United States and the Vietnam government for facilitating family reunifications, the Tran family arrived. The parents, Nhan and Lao Tran, 55 and 49 respectively, two sisters, Nguyet, 19, and Thu, 17, and younger brother Tai, 14, were welcomed by their older sons, both fully employed, self-supporting, and grateful for a reunited family and a life of freedom.

One of the most active agencies in this network was Lutheran Social Services of Minnesota. Its program for unaccompanied minors began in 1979. Gno Pham, a Vietnamese refugee, joined the LSS staff as a social worker in 1981 and in 1985 became director of the program. Gno Pham had first come to the United States as a student in the 1950s, but returned to Vietnam after graduating from St. Catherine's College in St. Paul, Minnesota, and earning a master's degree in social work from Loyola University. She married, reared a family of five children, and worked for the Vietnamese government for 20 years. When Vietnam collapsed in 1975, she was sent to a concentration camp as a collaborator. After her release three months later, she and her family escaped by boat to a Malaysian refugee camp. From there she contacted a classmate in St. Paul, and under the sponsorship of the Alumni Association of St. Catherine's College, she and her family came to the United States in 1979.

Within a period of five years as program director, Gno Pham supervised the placement of over 500 young people, about 25 percent in Vietnamese homes. As the refugee families became more settled in their new environment, such offers became more frequent. One Vietnamese family explained, "If the American people can care for our Vietnamese minors, why shouldn't we do the same? We are also refugees. We know them; we speak their language. Isn't it better for them to be with us so they have some link to the Vietnamese community?"[18]

In 1987 the Lutheran International Children Service (LICS) was established as an outgrowth of the children's program of LIRS. Founded in Dallas, Texas, with an initial membership of 22 Lutheran social service agencies, its primary goal, as stated by Marta Brenden, was "to meet the needs of children who are in vulnerable situations in both the United States and in other countries." The Association has been funded by private foundation grants and agency memberships. Lutheran Immigration and Refugee Services became one of the charter members.[19]

In recent years the number of unaccompanied minors has declined, and some of the placement agencies have been gradually phased out. Part of the responsibility for the decline must be borne by the U.S. Immigration and Naturalization Service offices in Southeast Asia which have rejected unaccompanied minors for refugee status. In some cases, even siblings of children already in the United States have been rejected as not having a "well-founded fear of persecution," and therefore not qualifying as refugees. The only remaining recourse for these children has been a special process called "humanitarian parole." Under this category the children are classified as immigrants, and no federal support is available for foster care or medical needs. LIRS strongly protested this procedure as detrimental to the welfare of children and as an improper way of saving refugee numbers from the Asian quota to be transferred to the quotas for other geographical areas.[20]

10

The Politics of Compassion

Ever since the Iron Curtain had descended across Europe in 1947, dividing East from West, the refugee policies of the United States conformed to the politics of the Cold War. The immediate postwar national antipathy to receiving refugees yielded in 1948 to citizen demands to open our doors to the displaced persons whose homelands were under communist control. Ethnic Germans, expelled from their homes in eastern European countries or from the German provinces annexed by Poland and the Soviet Union, were admitted if they could demonstrate clean political records. Hungarian "freedom fighters" were welcomed as heroes, and anti-Castro Cubans entered Florida by the thousands. The evacuation and admission of 130,000 Vietnamese and Cambodian refugees in 1975 was motivated in part by humanitarian impulses, but even more by a sense of guilt and an obligation to rescue as many as possible of the allies we had abandoned to the victorious North Vietnamese communist forces.

The Flight of the Chileans

During the early 1970s, U.S. policy consistently restricted the entry of refugees from right-wing regimes with which the United States was closely aligned. Cubans were welcomed; refugees from oppressive regimes in South Korea and the Philippines faced closed doors. A coup d'etat in Chile on October 11, 1973, in which the democratically elected Marxist government of Salvador Allende was overthrown by military forces led by General Augusto Pinochet, produced a wave of political refugees, many of whom sought asylum in the United States. Several thousand refugees who had fled authoritarian regimes in Brazil, Argentina, Uruguay, and other Latin

144

American countries and had been granted asylum in Chile during Allende's presidency, became immediate targets of the Pinochet government. Thousands of Chileans who had supported Allende were summarily imprisoned as enemies of the state. Many were tortured or shot.

International response was prompt. Several Latin American and European governments opened their embassies and offered asylum. The Nixon administration, however, which had contributed to the destabilization of the Allende government, made no protests to the Pinochet government regarding human rights violations. Instead, direct bilateral aid to Chile rose from $10.1 million to $177.3 million in 1975.

As early as September 1973, immediately after the coup, LIRS contacted both LWF/WS in Geneva and the U.S. State Department, indicating its readiness to resettle refugees admissible by the United States. In spite of the obvious lack of government interest, LIRS urged the U.S. and intergovernmental bodies to facilitate the movement of refugees to other areas that would offer asylum. Chilean pastors were generally supportive of the refugees, even at great personal risk.[1]

Almost immediately after securing control of the country, the Pinochet regime sought to rid itself of dissidents and improve its image abroad. International agencies such as ICEM and the International Committee of the Red Cross (ICRC) made arrangements for thousands of individuals in prisons and detention centers to leave Chile.

When the Pinochet government announced in September 1974 that most of its political prisoners would be released if foreign governments would offer asylum, the U.S. Office of Refugee and Migration Affairs urged the State Department to take some positive action. In April 1975, the State Department proposed a group asylum program to the Attorney General for 400 parole cases. When finally approved after a two-month delay, the program was hedged with requirements for the most rigorous political screening since the 1950s. Further delays occurred in the processing of cases. Each individual parolee had to be personally approved by the Director of the Immigration and Naturalization Service.

In July 1975, when the State Department finally approved its "400 Program," LIRS added an Argentinian Lutheran pastor, Osvaldo

Hirschmann, to its staff. The Standing Committee agreed to resettle 75 families if clearances could be secured. A special orientation brochure was prepared and several sponsorships were secured from Lutheran congregations. But by November 6, LIRS had received only two dossiers from the State Department, one of which was indefinitely delayed.[2] As of January 1976, seven months after the program began, only 76 persons had been approved for the parole program, and only 27 had arrived in the United States.

The family of Edmundo Barrera, including his wife and two daughters, ages nine and fifteen, did arrive. Barrera's "crime" had consisted of membership in the wrong political party when President Allende was overthrown. He had been beaten and tortured with electric shocks while his jailers told horror stories about the fate of his wife and daughters. The family was sponsored by two Chicago congregations, St. Luke's and La Primera Iglesia, a Spanish-speaking congregation. They were temporarily housed in a Roman Catholic rectory, together with a family of Vietnamese refugees. Barrera found employment at Augustana Hospital in Chicago.[3]

The efforts of private voluntary agencies and some public officials to make the U.S. response to refugee problems less overtly political and more explicitly humanitarian had little effect. No significant progress was made in securing the admission of Chileans until the Carter administration assumed office in January 1977 and began promoting human rights as an explicit element of U.S. foreign policy.

Late in 1976, with a more favorable climate prevailing in Washington, the number of referrals of refugees increased. By November, 57 Chilean families, a total of 196 persons, had arrived in the United States under LIRS sponsorship. Several other families, approved for entry to the United States, were awaiting exit permits from Chilean authorities. When the so-called "400 Program" concluded in February 1977, the United States had admitted about 1,100 refugees, of which LIRS had resettled a total of 278 persons.[4]

A second parole program, for 200 families, was opened by the State Department on February 28, 1977, mostly for Chilean refugees in Argentina, but also for a few still remaining in Chile, and some political refugees from Bolivia and Uruguay. Travel costs for these refugees, as for the earlier Chileans, were provided through loan funds of the Lutheran World Federation, administered by LIRS. At the conclusion of the "200 Program" the number of Chilean refugees resettled by LIRS had risen to 387.[5]

The early months of 1976 were a period of comparative quiet for the LIRS staff. The frenzied activities involved in the reception and placement of 16,000 Indochinese refugees in eight months had subsided. Government resettlement camps were closed. The American public lost interest in Indochina, hoping that the "Vietnam problem" would simply go away.

The Chilean program, for which the U.S. government had little enthusiasm, was virtually at a standstill. A new program for resettling Laotians was just beginning, but was in no way comparable in size to the huge Vietnamese program.

The Kurds from Iraq

An invitation from Ingrid Walter on February 27, 1976, to participate in a conference phone call dealing with Kurdish refugees in Iran probably came as an unexpected and somewhat exotic suggestion to members of the Standing Committee.[6] The Kurds were victims of a failed effort for ethnic autonomy in the Middle East dating from World War I. The unfulfilled Treaty of Sévres in 1920 had left twelve million Kurds divided among five countries: Iran, Iraq, Turkey, Syria, and the Soviet Union.

In March 1975 the Iraqi military crushed a long simmering struggle by Iraqi Kurds for greater autonomy within Iraq. More than 200,000 Kurds fled across the border into holding camps in Iran. Recognizing the danger to those who were directly involved in the autonomy movement and the fact that Iran was forcibly returning many refugees to Iraq, the U.S. government and several European countries, especially West Germany, agreed to admit a limited number of Kurdish refugees being held in Iranian camps.

Seven American voluntary agencies, including LIRS, agreed to resettle the 400–700 Kurds to be admitted by the U.S. government. As its share LIRS undertook to place up to 80 refugees and immediately began a search for sponsors. Because of the relatively small number of Kurds involved, LIRS decided to seek sponsors in only a few areas so the refugees would have opportunity for more frequent contacts with their countrymen.[7]

With the assistance of Lutheran church officials, cluster meetings with congregations were organized in the Red River Valley of North Dakota and Minnesota. LIRS staff prepared a special information brochure describing the character and customs of the Kurdish people and the political conditions that had forced them into exile. Within a single month sponsorships were offered for 75 people in North Dakota and in neighboring Moorhead, Minnesota. The ready response from these areas may have reflected a long-standing interest among midwestern Lutheran congregations in the work of the Lutheran Orient Mission, which for many years had operated a hospital among the Kurds in northern Iran.

In 1977 LIRS committed itself to the resettlement of 75 additional Kurdish refugees. Most of these joined relatives or close friends in North Dakota. Others were placed in clusters in and around Sioux Falls, South Dakota, and Mankato, Minnesota. As the program terminated in September 1977, a total of 145 Kurdish refugees had been resettled by LIRS.[8]

Welcoming the Loyal Laotians

Almost forgotten in the precipitous 1975 departure of the Americans—and those of their Vietnamese allies fortunate enough to escape—were the Laotians. These inland allies, whose landlocked country was bordered by Vietnam on the east, China on the north, Cambodia on the south, and Thailand on the west, had carried on a civil war against the communist Pathet Lao and against the North Vietnamese. The United States had provided Laos with large amounts of military aid, and the Hmong people, one of the Laotian tribes, cooperated with the CIA in training a secret army to fight the Pathet Lao. When the war ended, the Hmong refused to abandon their resistance and continued to fight. When their supplies were finally exhausted, they began to flee in large numbers. In three years, 300,000 Laotians, ten percent of the country's population, crossed the Mekong River to find refuge in Thailand.[9]

The U.S. government felt a special obligation to these embattled allies, but they were not easily rescued. A special parole program, however, was established in December 1975 for 3,466 Laotians who had been closely associated with the U.S. government, but had not been included in the massive Vietnam evacuation in April. U.S. State Department representatives came to New York to discuss a possible contract with LIRS to place a share of these special cases. LIRS agreed to seek sponsors for 450 persons.[10]

The securing of sponsors was made easier, according to one LIRS official, because the Laotian program "was able to ride piggyback on a high-powered LIRS Vietnamese and Cambodian resettlement program." At its beginning in December 1975 there were already over 200 unused assurances from congregations ready to sponsor refugees.[11]

Since the number of Laotians contemplated at the time was quite small, LIRS determined to place several families in clusters within a 30- to 40-mile radius. The first two Laotian families arrived at Kennedy Airport in New York on December 19, 1975, and were welcomed by their sponsoring congregation in Paramus, New Jersey. A few other families were also settled on the East Coast, but larger clusters were located in the Detroit-Ann Arbor area in Michigan and near Milwaukee, Wisconsin. Eventually, St. Paul and Minneapolis, Minnesota, became the virtual capital of the Hmong refugees.[12]

Unlike the Vietnamese, who were flown from a staging area on Guam to government camps in the United States for processing and orientation, the Laotians were sent directly to their sponsors. The burden of reception and orientation, therefore, rested directly with the sponsors. Later, when established family groups began to welcome relatives, this procedure was much simpler. In the early stages, sponsors received a letter and a special brochure from Robert Eledge, LIRS staff member in charge of the program. The brochure provided background information concerning the Laotian people and offered suggestions for their orientation. Since most Laotians were Buddhists, sponsors were encouraged to welcome them to participate in church activities and services, but were urged to respect their religious beliefs and practices.[13]

The initial group of Laotian refugees was limited to persons who had had close relations with U.S. activities in Southeast Asia. They were quickly approved for admission under the special parole of December 1975. The original LIRS share of 450 persons in this group was later raised to 550. The LIRS contract with the U.S. government allocated a per capita grant of $300 for each person resettled.

Aside from the special parole granted in 1975 for the relatively small number of loyal Laotians, the U.S. government took no further steps to admit Indochinese refugees until May 1976. While LIRS continued to seek placement for its quota of Laotians and to fulfill its obligations under the Chilean and Kurdish programs, it also pressed the State Department to admit additional refugees from Southeast Asia.

In December 1975, Worthington Linen, an LIRS consultant, visited refugee camps in Thailand as a member of a team representing the American Council of Voluntary Agencies. They reported "deplorable conditions" of crowding and deprivation in the camps and urged the U.S. Attorney General to extend the parole quota to relieve the mounting crisis. Eight voluntary agencies joined in sending a telegram to leaders of congressional committees, stating their willingness and ability to provide sponsorships and resettlement services for as many refugees as the United States would admit. Acting on strong support from the State Department and from several influential members of Congress, including Senator Edward Kennedy and Congressman Peter Rodino, the Attorney General announced the Extended Parole Program of May 5, 1976, authorizing the admission of 11,000 more Indochinese refugees. LIRS accepted a quota of 1,749 of the total 11,000 refugees to be admitted.[14]

LIRS immediately set into motion an intensive sponsorship procurement campaign. Letters explaining the new program were sent to district and synodical presidents of the three Lutheran church bodies, LSS executives, LCUSA standing committees, and LIRS regional consultants. An appeal letter was sent to all Lutheran congregations in the United States. A film strip depicting the refugee camps in Thailand was prepared for congregational use. Finally, the three church presidents signed a mailgram that was sent to congregations in areas targeted for sponsorship procurement.[15]

Separate desks for each of the nationality groups—Laotians, Cambodians, and Vietnamese—were set up in LIRS headquarters, each under the direction of an individual staff member. During June, speaking tours were arranged among congregations in the targeted areas, and a group of individuals selected from those areas met in New York to develop sponsorship strategies.

Members of the sponsorship teams found their tasks more difficult than in the previous year, when the Vietnamese and Cambodian evacuees were being resettled. The backlog of sponsorships from the Vietnamese program had been used up in the first Laotian program. Refugee concerns were no longer being highlighted by the media. Public interest was at a lower level. Many congregations were still assisting the previous year's refugees, and the rate of U.S. unemployment reflected a depressed economy. Nevertheless, by the end of 1976 congregational sponsors had been found for all the Indochina refugees assigned to LIRS under the Extended Parole Program. A total of 1,874 persons were resettled, including 191 Cambodians, 255 Vietnamese, and 1,421 Laotians.[16]

Vietnam's Boat People

Initially, American officials had thought the May 1976 parole of 11,000 Laotians would be the last and that any further Indochinese exodus would be small and could be handled under the 1965 amendments to the Immigration and Nationality Act. But no sooner had the Extended Parole Program been put in place than Vietnam tightened its military and reeducation policies and a new surge of refugees resulted.[17]

The "boat people" were mostly Vietnamese who left their country at great personal risk aboard small, privately owned vessels. If they successfully slipped through the screen of Vietnamese coastal patrols, they set sail for the nearest port of refuge in Malaysia, Singapore, Indonesia, or wherever their often unseaworthy craft could be safely brought to shore.

Typical of this group was Nguyen Hoang Cuong, a 49-year-old Vietnamese businessman who owned a radio and television assembly plant. Too old for military service and fortunate enough to escape a reeducation camp, he and ten members of his extended family, including his wife and three sons, slipped out of Tra Vinh village in the Mekong Delta in a 33-foot boat powered by a 10-horsepower engine. Without compass or charts, they ventured out into the South China Sea. Passing ships ignored their signals for assistance. They headed for Malaysia and eventually landed on the northeast coast where they got food and clothing from villagers and fuel from the police. Their attempt to enter Singapore was blocked, first by a marine police launch that towed them out to sea, and a second time by a naval vessel. They were given food and fuel, but appeals for repairs for their engine were refused, and they were left adrift at night in international waters. After several hours they succeeded in starting the engine, and by a stroke of luck beached the boat near a Malaysian refugee camp.

Cuong's party was one of the fortunate ones. Hundreds were lost at sea, victims of storms, shipwreck, starvation, or piracy. By 1979 more than 300,000 survivors had reached the dubious safety of Southeast Asian refugee camps. No one knows how many perished or were captured in their attempts to escape.[18]

While this surge of boat people from Vietnam increased during late 1976, swelling the population of refugee camps in Malaysia and Thailand, the stream of Laotians into Thailand also continued at the rate of 2,000 per month. By early 1977 the U.S. quotas established by the Extended Parole Program were filled, and there seemed no alternative but to ask the Attorney General for the fifth Indochinese parole program in two years.

On August 11, 1977, the newly elected Carter administration authorized 15,000 more admissions, including 7,000 Vietnamese boat people and 8,000 land refugees, mostly from Laos. Those with relatives in the United States, or formerly associated with the U.S. government, or with prewar non-communist governments in Southeast Asia, were given preference.[19]

Another new category was added for refugees presenting "compelling humanitarian reasons." Almost any Vietnamese or Laotian not specifically excludable under U.S. immigration law was admissible under the Indochinese Parole Program (IPP–77). LIRS agreed to resettle a quota of 2,250 refugees under this program, and began immediately to promote sponsorships among Lutheran congregations. In setting a goal of 600 sponsors, LIRS decided to approach the task on a long-term basis rather than as a crisis appeal.

Press coverage of the refugee situation since the mass evacuation of Saigon had been minimal, and congregations were generally unaware of the continuing plight of Vietnamese refugees or of the U.S. resettlement program. The sponsorship promotion plan, therefore, had first to raise consciousness of the needs and then to promote a response to the need.

LIRS regional consultants were instructed to approach church leadership on local, regional, and national levels. LIRS itself developed several direct mail promotional pieces, including a brochure, "Consider a Face to Face Ministry," and a flyer entitled "A Stranger Knocks—He Brings an Opportunity." These were sent in large shipments by first class mail to all congregations and church offices. Each of the national Lutheran church presidents was directly addressed with an appeal for his personal support.

LIRS had secured more than half its quota of sponsors when the U.S. government once again expanded the parole on January 25, 1978, to include 7,000 additional boat people. To supply its share of sponsors for these refugees, LIRS had to conduct an emergency campaign in selected areas of the country. LCA synod presidents and deans in Pennsylvania, for example, directed a phone campaign that produced 18 sponsors in three days and 20 more in the following four weeks. J. A. O. Preus personally contacted Missouri Synod districts, urging the formation of district task forces to secure sponsors. By June 1978, assurances were coming in at the rate of 70 per month, and LIRS had placed more than 2,300 refugees under the IPP–77 and IPP–78 programs.[20]

Much of the credit for the repeated extensions of refugee admission quotas in 1976–78 must be given to a Citizens' Commission similar to the group that successfully lobbied in 1948 for the passage of the Displaced Persons Act. Organized by Leo Cherne, Chairman of the International Rescue Committee (IRC), one of the most active of the private voluntary agencies engaged in resettlement work, the Commission enlisted support from religious leaders, business and labor leaders, journalists, and others with good Washington connections.

They focused on raising the consciousness of the American public to the rising refugee crisis in Southeast Asia through statements, appeals, and interviews in the press and on television. Congressional and staff delegations visited refugee camps in Thailand and brought back eyewitness accounts of human misery.

The Commission's work was largely responsible for President Carter's approval of a plan to put the Indochinese refugee program on a long-term basis, including new refugee legislation and another interim parole to admit 25,000 Indochinese over the course of a year, beginning in June 1978.

While discussion of this so-called Long Range Program was going on, Vietnam took steps to nationalize private trade and expelled thousands of its ethnic Chinese minority, who were the commercial entrepreneurs of the country. Between March and July 1978, 160,000 Vietnamese of Chinese origin left Vietnam and traveled overland to

China. When China closed its borders to Vietnam in July, the number of Vietnamese fleeing by boat to other Southeast Asian countries increased dramatically , from 2,800 in August to 21,500 in the month of November alone.[21]

In addition to the series of parole programs directed mainly to the Indochinese refugees, the U.S. was also admitting refugees from other countries under the provisions of the 1965 Immigration and Nationality Act. It authorized the admission of 170,000 regular immigrants annually from Eastern Hemisphere countries, according to a series of preferences spelled out in the law. The "seventh preference" provided admission for a limited number of refugees from communist or communist-dominated countries, or from the Middle East.

Under this provision, "conditional entrants" from eastern Europe and Hong Kong, Indochinese family reunification cases from Europe, some Indochinese humanitarian cases, and even a few Ethiopian refugees were eligible. Through these programs, called U.S. Refugee Program 1977 and 1978 (USRP–77 and USRP–78), LIRS placed 342 persons, mostly Indochinese family reunifications from Europe and humanitarian parolees, in 1977, and 808 in 1978. Under all programs, LIRS resettled a total of 2,726 persons in 1976, 942 in 1977, and 3,370 in 1978.[22]

As more and more boatloads of refugees arrived in Malaysia, Thailand, and Indonesia, the policies of these governments hardened. In 1978, Thailand's prime minister declared his country would receive no more boat people. Supplies and repairs would be offered, but boats would not be allowed to land their passengers. Those who did manage to get ashore were crammed into makeshift camps, without adequate shelter or sanitation.

Out of 94,000 boat people who had been given refuge in these countries of first asylum, only 38,000 had been resettled by November 1978. Twenty-one thousand had gone to the United States; 10,000 to Australia; and 3,000 to France. In the spring of 1979 war broke out between China and Vietnam, and even more ethnic Chinese left Vietnam for Malaysia, Thailand, Indonesia, and Hong Kong. In June the monthly departure rate was in excess of 56,000.

At last, in July 1979, an International Conference on Indochinese Refugees was convened in Geneva, with 65 countries in attendance. Placements for 260,000 refugees were committed, and conference members pledged international cooperation in effecting sea rescues. President Carter ordered the Seventh Fleet to seek out refugees in distress on the high seas and announced that the U.S. would double its intake of Vietnamese refugees to 14,000 a month. The boat people crisis reached a turning point in July 1979. The Vietnamese government clamped down on illegal departures, and the number of boat people declined for the first time in 18 months.[23]

LIRS in Hong Kong

In the spring of 1979 LIRS received a request from the U.S. State Department to open a resettlement office in the British Crown Colony of Hong Kong. At that time Hong Kong had the distinction of not having turned away any boat people, and 70,000 refugees had crowded into the holding camps of Hong Kong and the neighboring Portuguese colony of Macao. Most of these were Vietnamese and ethnic Chinese who had fled in 1978 when the Vietnamese government nationalized private businesses, and in early 1979, when war broke out between Vietnam and China. Many of them would be eligible for resettlement in the United States under President Carter's parole order of June 1978, admitting 25,000 refugees.

According to the State Department proposal, LIRS was asked to operate the Hong Kong office on behalf of all U.S. resettlement agencies, while other agencies placed Joint Voluntary Agency Representatives (JVARs) in other centers of refugee concentration in East Asia.

George Harkins signed the State Department contract for LCUSA and LIRS. Roger Shinn, LIRS regional consultant with LSS of Northern California and Nevada, and his deputy, Daniel Larsen, LIRS staff assistant in New York, flew to Hong Kong to open the office. At the height of the program the JVAR staff numbered 52 persons, including caseworkers, interpreters, and representatives from the U.S. Consulate. In the summer of 1980 the JVAR office processed 2,000 refugees a month for resettlement in the United States. Heads of families approved for entry to the U.S. were allowed to enroll for language instruction in a special ESL program also being administered by LIRS in Hong Kong.[24]

11

From Cambodia to Cuba

The best kept and most tragic secret of the Indochina wars was the systematic and ruthless destruction of the nation and people of Cambodia. This nation of quiet farmers, wedged between South Vietnam and Thailand, had managed to avoid direct involvement in the early stages of the civil war in Vietnam. But its chief of state, Prince Norodom Sihanouk, who favored the Hanoi government, allowed the North Vietnamese to construct sanctuaries inside Cambodia's eastern border, from which attacks were mounted against the South Vietnamese.

In 1969, President Nixon ordered a campaign of B–52 bombardments of these sanctuaries, followed in April 1970, by an invasion by U.S. army troops. For five years thereafter, Cambodia was ravaged by civil war between government forces under American-backed General Lon Nol and the communist Khmer Rouge, led by General Pol Pot and backed by North Vietnam and the People's Republic of China. American bombing continued until an act of Congress forced its termination in 1973.

Cambodian Holocaust

During 1974 reports of extreme brutality began to emerge from areas under Khmer Rouge control. But these grim stories sounded like fictional atrocity tales; few believed them. When the capital city of Phnom Penh fell to the Khmer Rouge on April 12, 1975, just two weeks before the fall of Saigon, the Khmer Rouge literally emptied the city, driving its inhabitants, including hospital patients, families, and schoolchildren, into the countryside at gunpoint. Then the Khmer Rouge closed Cambodia, renamed the People's Republic of Kampuchea, to the outside world. For the next three years, they embarked upon a bloody revolution whose brutality rivaled the horrors of the Holocaust. The country's borders were mined. Ter-

156

rorism, murder, and starvation decimated the Cambodian populace. More than a million people perished during the first year.

Not many refugees managed to escape from the country between 1975 and 1978. But there were enough eyewitness reports to warrant greater attention to this human catastrophe than was given by either journalists or national leaders. In retrospect, one candid analyst admitted, "Just as few people in the 1930s and 1940s had wished to believe in the Nazi elimination of Jews, . . so many people wished not to believe that atrocities were taking place in Cambodia under Khmer Rouge rule."[1]

The truth burst into the open in December 1978, when the Vietnamese, erstwhile allies of the Khmer Rouge, invaded Cambodia from the east and installed a rival regime in Phnom Penh. Cambodians fled by the thousands toward the border with Thailand, risking death in the mine fields or from either of the warring armies battling over their ruined land.

The Thai government, fearful of being overrun by refugees, closed its borders, and at one point forced more than 40,000 refugees quite literally over a precipice, back into the Cambodian jungle and into the hands of the Khmer Rouge. The incident precipitated an international outcry. The United Nations High Commissioner for Refugees eventually prevailed on Thailand to restore asylum and to set up holding centers along its frontiers, from which the refugees could be resettled or voluntarily repatriated.

Added to the very real dangers of physical violence at the hands of military forces, the Cambodian refugees faced the hazard of disease and starvation. Most rice fields had not been planted, and few of those that had, had been harvested. The spectre of widespread famine loomed over Cambodia in 1979 and for several years thereafter. Unprecedented relief efforts had to be launched by intergovernmental relief agencies before any significant action could take place for repatriation or resettlement.

When the confirmed reports of the Cambodian atrocities were acknowledged and publicized in the West, vigorous campaigns were launched to meet the impending food crisis and to offer resettlement opportunities for the Cambodians. Except for the relatively small numbers who had escaped from Thailand when Phnom Penh was captured and before the borders were sealed in 1975, few Cambodians had been able to benefit from U.S. or any other resettlement programs. But in December 1978, with the support of key members of Congress and the lobbying of voluntary agencies, legislation was approved directing the Attorney General to include 15,000 places for Cambodians in the Indochina parole program.[2]

The Refugee Act of 1980

While the Cambodian parole was being debated by Congress, discussions were also underway with the goal of bringing some order into U.S. government procedures for handling the refugee problem. The system of executive parole, intended as an interim means of handling one-time emergencies, was clearly out of control. As one emergency followed the other, ten separate paroles had been used to admit over 300,000 Indochinese between 1975 and 1979.

A congressional Select Committee on Immigration and Refugee Policy had been established by the Carter Administration in late 1978 to conduct a systematic study and make policy recommendations. But the parole of 15,000 Cambodians and the prospect of even greater numbers yet to come moved Congress to take more direct and immediate action to bring the system under control. Without waiting for recommendations from the Select Committee, Senator Edward Kennedy and Representative Peter Rodino drafted a sweeping new refugee bill. After numerous hearings and consultations between Congress and the Executive Branch, the Refugee Act of 1980 won approval in March.

The new law explicitly abolished the parole system and established a separate and independent immigration quota for refugees. A quota of 50,000 per year was set for each of the next two years, with provision for an annual allocation thereafter by the President "after consultation with Congress."

One of the most significant provisions of the law was a new definition of the term "refugee." Refugees were defined as persons unable or unwilling to return to their home countries "because of persecution or a well-founded fear of persecution on account of race, religion, nationality, membership in a particular social group, or political opinion." This definition was the same as that employed in the 1951 United Nations Convention relating to the Status of Refugees, to which the United States was a signatory. The Act also established an Office of Refugee Resettlement within the Department of Health and Human Services (HHS),* through which reset-tlement programs, such as employment training and placement, ESL, and cash assistance aimed at economic self-sufficiency, would be administered. It also regularized the procedure for handling grants and contracts with voluntary agencies for initial resettlement of refugees.[3]

The voluntary agencies welcomed congressional efforts to bring order into the refugee program. Throughout the entire series of government resettlement programs, the voluntary agencies had pro-vided the only system through which refugees had been brought into American communities. Without this service the programs could not have been carried out.

Call for Sponsorships

When the new U.S. refugee programs were created in late 1977 and 1978 for the boat people, and in 1979 for the much larger number of Cambodians, LIRS found itself facing serious problems in mounting an expanded campaign for sponsorships. During 1978 sponsorships had been secured on an average of 75 per month. But with the expanded quotas under the new U.S. parole programs, projections indicated 200 or possibly 250 sponsorships per month would be needed. As early as May 1978 the regional consultants had been asked to assist in soliciting sponsorships, and in early 1979 mailgrams were sent urging them to give first priority to this activity. Districts and synods of the national churches also organized vol-unteer task forces to promote sponsorships.[4]

Ellen Erickson, LIRS regional consultant, formerly in South Da-kota and now with Lutheran Social Service of Minnesota, described the work of a task force representing the Lutheran judicatories in Minnesota. "They were responsible for publicizing the refugee re-settlement program. It was their responsibility to heighten the awareness of individuals and to honor people or congregations within the synod or district who were involved in refugee resettle-ment. Just constantly keeping that in front of people and constantly

---

* (The Department of Health and Human Services was estab-lished by Congress on September 27, 1979, replacing the former Department of Health, Education, and Welfare.)

articulating from the Gospel what it means to care for people in need. They were to remind people that the congregation is in the forefront of a very special ministry."[5]

From Hong Kong came an eloquent appeal to Lutheran congregations from Roger Shinn, Joint Voluntary Agency Representative for resettlement. As a former regional consultant for LIRS, he knew how important it was to have sponsorships awaiting a refugee's arrival. "We in the church are blessed beyond what any of us really needs," he wrote. "Is it asking so much: a place to live, some clothes to wear, some personal guidance, and lots of love? When you're over here, you realize even more that the churches hold so many lives in their hands. Hands are made to reach out and serve. Let's do it!"[6]

An urgent appeal for sponsorships was sent to all congregations in a Christmas letter signed by Dr. John Houck, the new LCUSA General Secretary, and Ingrid Walter, LIRS Director. The letter asked each pastor to return an enclosed postcard designating a congregational contact person and requesting promotional material.[7]

One of the greatest assets of the Lutheran refugee program was the network of congregations and people who had been involved in refugee resettlement for nearly half a century. Congregations and pastors who had responded to every appeal since the DP program of 1948 needed no promotional materials to stimulate their response. They only asked for information.

Atonement Lutheran Church in Columbus, Ohio, with fewer than 200 members, had undertaken eleven different sponsorships. Grace Lutheran in Winter Haven, Florida, had welcomed 220 refugees. Trinity, in south Minneapolis, blessed with a devoted worker like Adeline Marty, whose home was virtually a way station for refugees, had found homes for at least 205 persons.[8] On a special Refugee Sunday, Trinity Lutheran in Moorhead, Minnesota, celebrated 25 families who had been resettled by the congregation and had subsequently joined the church. Congregations like these, and hundreds of others across the country, had responded again and again to the world's displaced persons. While lifting the burdens of Cambodians and Vietnamese, Hungarians and Ugandans, Germans, Latvians, and Estonians, they had lifted their own horizons as well.

In September 1978, the LIRS Standing Committee took action authorizing staff to accept refugee "anchor relatives," family members already established in the United States, as sponsors where congregational sponsors were not available. Such sponsorships required the recommendation and signature of a Lutheran pastor or an LIRS regional consultant.[9] This procedure opened the way for the reuniting of the extended Asian families. A small group of five members of St. Paul Lutheran Church in Melrose Park, Illinois, calling themselves the "Care Corps," discovered this after they sponsored four ethnic Chinese boat people from Vietnam in May 1978. "We've never put in a new application since then," recounts Renata Weiss, one of the Corps members. Subsequent cases were all parents, aunts, uncles, cousins, nieces, and in-laws of the four young men. "They gave us information about their relatives and friends in the refugee camps, and we sent for them." The Care Corps, declared Weiss, was able to meet all its challenges, including the arrival of twelve- and thirteen-member family groups at Chicago's O'Hare Airport.[10]

"Blanket assurances," issued prior to the development of a specific sponsor for a refugee and designating a regional consultant's office as the sponsor, were also authorized. This procedure speeded the process of placement by reducing the waiting time before arrival both for sponsor and refugee.[11]

Promotional efforts at every level in the LIRS system were stepped up. The February 1979 issue of the *LIRS Bulletin* went out to all Lutheran congregations as well as to the 22,000 addresses on its regular mailing list. Inserts announcing a Cambodian Day of Prayer on April 17 and a poster for the International Year of the Child were included.

The premier showing of the LIRS promotion film, "Room for a Stranger," was scheduled for March 5 at a meeting of Lutheran district and synod presidents. Prints were made available for churches, synods, and LIRS regional consultants. The 20-minute film subsequently received a Silver Medal at the 22nd Annual Film and TV Festival in New York.[12]

Public figures were often willing to lend personal support to the refugee program and the efforts to secure sponsorships. Minnesota Governor Albert Quie, a Lutheran, was particularly responsive to refugee issues. On one occasion the LIRS coordinator in Minneapolis received a telephone call from Gretchen Quie, the governor's wife, offering the use of a carriage house on the grounds of the governor's mansion in St. Paul as a temporary home for refugees. Several families benefited, and there were occasions when Mrs. Quie was seen walking on Grand Avenue in St. Paul with the refugee family currently resident in the carriage house. The governor himself held a reception for refugees, and during his administration formed a Governor's State Advisory Council for Refugee Concerns.[13]

Most effective in stirring the hearts and consciences of potential sponsors were the biographies of the refugees themselves. A 34-year-old refugee, Chey Rith, was among the 40,000 Cambodians forcibly repatriated from camps in Thailand in May 1978 into the desolate rock-strewn border jungle called the "Valley of Hell." After his family had been murdered by the Khmer Rouge regime in Cambodia, he fled across the border and reached an apparent haven of safety in a camp in Thailand. Together with several hundred others who had also made the crossing, he was forced at gunpoint onto a bus and taken back to the border. Thai troops herded them down a precipice so steep they had to hold on to vines and trees to keep from falling. Many who resisted were shot. After six days in the jungle, surviving on wild potatoes and fruit and nuts from the trees, Chey led a group back into Thailand. They were caught again and forced back into the valley. On a third attempt he and one companion made it to safety in Bangkok. Missionaries brought them to a transit center for refugees. In June 1979, Chey arrived at Kennedy Airport. With the aid of an LIRS translator, Phat Mau, he gave his story to journalists.[14]

A daily dramatic reminder to LIRS staff in New York of the Cambodian terror was the presence of Sichan Siv, assistant to the LIRS Social Services coordinator. At the time of the fall of Phnom Penh on April 12, 1975, Sichan was employed by the U.S. relief agency CARE in distributing food to refugees. He missed the last U.S. helicopter flight out of Phnom Penh and was caught up in the forced evacuation of the city by the communist Khmer Rouge. Especially at risk as an "intellectual," a former teacher, and an employee of an American organization, he threw away his glasses and personal papers and rode his bicycle toward the Thai border 500 miles away. When stopped for questioning, Sichan explained that he was looking for his family. He was commandeered by Khmer Rouge functionaries into working in rice fields, repairing roads, digging ditches, and driving trucks. At one point he was detained for eight months, working ten to twelve hours a day on the dikes surrounding rice fields, often standing in water up to his chest and at night listening to lectures on the revolution. He contracted a bad case of fever and diarrhea and spent two weeks in a military hospital. Finally, while riding on a truck load of timber near the Thai border, Sichan jumped off and plunged into the jungle. Three days later, after swimming a river and dodging patrols, he stumbled upon a group of people near a Buddhist temple and realized they were speaking Thai rather than Khmer.

Although Sichan had escaped from Cambodia, other hazards stood between him and freedom. Thai border guards took him into custody and confined him in prison, where he was robbed and beaten and charged with illegal entry into Thailand. Eventually he was placed in a refugee holding camp, from which he was able to send a letter to a friend in Bangkok associated with his former employer, CARE. Thirteen months after he left Phnom Penh, Sichan was interviewed by a U.S. immigration officer in Bangkok and given a parole number. A month later he landed at Kennedy Airport in New York.[15]

In September 1978, he joined the New York LIRS staff as Assistant to the Social Service Coordinator. In January 1980 Sichan Siv was awarded a scholarship by LIRS to study at the Columbia University Graduate School of International Affairs. Subsequently, he worked for the Institute of International Education. In 1989 President Bush appointed him to the White House staff as deputy assistant for public liaison, the first Southeast Asian refugee to become a ranking presidential assistant.[16]

The measures undertaken by LIRS in 1979 to expand the number of sponsorships for Cambodians and Vietnamese boat people produced encouraging results. From an average of 75 per month in 1978, assurances rose steadily in 1979, reaching 400 in August. Much of the increase came in the categories of anchor relatives and blanket assurances, marking a trend that continued into 1980 and 1981 as more refugee families became well enough established to sponsor members of their expanded families still in their home countries.[17] In 1980 36 percent of the 4,315 sponsorships received by LIRS were provided by anchor relatives.[18]

Arrivals by the Thousands

Arrivals also increased, especially in the latter half of 1979, when President Carter doubled the quota of Indochinese parolees to 14,000 per month. To accommodate the upsurge of numbers, the U.S. State Department set up a temporary transit center near the San Francisco International Airport and rented rooms from nearby motels to provide overnight respite for incoming refugees. Two members of an LIRS reception team were given office space with telephones to facilitate the movement of families to their sponsors in various locations throughout the country. Between July and December LIRS resettled 1,200 persons per month and completed the year with 10,801, three times the number placed in 1978.[19]

Among the arrivals during the summer of 1979 was Kao Lor, a Laotian farmer-soldier, who became the 100,000th refugee resettled by LIRS since World War II. He and his family were sponsored by the Refugee Task Force of Augustana College in Sioux Falls, South Dakota. Kao Lor was presented with a citation by LIRS. The Augustana Task Force, which had previously sponsored five other families, was recognized for "the devotion and humanitarian spirit displayed in its resettlement ministry."[20]

During the summer of 1980, a program was designed to place Cambodian refugees in twelve cluster sites throughout the United States. Developed cooperatively by voluntary agencies, local and state governments and local Cambodian Mutual Assistance Associations, the cluster plan was intended to prevent "secondary migration" to such impacted areas as Southern California.* LIRS agreed to concentrate its efforts in Boston, Chicago, and Jacksonville, Florida. By December 1981, it had placed 2,241 Cambodians.[21]

During 1980 the influx of Southeast Asians continued, reaching a figure of 200,000, its highest level since 1975. LIRS resettled a total of 13,574 persons, also its highest number since the first Vietnamese exodus.[22]

---

* (Secondary migration refers to the movement of refugees from their place of original sponsorship to another location in the U.S., often to join relatives or to seek better economic opportunities. Impacted areas were areas of the country with especially heavy concentrations of refugees.)

In 1980, the year in which the U.S. government approved a new Refugee Act intended to regularize the process of admitting refugees, the greatest wave of asylum seekers since World War II flooded across the borders of the United States.

The Landing of the Marielitos

Nineteen-eighty was the year of the Iranian hostage crisis, the first year of the Soviet invasion of Afghanistan, and an election year. It was perhaps understandable that the U.S. government was not prepared for the influx of Cubans and Haitians in April.

Under some pressure from the Carter Administration, Fidel Castro had agreed to release several thousand political prisoners for admission to the United States. Other Cubans, unhappy with conditions in their country, were eager to escape. In March 1980, a busload of dissatisfied Cubans rammed through the gates of the Peruvian embassy in Havana and were granted temporary asylum. Thousands more swarmed after them, many desiring to emigrate to the United States.

Instead of arranging an orderly emigration, as suggested by President Carter, Castro simply announced on April 19 that anyone wishing to leave Cuba for the United States could do so. He opened the port of Mariel as a point of exit and urged Cuban-Americans to come and retrieve their relatives. Hundreds of boats of all shapes and sizes left Miami for Mariel and returned with full loads.

What seemed at first to be a sign of the unpopularity of the communist regime in Cuba turned sour when it became known that Castro had used the opportunity to unload large numbers of social undesirables, even criminals, as part of the exodus. As the "Marielitos" continued to stream ashore—85,000 in the month of May— the public view of the boatlift became considerably more antagonistic. Miami was overrun. Jobs and housing were scarce, and tensions ran high.

A majority of the new arrivals would not meet the new definition of refugee contained in the 1980 Refugee Act. Most were fleeing to rejoin their families or to improve their economic status. Under the circumstances, it was impossible to carry out a screening process to determine the motives for the departure of each person. President Carter chose not to classify the new arrivals as "refugees" under the

Refugee Act, but created a new category called "entrant." Haitian boat people who had entered the United States before June 20 were included in this category. "Cuban-Haitian Entrants" were granted benefits equal to refugees, and state and local governments were assured of full reimbursement of costs.[23]

The Unwelcome Haitians

Both because of their race and their national origin, Haitians presented a special problem. Since 1972 several thousand Haitian boat people had arrived the United States, fleeing the brutal regime of the Duvalier family. But because of the close political relationship between the United States and the Duvalier regime, their claims to asylum on grounds of political persecution were consistently denied. President Carter's emphasis on human rights had brought about some changes in Haiti, but it had produced no change in the discriminatory practice of the Immigration and Naturalization Service toward Haitians in this country who applied for asylum.

In 1979 church and public interest groups successfully brought a class action suit again the INS to prevent the deportation of 4,000 Haitians. Federal District Judge James Lawrence King handed down a decision in July 1980 that charged the INS with discrimination and the denial of equal protection of the law to Haitians requesting asylum hearings. His opinion also refuted the government's claim that all Haitians were economic migrants and documented the prevalence of "stark, brutal, and bloody" political persecution in Haiti.[24] Indeed, during 1979, a particularly severe wave of human rights violation occurred in Haiti. Activists, lawyers, and critics of the Duvalier government were jailed or expelled from the country, and many took refuge in the United States.

Even when the Mariel boatlift took place in April 1980, INS policies toward Haitians were unaffected. Haitian refugees were still regarded as economic migrants. But in an election year it was politically unwise to relax the asylum process for Cubans to a formality, while using it to exclude black Haitians. President Carter included Haitians in the "entrant" category announced on June 20.

Prior to 1980, both LIRS and the Division for Mission and Ministry of LCUSA had supported the efforts of National Council of Churches' lawyers on behalf of Haitians threatened with deportation by the

INS. But their actual involvement with the Cuban-Haitian resettlement program began when LIRS sent Mary Nelson, a Chicago social worker, to Florida early in 1980, to evaluate the situation. While she was in Miami, the Mariel boatlift began, and she stayed on to help set up the LIRS operation there. The government immediately opened processing camps at Eglin Air Force Base in Florida and Camp Chaffee in Arkansas, and, shortly thereafter, two others, at Indiantown Gap, Pennsylvania, and Camp McCoy in Wisconsin, to accommodate the increasing influx of Cubans and Haitians.[25]

Upon Nelson's urgent recommendation, the LIRS Executive Committee initiated an emergency request for the release of $50,000 from reserve funds and drew up a preliminary budget to begin the program.[26] Since there were no government reception and placement grants when the Cuban program began, a request for financial support was sent to the Lutheran World Federation. Churches in Canada, West Germany, and Scandinavia responded with emergency grants. The Annual Meeting of LCUSA requested special funding of $300,000 from its constituent church bodies.[27]

With the understanding that the government would provide modest salaries for processing staff and transportation costs for refugees from camps to resettlement locations, LIRS and six other voluntary agencies opened offices in each of the four camps and in Miami. At the peak of the program LIRS employed a staff of 40 people in the camps. At the national offices of LIRS, Livingston Chrichlow was appointed program coordinator.[28]

Since it was the intent of the government to move the refugees out of the camps as rapidly as possible, the voluntary agencies accelerated their efforts to secure and verify sponsorships. During July, LIRS sent a mailing to the 18,000 Lutheran congregations in the United States. Requests for more information and materials came in response to the mailing, but in the face of the continuing effort to secure sponsors for Indochinese and other refugee programs, congregational offers of sponsorships for Cubans and Haitians were few.

Families and friends already living in the United States were the most productive sources of sponsorships for both Cubans and Haitians. A few families were sponsored by Lutheran agencies. Lutheran Family Services of Greensboro, North Carolina, found a place for Victor and Yolanda Menéndez and their four children in High Point,

North Carolina. They had joined the "freedom flotilla" after Victor, a hospital administrator, had been ousted from his job and jailed as a political prisoner. During their flight, the family was accidentally separated, and they found each other only after being processed in different camps in Florida and Arkansas.[29]

Many of the Haitians were young male adults, and the traditional model of congregational sponsorship did not work. Moreover, Haitian refugees were black. The cluster model was suggested, involving predominantly black inner-city churches in Chicago and Houston. Several congregations responded, offering living quarters and orientation programs with primary emphasis on employment and language instruction.

Christian Airey, a Haitian native who had lived in the United States since 1975, was pastor of St. Stephen Lutheran Church in a middle-class black neighborhood on Chicago's South Side. His congregation sponsored about 100 Haitian refugees, most of them single men. "We were able to get three houses which were almost abandoned," he recalled. "We spent days and days repairing, cleaning, and painting them." He and members of his congregation helped the Haitians over their first weeks in a strange city and a strange language. "But," said Pastor Airey, "most of them are doing well. They have jobs, are out on their own, are feeling great, and are really grateful."[30]

Bethel Lutheran Church, located in a black neighborhood on Chicago's West Side, established a cluster of 65 Haitians. Since the congregation operated a housing development program, it had access to several apartments where Haitian refugees could have temporary shelter. A supporting network equipped the apartments with basic furniture and utensils. Nobody at Bethel was wealthy, but as Mary Nelson, the housing coordinator, said, "You have a cluster of people who know the joy that comes from sharing."[31]

The initial Cuban-Haitian resettlement process was largely completed during 1980, but some activity continued throughout 1981 and 1982. According to a report on August 30, 1982, LIRS resettled a total of 10,555 persons, including 8,298 Cubans and 2,257 Haitians. Sponsorships for 8,881 persons were arranged by LIRS with relatives or friends of the refugees. Congregations provided sponsorships for 197 persons.[32]

Ongoing services for Cubans and Haitians were provided

through the LIRS network of LSS-related consultants and through other Lutheran agencies. President Carter extended the special "entrant" status to Cubans and Haitians who had arrived in the U.S. and announced themselves to the INS prior to October 10, 1980. Those arriving later had until July 15, 1981, to register and receive an "entrant status pending" classification. INS proceedings would determine whether they received asylum or were placed in detention, subject to deportation.[33] Both the Florida Lutheran Ministries and LIRS engaged in vigorous advocacy efforts to secure the legal rights of these refugees and to support their claims for asylum under the terms of the Refugee Act of 1980.

12

The New Advocacy

Just as it was impossible to regularize the production and flow of the world's refugees, so it was impossible to lay out long-range projections and strategies for dealing with them. Refugees were created in unpredictable numbers, in unpredictable places, by unpredictable situations. Moreover, the extent to which any resettlement agency might become involved depended in most cases on the policies and decisions of the U.S. government, whether or under what conditions it chose to admit the refugees to this country.

Each time a new program was initiated, usually in response to a crisis, LIRS (or its predecessor agencies) had to decide whether to participate. If it decided to go ahead, it had to map out a strategy, find adequate financing, rally its network of congregational sponsors, and expand its personnel. When the program was over, it contracted its staff until the next emergency arose.

During the years following World War II, when LIRS' predecessors were resettling DPs, ethnic Germans, Hungarians, and a variety of other refugees, program costs were borne by Lutheran church bodies, the National Lutheran Council, and The Lutheran Church—Missouri Synod, with significant assistance from the travel loan funds of the LWF and ICEM. Congregations rose to each new crisis to sponsor refugee families. As one emergency followed another, the supporting church bodies sought faithfully to meet the financial needs, even when carefully planned budgets had to be revised.

Working for the Government

With the coming of the Vietnam emergency in 1975, profound changes occurred, both for the voluntary agencies and for the U.S. government. Some things remained the same: the climate of crisis, the lack of preparation by the government, the frantic search for funds and personnel. But in the process of implementing the Vietnam program, new elements were introduced that altered the role of the government and substantially changed the style of operation of voluntary agencies. The major factor in these changes was the assumption by the government of financial responsibility for the resettlement of refugees.

Funding by the government initially caused some internal administrative problems for LIRS and its parent agency, LCUSA. It also raised questions about refugee resettlement as a ministry of the church. If the government paid the bills and set the rules, the sense of congregational involvement that had been the central theme of Lutheran refugee work might be eroded or even lost.

Equally critical was the political issue. U.S. refugee policy since World War II had been shaped by the Cold War. Refugees from communism were given official preference under the 1965 revision of the Immigration and Nationality Act, while those fleeing rightist oppression in countries such as Chile and Haiti were denied asylum. Was the church becoming a paid agent of the government, contracting for services only to those refugees who were politically acceptable?

These issues were raised and examined by LIRS staff and its governing committees and were also given public exposure by sensitive and sympathetic critics. Definitive resolutions of issues involving church and state relations are extremely rare, and LIRS made no new breakthroughs. But the discussions that took place served to maintain honesty, nurture healthy tensions, and encourage continued efforts to achieve justice.[1]

Internally, the LIRS Standing Committee continued to chafe under the structural complexities of the LCUSA organization. Studies that had begun during the administrative crisis of 1975, aimed at finding an optimal pattern for refugee services, were extended for several years. Suggestions that a separate division of social services be created, or that LIRS become a separate agency or an adjunct agency to the Council, were considered again and set aside again. Changes in personnel occurred in both the Division for Mission and Ministry and in the leadership of the Council, but LIRS remained as a department within the DMM.[2]

A New Director for LIRS

Effective January 1, 1977, Ingrid Walter, a veteran of 27 years' service, was appointed Director of LIRS. Walter had served as Acting Director since October 1975, replacing Donald Anderson at the height of the Vietnam program. She was the senior member of the LIRS staff and, more than anyone else, embodied the essence of the Lutheran ministry to refugees.

An Estonian refugee who fled her country in 1943, Walter had worked for three years in Germany with United Nations Relief and Rehabilitation Administration. She came to the United States as a displaced person in 1949, sponsored through Church World Service, and was invited by Cordelia Cox to join the Lutheran Resettlement Service in August 1950 as a stenographer. In the following years Walter pursued studies at New York University, earning both bachelor's and master's degrees. In 1983 Wartburg College recognized her with an honorary doctorate.

From 1950 until her retirement in 1985, she was involved in every aspect of refugee resettlement, rising in the organization from administrative assistant to assistant director, and finally to the head of the agency. She developed a wealth of experience and expertise in dealing with governmental and voluntary agencies, congressional committees, congregations, and, not least, individual refugees from every corner of the world. Her appointment was both a recognition of her record of distinguished service and a reflection of LIRS' determination to maintain the focus of its program on refugees as persons.[3]

Two officers of the LIRS Standing Committee also distinguished themselves during these critical years by their continuity and faithfulness of service. August Bernthal, pastor of Grace Lutheran Church in Winter Haven, Florida, was first appointed to the Committee by J. A. O. Preus of The Lutheran Church—Missouri Synod in 1970, and served continuously for 20 years, 17 of them as president. His colleague for 14 of these years (1974–1988) was Merill Herder, pastor of Central Lutheran Church, Mondovi, Wisconsin. Herder served as secretary of the Committee for 11 years and for three years as president, exchanging positions with Bernthal.[4]

Advocates for Advocacy

A few days after Ingrid Walter formally assumed responsibility as Director of LIRS, a meeting took place in New Orleans that presaged a significant new program development within LIRS. On January 5–6, 1977, LIRS New York staff and members of the Standing Committee met with regional consultants to discuss ways to phase down the federally funded LIRS regional offices, but, if possible, still maintain basic services to refugees and sponsoring congregations. The regional consultants were LIRS field staff attached to Lutheran social service agencies in areas of active resettlement. While urging continued federal support for their work, they expressed willingness, if necessary, to provide some services even without special funding. One of their recommendations was that a nationwide network of persons be established to serve as advocates for both public and private support for refugee concerns.

Ingrid Walter was also concerned about continued services to refugees and sponsors. She told the Standing Committee in February that it would be a tragedy if LIRS should lose the network of talented, active, and concerned individuals developed during the course of the Indochina program. But since government funding would not be available after September 30, 1977, she could only hope that at least some of the Lutheran social service agencies would be able to absorb the costs of the regional consultant services, with possible aid from New York on a case-by-case basis.[5]

Meanwhile, with their recommendations on advocacy in mind, the consultants set up an ad hoc task force to prepare resolutions seeking to enlist support from the Coalition of Executives of Lutheran Social Service Agencies, meeting in Minneapolis in April. They won unanimous endorsement for a request to the Standing Committee of LIRS to take the lead in establishing a national advocacy network and to designate an LIRS staff position to be filled by a person who would maintain such a network. The task force also requested Lutheran social service agencies to identify persons within their staffs to carry special responsibility for refugee concerns. An almost immediate response came from Lutheran agencies in Ohio and Iowa, which expressed their readiness both to continue refugee services and to participate in advocacy work. Another resolution called upon Lutheran church bodies to join in "active advocacy" in support of LIRS work on behalf of immigrants and refugees.[6]

The new director's major concern at the moment was the pending expiration of federal funding and the possible closing down of the regional consultants' offices. Advocacy to prevent this would be welcome, but the establishment of a national network for general advocacy seemed to her to be premature. Moreover, as the Vietnam resettlement program was moving toward completion in March 1976, the Standing Committee had directed staff to undertake a comprehensive policy review and to prepare recommendations for the future direction of LIRS in the event of possible new refugee programs. This was a crucial matter that needed immediate attention before the September funding deadline.

In view of the urgency of these concerns, Walter was reluctant to wait for the next regular meeting of the Standing Committee in June. She therefore called a telephone conference on May 10 to bring an important request before them. Citing the long-postponed policy review as uppermost, she asked authorization for the temporary appointment of a full-time staff person as Coordinator for U.S. Immigration Concerns. No fiscal adjustments would be needed until the following year, she explained, since the position of Assistant Director had been vacated. This person, she added, could also work with the regional consultants to establish an advocacy network.[7]

Authorization was promptly given for the appointment of Kenneth J. Stumpf, a lawyer and an ordained clergyman of The Lutheran Church—Missouri Synod.[8] Ingrid Walter welcomed Stumpf to the staff at the June 16–17 meeting of the Standing Committee. Her introduction made it clear that the formation of an advocacy task force would be his responsibility, but she indicated that the idea would require careful preliminary study. Copies of an "Advo-Kit," prepared at the request of the ad hoc task force and containing their suggestions for developing this new activity, were distributed to the Standing Committee. The Committee gave its approval to a definition of advocacy as "a system of churchwide organizations, congregations, and individuals to enable creative action in the area of immigration and refugee concerns for human justice, by encouraging discussions of and education on specific issues, by disseminating materials, by enlisting and promoting actions, and by participating in feedback through the network."[9]

The Committee also identified areas of immediate concern to which advocacy efforts might be directed, notably the adjustment of status for Indochina refugees and the continuation of the Indochina Refugee Assistance Program beyond September 30, 1977. Others of longer range were world refugees, undocumented aliens, U.S. refugee policy, and immigration law.

Eager to move ahead, the regional consultants took action at their next meeting in October, recommending personnel for the projected task force. Subject to confirmation by the Standing Committee, they nominated four of their members to represent four areas of the country: East Coast, Central, North Central, and West Coast. Four additional positions were suggested, to be filled by LIRS, to assure representation from churchwide agencies, judicatories, and Lutheran social service agencies.[10]

The initial meeting of the task force was held in New York on February 7–8, 1978, more than a year after the first request was made for its establishment. In preparation for the meeting Walter and Stumpf scheduled a series of meetings with all regional consultants to discuss goals and methods. Each area coordinator was asked to provide a core list of names to be included in network mailings. National church organizations, such as Lutheran Church Women and the Lutheran Human Relations Association, were also asked for names of contact persons.

Following their New York meeting, members of the task force appointed other interested regional consultants as "enablers" to complete the structure of each area of the network. They also agreed to send ideas for advocacy actions to the New York office to be shared with other task force members and, when appropriate, with all regional consultants.[11]

One of the first uses of this reporting process occurred in September 1978, when Kenneth Stumpf returned from area meetings with recommendations for actions by the Standing Committee. One request was for special legislation to admit 15,000 additional Cambodian refugees to the United States. The second was a request based on the 1969 LCUSA statement on "Immigration Policy: Moral Issues and the National Interest." That statement declared it to be an obligation of U.S. immigration law that the U.S. accept a fair share of international responsibility for the resettlement of persons urgently in need of a safe haven. The request was for legislation to admit 50,000 refugees each year. The Standing Committee passed resolutions supporting both requests.[12]

Declarations of support for such causes were not new to Lutheran refugee agencies. For nearly half a century they had issued statements of policy and urged particular actions upon the Congress and the President of the United States. What was new was that for the first time, the Lutheran Immigration and Refugee Service had an organized network of people and agencies in the field through which such concerns could be communicated both at governmental and grassroots levels.

Ingrid Walter's initial concerns for a policy review and her fears of budget restraints were swept aside when the new U.S. refugee programs from 1978 to 1980 practically determined LIRS policies for the immediate future. Resettlement matters dominated the agendas of LIRS and also overshadowed the effort to establish an advocacy network. Federal funds were available for processing and placing refugees, but not for advocacy. There was money to support the work of the 39 LIRS regional consultants, but their services were urgently needed for soliciting sponsorships or verifying offers from "anchor relatives."

The net result was that the formation of an LIRS advocacy network was temporarily set aside. Regional consultants continued their resettlement and casework activities for LIRS. Some consultants became involved in advocacy efforts on behalf of programs especially related to the groups of refugees with whom they were working. Meanwhile, LIRS and LCUSA continued their established patterns of advocacy, directing carefully crafted and pointed statements on issues of crucial importance to appropriate agencies and persons within the U.S. government.

Discovering the Undocumented

The LIRS had first become involved in the nationwide debate over the issue of undocumented aliens in 1976 when Congress amended the 1965 Immigration and Nationality Act, limiting the number of immigrants eligible to enter the United States from Mexico and Central America. Traditionally, the borders of the United States had been open to neighbor countries of the Western Hemisphere. The 1976 amendment, however, established a limit of

176

20,000 immigrants a year from any single country in the hemisphere. Since 62,205 immigrants had entered the United States from Mexico in 1975—the year before the limit was imposed—it seemed likely that the legal limit would be exceeded in 1976 and that the number of "illegal aliens" from Mexico, resident in the United States, would increase from year to year.[13]

LIRS opposed the 1976 amendment as discriminatory because it imposed the same limit on Mexico as on other Latin American countries. This provision ignored the fact that as our nearest neighbor, Mexico normally sent more immigrants to the United States than any other country. In January 1977, President Carter proposed reforms that would assure fair treatment both for newcomers and for the estimated three to six million undocumented persons already in the country. Congress established a Select Committee on Immigration and Refugee Policy to investigate and hold public hearings on the laws, policies, and procedures by which refugees entered the United States.[14]

In 1980, after two years of intense involvement with settling refugees from overseas, LIRS reentered the national debate on undocumented aliens. On February 6, the Standing Committee adopted "A Study Document of Principles on the Undocumented Alien Issue." After reaffirming the objectives of the 1969 LCUSA statement on "Immigration Policy: Moral Issues and the National Interest," the document offered a theological framework for the humane treatment of "strangers" entering a foreign country, followed by a series of specific recommendations.[15] The Lutheran Council affirmed the statement and distributed it, together with the recommendations, for discussion by churches and agencies. The Council called for (1) a contemporary update of registration for undocumented aliens; (2) an increase in admissions limits for neighboring countries; (3) primary preferences for family reunifications; (4) developmental aid to neighbor countries to raise economic standards; (5) no employer sanctions for hiring aliens; (6) full protection of the Bill of Rights for aliens; (7) further study of the merits of a temporary worker program; and (8) full benefits of the social welfare and educational system for aliens. The church was urged to exercise its prophetic role as an advocate of justice and a foe of exploitation.[16]

Closely related to the issue of undocumented aliens from Mexico and Central America was the continued effort to secure fair and just

177

treatment for Haitian asylum seekers. In spite of the clear documentation provided in the courtroom of Judge King, the Reagan Administration still refused to acknowledge Haitians as political refugees. Consequently, when their "entrant" status expired, their individual requests for asylum were regularly denied. Almost 2,000 Haitians remained in detention, many in the dingy Krome Camp in Miami. Both LIRS and LCUSA issued statements urging Lutherans to address letters to congressional representatives or to the Justice Department in Washington, objecting to the incarceration of the Haitians while they awaited asylum proceedings before the Immigration and Naturalization Service. "Due process," according to an official statement by LIRS, "should be guaranteed for those seeking asylum in the United States ... without regard to race, political persuasion, or other discriminatory factors." Efforts on behalf of the incarcerated Haitians were rewarded on June 29, 1982, when Judge Eugene Spellman of the Federal District Court in Miami ordered the release of the Haitians, with assurance of legal counsel during their asylum hearings.[17]

In February 1981, the Standing Committee held its meeting in El Paso, Texas. Committee members visited the INS processing center at the Mexican border and drove along the American side of the Rio Grande, where many illegal crossings into the United States were made. They looked at the fence erected by the U.S. government and observed the contrast between the affluent and the poverty-stricken areas of Juarez, Mexico, just across the border from El Paso.

These experiences provided a better understanding of the conditions at the border and moved the Committee to ask its subcommittee on undocumented alien policy to prepare an analysis of the forthcoming report of the Congressional Select Committee, to formulate responses and to develop a procedure for advocacy on behalf of the undocumented.[18]

A Look at the Salvadorans

While in El Paso, members of the Standing Committee also became aware of the vastly increased numbers of first asylum refugees from El Salvador entering the United States. Political upheavals in 1979 and 1980 had produced refugees from the brutal military regime in that country, fleeing because of threats to their lives. These were "asylum seekers," in contrast to the thousands of Mexicans who were temporary workers or persons seeking to join their families in the United States.[19]

Estimates placed 100,000 to 300,000 Salvadorans already in the United States. But most disturbing were the reports that virtually all Salvadorans who were apprehended at the border were being sent back, their claims for asylum under the 1965 revision of the Immigration and Nationality Act systematically denied. In 1980 no Salvadorans were granted asylum, and 12,000 were deported.

In August 1981, to ascertain the actual facts, the Standing Committee engaged Mary Solberg, former editor and a graduate of Adelphi University School of Social Work, to prepare a study of Salvadoran refugees as a basis for possible action by LIRS. Solberg's report described the situation of violence and repression in El Salvador, the treatment Salvadoran refugees were receiving at the hands of the INS, and the grim prospects awaiting them upon deportation. It also outlined some of the responses church people in the Southwest were beginning to make, on an ecumenical basis, to the influx of Salvadorans. One of the recommendations of her report was the establishment of a vigorous program of public education and of advocacy on behalf of the refugees for the granting of asylum as bona fide refugees in demonstrable danger if they were returned to their country.

The assassination of Roman Catholic Archbishop Oscar Arnulfo Romero in March 1980, as he said mass in a hospital chapel in San Salvador; the rape and murder of four American church workers; and other brutal activities perpetrated by death squads sponsored by Salvadoran security forces—as well as the consistent denial of asylum to Salvadorans on the grounds they were economic rather than political refugees produced angry outcries from U.S. churches and humanitarian agencies. Not only were bona fide refugees being sent back to imprisonment or death, but the United States government was sending millions in aid to El Salvador, to a government that failed to bring to justice the perpetrators of violence.[20]

Likewise, the spectacle of the U.S. Coast Guard intercepting Haitian refugee boats on the high seas, bound for the United States— in clear violation of the 1967 United Nations Protocol relating to the Status of Refugees—brought vigorous public protest. While condemning Southeast Asian governments for driving boat people from their shores, the United States was doing the same to Haitians.

A Step Forward for Advocacy

Lutheran resettlement agencies had long advocated liberal and just immigration laws and had frequently been critical of proposed or existing legislation, including the political interpretation of laws governing asylum for refugees. But the new injustices, occurring on American soil, drew from many LIRS-related staff, especially those in the field who were providing legal and humanitarian aid to Haitian, Cuban, or Salvadoran refugees in danger of deportation, a demand for a more comprehensive program of advocacy.

In response to this demand, LIRS scheduled a consultation in November 1982, with representation from Lutheran agencies, regional consultants, church bodies, LCUSA's Office of Governmental Affairs (OGA) in Washington, the LIRS Standing Committee, and New York staff. The stated purpose of the consultation was to assess the status of advocacy in the church and to explore ways of dealing with public issues. As members of the consultation reported on the activities of the organizations they represented, it became clear that organized advocacy was widely accepted and was already being implemented both by church bodies and by church-related agencies. Both the LCA and the ALC had concluded that a biblically-based distinction could be made between advocacy and lobbying. Lobbying was directed toward personal or corporate interests, while advocacy connoted educational and political efforts on behalf of justice and human welfare. The LCA operated a Public Policy Coalition, especially focused on issues of state government. The ALC assigned advocacy responsibilities to its Office of Church and Society, and in Washington, the LCUSA Office of Governmental Affairs served its member churches as ears and eyes in the nation's capital. Specific actions had been implemented by all the networks.[21]

Nevertheless, another consultation was scheduled for April 1983, to continue the discussion of an advocacy structure for LIRS. In January, Kenneth Stumpf reported to the Standing Committee that he felt it necessary to meet with each of the church body leaders who, he felt, might be hesitant about setting up an extensive advocacy program when existing networks could accomplish the same purpose.[22]

180

At the April consultation a plan for a regional network similar to that proposed by the regional consultants in 1977 was approved and recommended to the LIRS Standing Committee. The Committee in turn approved the proposal and established a budget of $80,000 for nine months, beginning June 1, 1983. Five percent of the time of each regional consultant was to be set aside for advocacy work. Four of the consultants would be designated as "area enablers" for each of four regions of the country. Additional time would be allocated for them to coordinate advocacy efforts by other consultants. The entire action, however, was conditioned upon the acquisition of additional nongovernmental funding.[23]

The Standing Committee also approved the appointment of an Advisory Committee on Advocacy. Its twelve members included church body representatives, "key immigration and refugee advocates," a Standing Committee member, an OGA representative, and a staff member from the LIRS Policy Development Section. The stated purpose was to act as an advisory and review body for advocacy positions and maintain contacts with other key networks. Procedurally, LIRS would disseminate information through the regional consultants located in LSS offices throughout the country.[24]

Only one part of the plan was formally implemented. Zdenka Seiner, an LIRS staff member in New York, was deployed to the LCUSA Office of Governmental Affairs in Washington for two days each week. Very quickly, however, this assignment developed into a full-time position, through which LIRS was able to monitor the progress of refugee and immigration matters in Congress and in the Departments of State, Justice, and Health and Human Services. In 1985 John Fredriksson, who had served as LIRS coordinator at Camp Chaffee during the Cuban program and later as coordinator of the Haitian program in Chicago, became the LIRS staff person in Washington. He became the major conduit for information about what was occurring in the capital, both for the New York staff and for the "enablers" of the LIRS advocacy network.[25]

13

Ministry to the Undocumented

With the advent of the Reagan Administration in January, 1981, the staff and Standing Committee of LIRS concluded that the agency must look carefully at its long-range projections. With fewer refugees being admitted, government funding would also decline, and LIRS would have to decide which programs to maintain and what staff it could afford.

Consequently, when budget proposals from LIRS regional consultants and agency executives were submitted in November 1981, the Standing Committee declared an immediate budget freeze and engaged a consultant to make a programmatic and financial analysis. After an extended review of operations both in New York and in the field, a Long Range Planning Task Force was appointed in mid-June 1982, with representation from the entire LIRS network. Their work resulted in major changes in management patterns and in the operational structure of LIRS.[1]

A Problem of Balances

The financial pressures opened the way for the resolution of a long-standing uncertainty about the use of accumulated balances in its resettlement funds. According to the contracts it made with the federal government, government funds were to be used for expenses incurred only under the program for which those funds were granted. For this reason, LIRS maintained a separate account for each program subsidized by a government contract. Such expenses included staff salaries, processing costs, and follow-up services to refugees.[2]

Substantial balances accumulated in these accounts during the resettlement process and were gradually spent during the follow-up period that extended over two years. Under the original Vietnam program, nearly $8 million in per capita grants had been paid to LIRS by the government. Accumulating interest, in a period of high interest rates, helped to maintain a substantial balance, even after both processing costs and follow-up services had been reimbursed.[3] In 1981 LIRS requested the State Department to release these funds for use in connection with any of the U.S.-supported programs, rather than only for refugees resettled under the original grants.[4]

While its request was pending, LIRS was subjected to some unpleasant publicity over the $6 million balance in its resettlement fund. A study of resettlement programs by an independent foundation commissioned by the State Department reported this figure, and it caught the attention of the House Subcommittee on Immigration and Refugees of the Committee on the Judiciary. LIRS was requested to provide an explanation.[5]

August Bernthal, chairman of the Standing Committee, appeared before the Subcommittee and explained that during the resettlement of the Vietnamese refugees LIRS had not made direct grants to refugees, as some agencies had done. Instead, thousands of nongovernment dollars and services had been provided to the refugees by the churches and sponsoring congregations, making it possible for LIRS to support a longer-term program of follow-up services. Since these Vietnam funds could not be used for other subsequently authorized programs, LIRS was actually operating currently on a deficit budget. Only in January 1982 had the State Department given permission to use funds accumulated during the Vietnam program in other resettlement operations. Bernthal assured the Subcommittee that the funds were now being rapidly and responsibly spent.[6]

Ingrid Walter, too, was called to testify before a Senate subcommittee and was also interviewed for television by an NBC reporter. Only brief edited excerpts from the interview were aired, which did little either to explain or clarify the situation.[7] Some months later the *Reader's Digest* published an article referring to the LIRS fund balance and assailing the integrity of all voluntary agencies engaged in resettlement. LIRS responded by publishing a "Fact Sheet," refuting the charges.[8]

Budgetary concerns for the fiscal year beginning March 1, 1982, were greatly alleviated by the freeing of the restricted funds. The Standing Committee elected to use them for developing job opportunities for refugees and promoting congregational sponsorships. For 1982–83, the Committee allocated $1,100,000 of the residual funds to supplement current funds already budgeted for regional projects. Consultants and congregations were instructed to prepare special grant requests for these purposes. Over the following two years, similar program grants for refugees, administered through Lutheran social service agencies and congregations, substantially exhausted the residual funds.[9]

Reviewing Management and Mission

To achieve necessary additional economies, the Task Force on Planning recommended that the management model of the New York office be revised. Accordingly, a new structure became operational on November 1, 1982, reducing the New York office staff from 50 to 39 persons.

In view of the anticipated reductions in the number of incoming refugees, the Task Force also recommended that sponsorship recruitment efforts be concentrated in those areas of the country that experience had shown to be most responsive to refugee needs. They therefore proposed a consolidation of areas, reducing the number of regional offices from 34 to 23, beginning March 1, 1983.[10]

Four senior staff constituted the new management team in New York: the Director, a Director for Policy and Program, an Associate Director for Policy Development, and an Associate Director for Program Services. Ingrid Walter continued as Director, carrying primary responsibility for relationships with U.S. government and international agencies and with the American Council of Voluntary Agencies for Foreign Service. Franklin Jensen, who had been in charge of church and agency relations, became Director for Policy and Program. He was responsible for overall administration and coordination of national resettlement operations and the network of regional offices.

Program Services were managed by Associate Director Marta Brenden. She supervised a staff of four regional program coordinators responsible for refugee casework, screening of personnel data, reviewing sponsorships, and providing consultation or referral for unusual problems.

The Associate Director for Policy Development, Kenneth Stumpf, monitored immigration legislation, advocacy efforts, and supervised programs for Cuban-Haitian and Central American concerns. Following his resignation in November 1983, these areas were absorbed by Jensen, the Director for Policy and Program.[11]

Accompanying the reorganization of its staff patterns, LIRS undertook a careful review of its long-range goals and objectives. At its meeting on May 4, 1983, the Standing Committee adopted a Mission Statement, reaffirming the historic commitment of LIRS as an outreach ministry of the churches and the congregations. The intent of its program was

> To implement the concerns of Lutheran churches and their congregations for refugees and immigration policies and programs by
>
> 1. Encouraging Lutheran congregations, inspired and motivated by the mandate and example of Jesus Christ, to respond to needs of refugees, immigrants, undocumented persons, and other aliens as an integral part of their total ministry.
>
> 2. Enabling congregations to effectively carry out such a ministry by providing necessary support services.
>
> 3. Promoting the emotional well-being and economic self-sufficiency of refugees and advocating for the needs of undocumented persons and other aliens.
>
> 4. Alerting Lutheran church bodies, synods, districts, congregations, and constituents to the needs of refugees, undocumented persons and other aliens.
>
> 5. Serving as advocates between government and theimmigrant or refugee in matters of legislation and its administration.[12]

In listing immediate objectives based upon the mission statement, the Standing Committee left no doubt, even in the face of declining numbers of refugees being admitted to the United States, that refugee resettlement would continue to be a major part of the LIRS program. But beginning in 1980 and 1981 concerns relating to the movement of people to the United States as a country of first asylum had commanded increased attention from all voluntary agencies. LCUSA itself had adopted a "Statement on Undocumented Persons" in May 1981. The denial of asylum to Haitians and Salvadorans and the presence of thousands of undocumented aliens in the United

States, fearful of deportation, raised issues of justice and fairness that could not be ignored. New prominence was therefore given to the intention of LIRS to propose and advocate more humane policies for dealing with world refugees and to make representation to the U.S. government for more equitable immigration laws.

The acceptance of this challenge by LIRS was not only reflected in its statement of goals. The new administrative structure established a major departmental unit for policy development, with special responsibility for advocacy and for programs dealing with the problems of asylum seekers and undocumented aliens. This step also had financial implications for an organization facing fiscal problems because of declining government subsidies.[13]

Central American Concerns

The leadership of LIRS had already begun to face the issues of first asylum when it decided to establish a program of Central American Concerns. Their action followed the LCUSA Statement in May 1981 (and Mary Solberg's graphic reporting in August 1981) of the presence of 200,000 undocumented Salvadorans in the United States and the refusal of the U.S. government to grant them safe haven. In a series of actions on September 24, 1981, the Standing Committee voted to give wide circulation to Solberg's report and to cooperate with other voluntary agencies in providing legal aid and social services to asylum seekers, and in advocacy efforts on behalf of the Salvadorans. They also voted to create a new position, Coordinator for Central American Concerns, and shortly thereafter invited Solberg to accept the appointment.[14]

Recognizing that a program directed to serving people who were not regarded by the government as bona fide refugees could not be supported by government funds, the Standing Committee transferred $100,000 to Central American Concerns from funds contributed by the churches for the Cuban-Haitian program. They also urged that an appeal be made to the church bodies for additional funds and that a similar request be directed to the Lutheran World Federation, Department of World Service, on an emergency basis "to provide life-saving legal services to Salvadorans." Lutheran churches in Europe and Canada responded with commitments totaling $80,000.

The office for Central American Concerns (CAC) began its operation in October 1981, with a threefold agenda: funding for legal representation and social services for Salvadoran refugees, education of Lutheran constituencies concerning the Salvadoran situation, and advocacy with U.S. government offices and agencies on behalf of Salvadoran refugees.[15]

In spite of U.S. constitutional assurances that any person apprehended and charged with violation of the law is guaranteed legal counsel and a judicial hearing, Salvadorans by the thousands were being detained and summarily returned to their country without opportunity even to apply for legal asylum. It was common practice for INS officials to urge a refugee to accept "voluntary departure" rather than run the risk of deportation by the INS, which would bar any subsequent legal entry into the United States. If the option of voluntary departure were not accepted, the refugee was still entitled by law to file an application for asylum. But until a court hearing could be scheduled, the refugee was placed in detention unless a bond were posted, usually not an easy matter to arrange. When the hearing finally took place, it was virtually certain that the application would be rejected.

In the course of proceedings such as these, the availability of friendly legal counsel was crucial. Privately supported ecumenical organizations such as El Rescate (The Rescue) in Los Angeles, the Valley Religious Task Force in Phoenix, Lutheran Latino Ministries in San Francisco, and the Border Association for Refugees from Central America in south Texas offered legal assistance as the centerpiece of their aid programs.[16]

The office of Central American Concerns made its first grant of $10,000 to El Rescate in Los Angeles, a new organization that subsequently developed into the most effective agency for aid to Salvadorans in Southern California. When the check was ready for mailing, Mary Solberg and several of her colleagues carried the envelope to the postbox on the corner of 25th Street and Park Avenue South, just outside the LIRS office. They gathered in a circle around the postbox, and as the envelope was dropped in, joined in prayer for those who would be aided through the gift and for all persons in the world suffering persecution and violence. During its first year of operation, Central American Concerns distributed $112,000 for selected projects of seven agencies and organizations in Los Angeles, San Francisco, Phoenix, Tucson, New Orleans, southern Texas, and New York City.

The promotion of constituency education took a variety of forms. The Report on the Salvadoran Situation was circulated throughout Lutheran church offices and the LIRS network of regional consultants and among other denominations and voluntary agencies. The Coordinator produced articles for church publications. Radio, television, and press interviews were scheduled in major cities. Presentations were given at conferences, churches, and church conventions, explaining the problem of the undocumented alien, and particularly the Salvadoran refugee. Solberg played a key role in organizing and facilitating the first major gathering of church-related and legal advocates for Salvadorans, national and local, at Encino, California, in February 1983. This consultation generated several ecumenical projects, including a ten-city tour, "Let the People Speak: Salvadoran Refugees Take Their Story to the American People"; a resource packet for distribution through national church bodies; and the endorsement of a national petition for "extended voluntary departure."[17]*

At the outset advocacy was focused primarily on Washington, D.C. The LCUSA Office of Governmental Affairs arranged interviews with officials of the State Department, the Bureau of Human Rights, the Coordinator for Refugee Affairs, the INS, members of both houses of Congress, and Washington representatives of other voluntary agencies. The thrust of these efforts was to call attention to the discriminatory policy being employed against Salvadoran refugees by the U.S. government, based upon its political and military support of the Salvadoran government. Although killings and death threats against civilians were daily occurrences in El Salvador, the U.S. government chose to maintain the fiction that Salvadoran refugees were simply looking for a better economic situation.

An article in the *Los Angeles Times* on July 15, 1981, reported a typical case in which a judge's decision was based upon political policy rather than the "well-founded fear of persecution" experi-

---

* (Extended voluntary departure is a temporary and renewable legal status of "safe haven," granted by the federal government to all citizens of another country present in the U.S. who would be in grave danger if they had to return to their country of origin.)

enced by the refugee escaping from his country. The report recounted the experience of Ricardo Ernandes, 21, a trade union organizer, who claimed political asylum because of his union activities. "In his petition he said he had been shot at three times in El Salvador and that his cousin had been mistaken for him, and shot and killed. The killer had left a note on the cousin's chest, saying that they had been seeking Ernandes. 'The judge wanted concrete proofs!' said Ernandes, who has been in the El Centro (California) detention camp for eight months. 'How am I supposed to give him concrete proofs? Three times they came looking for me because I was active in a labor union in my factory. The last time they shot at me, but they missed. I know who they were, they were National Guardsmen in civilian dress, and they had government guns. Everybody in El Salvador understands these things.' "[18]

At the encouragement of CAC, LCUSA joined other religious and legal advocacy groups in a Freedom of Information lawsuit, calling on the INS to provide names and addresses of Salvadorans returned to their country between March and August 1981. The Council also joined as a cocomplainant before the Organization of American States Human Rights Commission in protesting human and legal rights violations against Salvadoran refugees in the United States. Persistent efforts to secure legislation for "extended voluntary departure" for all Salvadoran refugees in the United States until a Presidential study could determine the presence or absence of persecution in El Salvador finally produced a bill in Congress, sponsored by Representative Joseph Moakley of Massachusetts and Senator Dennis DeConcini of Arizona, but it was unable to gain the necessary votes for passage.[19]

The Sanctuary Movement

By the fall of 1982, the issue of undocumented persons in the United States had become as important as the resettlement of refugees from overseas. The Standing Committee requested staff to prepare a draft statement of the position of LIRS regarding asylum issues. Press reports described increasing migrations across the border, not only of Mexicans and Salvadorans, but Guatemalans and Hondurans as well. On March 24, 1982, the second anniversary of the assassination of Archbishop Romero in San Salvador, churches of several denominations in the United States launched what became known as the sanctuary movement. Eventually, scores of congregations offered physical sanctuary and support to Salvadoran and Guatemalan refugees, while many other churches gave support to a designated "public sanctuary church" in their community. Among Lutheran congregations, Angelica in Los Angeles, University Lutheran in Berkeley, and Luther Place Memorial in Washington, D.C., were the first to announce participation.[20]

Advocates of sanctuary affirmed the practice as a ministry of compassion with roots in an Old Testament tradition, according to which certain cities were set apart as places where an accused person could find refuge from avengers until fair judgment could be rendered by proper authorities. American history provided the example of the Underground Railroad, through which slaves were sheltered and assisted in their flight to freedom. Salvadorans or Guatemalans, it was declared, were not criminals, but were merely seeking a haven of protection from life-threatening conditions in their homeland until it was safe for them to return. To compel such refugees to return to the brutality and repression from which they had fled would be in itself an act of callous legalism, if not outright criminality.[21]

In a mail ballot on March 25, 1983, the Standing Committee voted unanimously to affirm the ministry of congregations providing sanctuary to Central American refugees.[22] Church body presidents, however, were more cautious about "encouraging civil disobedience." They advised the Lutheran Council to "inform its participating church bodies" of the actions of LIRS and the Division of Mission and Ministry affirming the use of churches as sanctuaries for undocumented refugees, but declined to endorse the actions.[23]

When the budget preparations were begun for 1983–84, the first full year of CAC, the Standing Committee again faced a financial problem. Once more Cuban-Haitian program funds were transferred to CAC. Church bodies of LCUSA provided some additional funds, and member churches of LWF committed $93,000 to complete CAC's budget of $295,400.[24]

Each succeeding year CAC struggled to maintain its operating budget and its grants programs. Consistent annual support from member churches of the Lutheran World Federation reflected their understanding of the Central American crisis as an international issue. In April 1983, when the Department of World Service decided to open an office in San Salvador, El Salvador, as a part of its world-wide program, it chose Mary Solberg as the first LWF representative for Central America.

Under the direction of Lauren McMahon, the CAC continued its threefold agenda of legal and social services aid, education, and advocacy. Using only privately contributed funds, it was able each year to award grants totaling from $100,000 to $150,000 to agencies engaged in direct services to undocumented refugees. In 1985 the Ford Foundation approved a $400,000 grant to the CAC program over a three-year cycle, to be matched by church funds.[25]

Legislative advocacy continued as a regular feature of the CAC agenda. From 1982 until 1986 much of its effort was focused on the Immigration Reform and Control Act, known during its tortuous congressional odyssey as the Simpson-Mazzoli Bill. The growing numbers and greater visibility of first asylum seekers and the in-creasing use of the political asylum process caused alarm among some members of Congress and segments of the public. Many felt the United States should insulate its borders more effectively and administer its immigration quotas and refugee admission proce-dures more strictly.

First introduced by Senator Alan Simpson of Wyoming, the bill emphasized "control" of U.S. borders and immigration policies. One of its provisions made it possible to "summarily exclude," that is, not admit at the border, persons seeking to enter unless they artic-ulated a claim to political asylum satisfactory to the Border Patrol Officer. The role of the judicial system would thus be replaced by the administrative structure of the Immigration and Naturalization Service.[26]

Legalizing the Undocumented

Other key elements of the law were the legalization of undo-cumented aliens, sanctions against employees who hired undocu-mented aliens, substantial changes in asylum laws, and major revisions of the legal immigration process.

LIRS supported the principle of legalization, but favored setting an arrival date later than 1980 for undocumented aliens to register for "temporary residence status." The granting of legal status to a larger number of persons already in the country would, in LIRS' view, reduce both fears and tensions and promote the economic and social well-being of the entire country.

LIRS stongly opposed the provision in the Simpson-Mazzoli bill imposing fines or prison sentences on employers who knowingly hired undocumented workers. The costs of supervision and enforcement of such a law, it contended, would be exorbitant both for businesses and for government. Most employers would try to avoid sanctions by avoiding hiring "foreign-looking" workers. Discrimination against both U.S. citizens and legal immigrants might easily result, simply because they "looked foreign" or did not speak English well. Moreover, on the basis of a 20-country study, the Government Accounting Office (GAO) had concluded that the system was simply not workable.

These weaknesses in the bill, unless amended, were sufficient in the judgment of LIRS to neutralize its effectiveness in meeting the basic problems of first asylum and the thousands of undocumented aliens living illegally in the United States. When the bill finally passed on November 6 as the Immigration Reform and Control Act of 1986, a coalition of voluntary agencies registered disappointment that although the eligibility date for legalization had been moved from 1980 to 1982, their efforts to remove the provision for employer sanctions had not been successful.[27]

As a long-time advocate of legalization, LIRS was prepared to participate in the processing of eligible applicants. Following approval of the legislation, LIRS staff conducted a preliminary survey of interest among its affiliated Lutheran social service agencies. It found a strong consensus of support for Lutheran involvement. Numerous meetings were conducted by the INS to explain the program and procedures to be followed.[28]

The law established a twelve-month period beginning May 5, 1987, during which applications were to be received. To implement the program, the INS entered into cooperative agreements with "qualified designated entities" (QDEs). QDEs could include voluntary agencies such as LIRS, or any agency recognized by the Board of Immigration Appeals as having staff qualified to represent individuals before the INS and immigration judges.

The INS provided limited funding to designated agencies at the rate of $16 per local application. Two dollars were retained by the central agency, and $14 were passed on to the direct service providers (DSPs). Processing fees levied upon the applicant by the INS and the local DSP were expected to average about $100 per person.

On January 22, 1987, the Standing Committee endorsed full participation in the legalization program and authorized additional staff to coordinate the activities of 42 field offices (DSPs) in which the actual processing would take place. Administration of the program was handled by a special team of LIRS staff, headed by Carol Smalley, and assisted by a part-time consultant, Estelle Strizhak, an experienced immigration practitioner. As a "national coordinator," the LIRS team in New York provided training, technical assistance, and supervision for the DSPs.[29]

The program opened on May 5. During the first 90 days the Lutheran network responded to 23,000 inquiries. Before the program was terminated one year later, LIRS had assisted more than 5,000 persons to secure legalization papers.

14

Strengthening Home Resources

Over a period of 14 months, between January 1984 and March 1985, LIRS experienced sweeping changes in its administrative leadership. Having guided the agency through a review of its long-range goals and a reorganization of its staff patterns in 1982 and 1983, Franklin Jensen retired as Director for Policy and Program on January 15, 1984. Jensen had joined LIRS in 1979 as Director for Church and Agency Relations, after 26 years as a parish pastor and ten years as executive of the Department of Church and Society in the Lutheran Church in America. He was succeeded by Donald H. Larsen, Executive Director of LCUSA's Division of Mission and Ministry, of which LIRS was a department.

When Larsen was invited to join LIRS, he did so with the understanding that he would succeed Ingrid Walter as director upon her retirement. Walter retired on January 1, 1985, after 35 years of service with LIRS, and Larsen became the new LIRS director. As a pastor of The Lutheran Church—Missouri Synod, Larsen had joined the staff of the Lutheran Council when it was first established in 1967. He had served as Secretary of the Department of Church and Community Planning and as Executive Director of the Office of Research, Planning, and Development before becoming Executive Director of DMM.[1]

As he assumed leadership of LIRS, Larsen gave his attention to three major tasks: the reorganization of staff, budgetary concerns, and LIRS relations with its supporting church bodies. As the former Executive Director of DMM, the administrative supervisor of LIRS, Larsen was already familiar with these concerns, and his year as Director for Policy and Planning for LIRS had brought him into even more direct contact with them.

To manage daily operations, Larsen chose three associate directors to head three national staff units: Program Services, Marta Brenden; Planning and Development, John Griswold; and Administration and Finance, Karl Fritch. The Washington-based Associate for Governmental Affairs, Zdenka Seiner, also reported to the Director. The Director and three associates constituted the management team. They met twice each month and the full staff once a month.[2]

The new unit for Program Services, under Marta Brenden's direction, carried responsibility for resettlement and services to refugees. Sponsorships continued to be sought. New refugees were arriving. Special needs of refugee families were being cared for by congregations and LSS agencies. But the climate in which resettlement was being conducted had undergone significant changes.

The issue of first asylum, dramatized by the Cuban-Haitian movement in 1980, followed by the flood of illegal entries from El Salvador and Guatemala, placed the refugee question in a new context. Since World War II, the U.S. government had enjoyed the luxury of deciding which, how many, and under what conditions refugees should be admitted to this country. After 1980, the United States had to be concerned about how and how much to try to maintain the integrity of its own borders against illegal infiltration by thousands of asylum seekers fleeing oppression in their home countries.

Voluntary agencies such as LIRS, involved in the resettlement of refugees, were also affected by this change. As long-time champions of just and nondiscriminatory immigration laws, they could not remain silent when persons who were under threat of persecution or death at home were denied asylum by the United States government and in many cases were denied even the right to request it. Advocacy took on new importance, as the staff and the Standing Committee of LIRS contended for the civil rights of refugees at the border and for the rapid legalization of millions of undocumented aliens already living in the United States, but fearful of apprehension and possible deportation.

These developments did not signal any diminution of the world refugee problem. More than 14 million of the world's population were still in exile. Partly because of its new involvement with refugee problems of its own and partly because of the overall budgetary cuts imposed by the Reagan Administration, the United States drastically reduced the number of refugees admitted each year.[3]

Although the regular programs and procedures of the government continued, including the per capita reimbursement of the voluntary agencies, fewer refugees were available for resettlement. From a high point of 13,574 in 1980, LIRS placements dropped to 4965 in 1983.

The largest numbers processed by LIRS continued to be Vietnamese and Cambodians, but in 1983, 22 percent came from Europe and Africa. Famine and civil war in Ethiopia drove refugees by the thousands westward into the Sudan. LIRS was able to find sponsors for 74 emergency cases. Nearly 700 Europeans came from Poland, Hungary, Czechoslovakia, Romania, Bulgaria, Albania, and the Soviet Union.[4]

According to Tatiana Trelin, Records Manager, the number of placements increased to 6,070 in 1984, but declined steadily during the three succeeding years. In 1985, 5,760 persons were resettled, 4,998 in 1986, and 4095 in 1987.[5]

Special Refugee Programs

One of the special programs for the placement of Vietnamese refugees was the Orderly Departure Program (ODP), an arrangement developed by the United Nations High Commissioner for Refugees under which the Vietnamese government allowed certain of its citizens to emigrate. Family reunions were often facilitated through the ODP; and after 1982, a small number of Amerasian children were permitted to emigrate. ODP cases generally were processed through Bangkok in Thailand before coming to the United States. LIRS arrivals under this program increased from 125 in 1983 to 708 in 1986, but its continuation remained uncertain, depending to a great extent upon the status of relations between the U.S. and Vietnamese governments.[6]

Although LIRS continued to emphasize the role of congregations as sponsors, anchor relatives and the Lutheran social service agencies provided most sponsorships. As more refugees became established in this country, they were able to sponsor their compatriots. Lutheran social service agencies that undertook "blanket sponsorships" often were able to place families within Lutheran congregations. The largest percentages of church-sponsored refugees were found in Minnesota, Pennsylvania, and North Dakota. During 1983,

28 percent of all cases were welcomed by church sponsors.[7]

Because of the development of so-called impacted areas, such as southern California or southern Texas, with heavy concentrations of refugees, the U.S. Office of Refugees developed a project called Favorable Alternate Site Placement (FASP). Special advance studies of available housing and jobs were conducted with the aid of state or local governments. Participating voluntary agencies agreed to place a certain number of refugees at the site within a specified period of time. The U.S. Office of Refugees made funds available for social services. In the summer of 1983 LIRS participated in a project in Phoenix for 50 Vietnamese and another in Greensboro, North Carolina, for 200 Cambodians.[8]

Another community resettlement project involved the placement of a Vietnamese group called "Montagnards" in three cities in North Carolina. In recognition of its "excellent record of resettling refugees," LIRS was selected by the U.S. State Department as the sole voluntary agency to resettle the first Montagnard community in the United States.

During the Vietnam war the Montagnard people from the highlands of Southeast Asia had been close allies of the United States, fighting alongside the Special Forces known as the Green Berets. After the United States withdrew, the Montagnards continued their resistance, believing they were fulfilling the wishes of the U.S. government. In 1980 the resistance force of 4,000 Montagnards began a trek through Laos and Cambodia. Many died from combat, sickness, and starvation. In 1984, after surviving the labor camps of the Khmer Rouge, they escaped to a refugee camp in Thailand. About a year later, under pressure from private groups, former Green Berets, and the news media, the State Department was able to secure their release.

Representatives of the Lutheran Family Service agency in Greensboro, North Carolina, traveled to Bataan in the Philippines, where the Montagnards had been placed in a relocation camp, to learn more about these mountain people from Vietnam's southern highlands.

In November 1986, the 201 Montagnards were met at the Greensboro airport by hundreds of sponsors and by the press. Their sponsors were 50 congregations, 16 of them Lutheran, civic groups, and individuals in Greensboro, Charlotte, and Raleigh. Most of the

Montagnards were single men. By mid-December, all were studying English, many were already employed, and plans were underway for the formation of a mutual assistance association. John Griswold, LIRS Associate Director for Planning and Development, who coordinated the project, described it as a unique episode in immigration history. "This is special," he said, "since there is no other Montagnard community in the United States."[9]

Cultivating Lutheran Social Service Agencies

Fully as crucial to the effective operation of LIRS as its New York staff was the network of regional consultants. From a very tentative beginning during the Vietnam resettlement program of 1975–76, the regional consultants network had developed into an integral part of the LIRS system. This group of men and women, with offices in Lutheran social service agencies across the country, gave the Lutheran operation its distinctive character. Not only were they the partners of Lutheran congregations in securing sponsorships for refugees, but they brought to the follow-up services the resources and expertise of social service professionals.

The strengthening of a mutually supportive relationship between LIRS and the regional consultants network was a constant concern as the range of services expanded and became more complex. The regional consultants—or RCs—developed a coordinating committee with a representative from each of three geographical regions. This so-called RC–3 met three times a year as a channel for communication with the New York office and as an agenda committee for area and national conferences of regional consultants.

Relations of the Lutheran social service agencies themselves with LIRS grew closer because of the interaction of the RCs with both LIRS and the Lutheran social service agency executives, especially through the annual process of preparing budgets and funding requests. LIRS executives were invited to appear at meetings of the Coalition of Lutheran Social Service Executives to share information on LIRS programs and deepen personal relationships. Similar opportunities were extended to meet with agencies' boards of directors.

The Standing Committee of LIRS, in turn, developed a Peer Group Analysis Team, made up primarily of agency executives. They became a part of the LIRS planning process and were able to offer helpful counsel on financial matters. Beginning in 1983 LIRS staff teams, including one regional consultant on each team, conducted formal on-site visits to each regional office. They collected information about regional programs and sought to strengthen the sense of partnership in ministry. LIRS staff also conducted periodic orientation seminars for new regional consultants, to provide both a solid technical introduction and a broad perspective for the work of LIRS.[10]

While efforts were being made to strengthen relations with Lutheran social service agencies and the regional consultants, LIRS also laid strong emphasis upon its traditional relationship to the churches and their congregations. Mission executives of the member churches of LCUSA were invited to participate in the national conference for regional consultants, and to share their church's understanding of refugee resettlement and immigration concerns in its life and work.[11]

To provide a specific focus on refugee ministry, LIRS requested each of its supporting church bodies to appoint a Supplemental Staff Person. Initial appointments were made by all three church bodies, but only The Lutheran Church—Missouri Synod continued the appointment beyond the first year. Eugene Gunther began his work in January 1983, and the LCMS Board of Social Ministry agreed to share an operating budget of $10,000 with LIRS. One of Gunther's first projects was the establishment of a churchwide observance of a Refugee Concerns Sunday throughout the LCMS on April 17, 1983. Lily Wu, LIRS Associate for Information Services, provided material for every congregation. Hundreds of congregations requested additional pieces for their general use. The observance has since become an established annual event within the LCMS.[12]

Anticipating the ELCA

Anticipating the forthcoming merger of The American Lutheran Church, the Lutheran Church in America, and the Association of Evangelical Lutheran Churches, LIRS prepared a paper on the future directions and shape of refugee ministry in the Lutheran churches. They submitted the paper to the Task Force on Social Ministry of the Commission for a New Lutheran Church (CNLC), giving notice to the churches that LIRS "intends to start planning in 1984 to assure inter-Lutheran participation in this work beyond 1988."[13]

The following year the Commission for a New Lutheran Church established a joint committee with the LCMS and prepared a preliminary document describing a basic structure for future cooperation between the new Lutheran church and the LCMS. Since the Lutheran Council in the USA would be dissolved with the merging of three of its member churches, some special arrangements were necessary for carrying on work in such areas as refugee services, in which continued inter-Lutheran cooperation was desired.

The joint CNLC-LCMS Committee on Cooperation submitted its report to LIRS in November 1985, proposing general principles and guidelines to govern inter-Lutheran activities after the formation of the new church.[14] Following consultation with the management staff of LIRS, Donald Larsen responded, outlining his proposal that LIRS be incorporated as an independent cooperative agency. He suggested that the agency be governed by a board of directors, elected or appointed by the supporting Lutheran church bodies, and that annual financial support from the churches be continued. He expressed the hope that governing documents, including articles of incorporation, bylaws, and a policy manual could be drawn up by the end of 1986, anticipating the transition date of January 1, 1988.[15]

Under Budgetary Restraints

As the transition date approached, it was finally a financial problem rather than the future legal and functional relationship of LIRS to the new configuration of Lutheran churches that caused LIRS leadership the greatest concern. In November 1986, Larsen presented a paper to the Executive Committee of LCUSA, describing the fiscal crisis confronting LIRS and the circumstances which had produced it.[16] His request for $190,000 to meet an anticipated Resettlement Fund deficit for the fiscal year ending February 28, 1987, was declined by the Council and referred back to the Standing Committee of LIRS and its advisory groups to explore ways of resolving the crisis.

In a sharp response, the Standing Committee reminded the Council that LIRS had been mandated by the churches to operate a viable program to meet the needs of the world's uprooted people in response to God's love in Jesus Christ, and in partnership of service with the U.S. Department of State in refugee resettlement. On the instruction of the churches, LIRS had used its own reserve funds to meet the annual deficits since 1982. With the contribution of $500,000 to the current budget, LIRS' reserves were exhausted. The Committee and its advisory task force on finance concluded that without additional funding from the churches, further budgetary cuts would "oblige the beginning of the phase-out of Lutheran involvement in resettlement."

Moreover, with reserves no longer available, the Committee pointed out that the LIRS program for 1987 was also in jeopardy. To operate a viable program in 1987, an increase in annual church support from the current $270,000 to $438,000 would be required. It proposed several possible options for raising this amount, including the establishment by the churches of a $500,000 line of credit for LIRS to borrow against, requests to the Aid Association for Lutherans (AAL), or to the Lutheran World Federation for grants, or the hiring of a professional fund raiser to solicit $438,000 from private donors. The total amount needed for the calendar year of 1987, including the $190,000 deficit for 1986–87, was $628,000.[17]

The church bodies eventually accepted both the reality and the validity of the LIRS crisis and its serious implications for the continuation of the ministry to refugees. Through the exercise of stringent economies and about $100,000 in additional income from active government contracts, LIRS was finally able to fulfill all its obligations for the fiscal year 1986–87. Each of the churches agreed to meet a proportionate share of the shortfall for 1987. But as a condition of its $100,000 special grant, the LCMS Board for Social Ministry Services called for a management audit of LIRS "to determine program revisions and staffing considerations that will make LIRS more effective and efficient."[18]

An auditing team headed by Carl Thomas, Executive Director of Lutheran Social Services of Michigan, undertook the assignment. In September 1987, it submitted its report expressing full confidence in the leadership and staff of LIRS. The positive response of the churches to the special budget request of 1987 provided further encouraging evidence of their intention to provide increased financial support when LIRS began a new chapter in its life on January 1, 1988.

The Fiftieth Year

Any stranger entering the office of LIRS at 360 Park Avenue South in New York City on a morning in early January 1988, would have seen little evidence of newness or change. Most of the same people were at their desks. Telephones rang and questions were answered, much as they had been on any previous day. But despite appearances to the contrary, January 1, 1988, was a day of new beginnings for LIRS and for the entire Lutheran community in the United States.

A merger of historic proportions had brought together three church bodies representing two-thirds of all Lutherans in the United States, forming the Evangelical Lutheran Church in America, with five million members and 11,000 congregations. The merger of three of the member churches of the Lutheran Council in the USA brought within the new church body many of the functions that LCUSA had previously performed as an interchurch agency. The Council had therefore been dissolved, with the understanding that continuing cooperative activities involving the ELCA and the LCMS be handled through bilateral agreements.

LIRS' New Identity

At its final meeting in November 1987, the Lutheran Council gave its official approval to the incorporation of the Lutheran Immigration and Refugee Service as an independent agency under the laws of the State of Minnesota. They also approved a set of bylaws and a policy statement under which LIRS should be governed.[1]

The Standing Committee was replaced by a nine-member Board of Directors, nominated by the ELCA, the LCMS, and the Latvian Evangelical Lutheran Church in America, and elected for three-year terms. Initial membership of the Board included four ELCA directors: Charles Miller, Carl Thomas, Sarah Naylor, and Thomas Hurlocker. Representing the LCMS were August Bernthal, Eugene Linse, and Richard Alms. Vilis Varsbergs represented the Latvian Evangelical Lutheran Church. Tekle Haileselassie was nominated by the former Standing Committee of LIRS to fill a newly created place on the Board for a representative of the refugee community. The Board held its first meeting on February 10–11, 1988, electing August Bernthal chairman and Sarah Naylor secretary. It also formally ratified its governing documents and elected Donald H. Larsen to a four-year term as Executive Director.

There was little change in the program of activities at LIRS, but some new staff appeared, and others were assigned new tasks. John Griswold, who had joined LIRS in 1975 when the Vietnam program began, and had been involved in virtually every aspect of refugee resettlement, became Director for Programs. He supervised the major program areas, such as resettlement, first asylum concerns, immigration and legalization, unaccompanied refugee minors, communications, and the Washington office for advocacy. Arthur Thompson joined LIRS in September 1988, as Director for Administration and Finance.[2]

Refugees in World Context

A personal distinction for the Executive Director, as well as a recognition of the high esteem in which LIRS was held by its peer organizations, came in early 1988 when Larsen was elected chairman of the Committee on Migration and Refugee Affairs at InterAction. Also known as the American Council for Voluntary International Action, this group carried responsibility for representing the voluntary agencies in their consultations with Congress and the Administration of the U.S. government. One of InterAction's major priorities in 1988 was to urge the increase in the number of refugees to be admitted to the United States, from the 1988 limit of 68,500 to 103,500 in 1989. A paper prepared by InterAction in March 1988 pointed out the areas of continuing and increased pressure from refugees in Africa, Afghanistan, and the Soviet Union. Relief for the so-called long-stayer populations, especially in Hong Kong, Malaysia, and Thailand, InterAction declared, was long overdue.[3]

Of immediate concern was a new wave of Vietnamese boat refugees arriving on the shores of Thailand, precipitating the closing of the Thai borders. Boats filled with refugees were being towed out to sea. Others were being intercepted and turned back. Many lives were lost. Such harsh acts demonstrated the desperation of the Thai government and reminded Western countries of their commitment to help relieve Thailand of its burden. As a representative of InterAction and as Executive Director of LIRS, Larsen visited processing centers in Thailand and the Philippines, as well as Hong Kong, in October. In Hong Kong he encountered the growing imbalance between arrivals and those leaving for permanent resettlement in a third country. During the first six months of 1988, 8,001 new refugees entered Hong Kong, while only 1,351, or one out of six, left for resettlement. During the first six months of 1989, the refugee population in Hong Kong doubled, exceeding 50,000 by September.[4]

That month Larsen testified on behalf of InterAction before the Subcommittee on Immigration, Refugees, and International Law of the House Committee on the Judiciary, recommending the admission of 140,500 refugees to the United States in 1990, a substantial increase over the 90,000 ceiling of 1989. The quota for 1990 was ultimately set at 125,000.[5]

During 1988 the largest number of refugees resettled by LIRS came from Southeast Asia; they were mostly Hmong people and Vietnamese. With the reactivation of the Orderly Departure Program, the number of Vietnamese increased. Many of those approved by the Vietnam government were political prisoners who had served their time in reeducation camps or prisons and were released to rejoin their families in the United States.

The continued deterioration of first asylum protection in Southeast Asian countries led finally to an International Conference on Indochinese Refugees in Geneva in June 1989. For the first time on record, the official delegation to a major international meeting of governments on refugee solutions included a representative of voluntary agencies. Representing InterAction, LIRS Executive Director Larsen was able to contribute the viewpoints of the private sector on world refugee issues.

As the largest recipient of Vietnamese refugees for resettlement, the United States played a significant role in shaping a Comprehensive Plan of Action, adopted by the International Conference in Geneva. The plan opposed the repatriation of Vietnamese asylum seekers, called for the international sharing of long-stayers, and supported more humane treatment for all asylum seekers in Southeast Asia. The United States itself agreed to accept 22,000 of the 50,000 refugees in the camps in Hong Kong.

However, even commitments made under the Comprehensive Plan of Action were difficult to maintain, as the flow of asylum-seekers continued and the camps became even more congested. Even Hong Kong, which had never turned away a refugee, seriously considered involuntary repatriation of Vietnamese refugees as a last resort.[6]

Afghans, Armenians and Soviets

LIRS also took its share of refugees from other troubled countries and regions. Before the Soviet withdrawal from Afghanistan, the number of Afghans who had chosen exile, mostly in neighboring Pakistan, was among the highest in the world. Religious and ethnic minorities from Iran continued to flee the excesses of the Islamic fundamentalist theocracy of the Ayatollah Ruhollah Khomeini. Historic persecutions of Kurds and other ethnic minorities in Iraq and Turkey had not abated. Neither the end of the Soviet occupation of Afghanistan nor the cease-fire between Iran and Iraq materially altered the hazards to human rights or to life itself in those countries. As civil war in Afghanistan continued unabated, the number of Afghan refugees registering with the U.S. Embassy in Pakistan reached its highest level in three years.

Although U.S. refugee quotas for the Near Eastern region were very limited, LIRS was able to resettle a few families and individuals from these countries each year. Yusuf Atef-Bakhtari, 39, was a former language teacher in Afghanistan and a graduate of the University of Kabul. With the assistance of LIRS he arrived in Falls Church, Virginia, in February 1988, with his wife Tahera, a former stewardess with Air Afghan, and their four children—Ajmal, 7, Mustafa, 5, Sahar, 4, and Shahnam, 3. They were sponsored by Holy Trinity Lutheran Church in Falls Church and the Unitarian Church in Reston, which located and furnished a home for them.

Yusuf had served in the Ministry of Education in Kabul, preparing textbooks for children and adults. He came under increasing suspicion because of his earlier friendships with U.S. Peace Corps workers and because his two brothers had joined the resistance forces of the Mujahadeen. Yusuf and his family fled the country in 1986, joining the 3.1 million Afghan refugees in Pakistan. They settled in the Pakistani capital of Islamabad, where Yusuf prepared and published materials for the Afghan resistance forces. Upon arrival in the United States, his linguistic abilities got him his first job, translating into the Farsi language an orientation booklet for refugees on "Facts of Life in the United States." The preparation of this booklet in 16 languages was a joint project of LIRS and the U.S. Catholic Conference.[7]

Beginning in 1988, a critical situation developed with respect to refugees from the Soviet Union. After years of restriction on their emigration, large numbers of Soviet Jews were finally given the opportunity to leave their country. Many of them traveled first to Vienna, Austria, and there sought entry visas either to Israel or to the United States. Current U.S. refugee quotas, limited because few Soviet citizens in recent years had been allowed exit permits, were inadequate to meet the new demands. Early in 1989, President Reagan agreed to increase the quota for the Soviet Union by 39 percent, to admit 25,000 refugees. In order to avoid the administrative expense in processing additional numbers of refugees, the increase of 7,000 places was balanced by a corresponding reduction of Asian quotas.

Most of the Soviet emigrés were Jews, but the relaxation of restrictions by Moscow also afforded opportunity to Armenians and evangelical Christians to seek religious freedom outside the Soviet Union. By mid-1989 nearly 1,000 Soviet Baptists and Pentecostals and smaller numbers of Armenians were arriving in Vienna each month, most of them hoping for resettlement in the United States.

LIRS processed both Armenians and Soviet evangelicals for resettlement during 1988 and 1989. Most of the Armenians had relatives in the Los Angeles area, and LIRS placed more than 1,000 people there, processing 300 cases during a single 30-day period in mid-1988.

Among the Pentecostals resettled by LIRS was Adam Bondaruk, 47, a lay pastor, and his extended family. In addition to his wife Galina and 11 children, Adam brought his parents, Semyon and Kseniya, 69 and 71, respectively; his wife's parents, Ivan and Nadezhda Gurin, both 66; and an unrelated family, Viktor and Iria Ukrainets, 24 and 26, and their four children, ages 5, 3, 2, and 1.

Ivan Gurin, Galina Bondaruk's father, had been a bishop in the underground church, which got its start in the 1920s. Twice he was sent to forced labor camps because of his faith. Pastor Bondaruk made his living by operating heavy excavation machinery. His father was a machinist in a coal mine.

"They're such gracious people," observed Richard Miesel, pastor of the Lutheran Church of Our Savior in South Hadley, Massachusetts, which sponsored them. Miesel must have been endowed with a generous supply of the same quality of grace. At one point he housed 15 of the Bondaruks under his own roof.

To add an ecumenical dimension to this sponsorship, two other parishes in South Hadley assisted Our Savior's: St. Patrick's Roman Catholic Church and St. Michael's Byzantine Catholic Church. One of the members of St. Michael's, Edward Zawistowski, who was fluent in Russian, provided assistance as a translator.

A sequel to the story of the Bondaruks' resettlement began in September 1988, when Adam and Galina Bondaruk and eight of their children moved to Sacramento, California, where Adam was called to lead a congregation of Soviet Pentecostals.[8]

First Asylum Concerns

One of the most serious and sensitive aspects of the world refugee problem in 1988 was the issue of first asylum: What happens to the refugees who flee persecution in their own country and seek refuge in the nearest available port of safety? Will they be well treated—or at least permitted to enter? This was the major theme of the International Conference on Indochinese Refugees in Geneva in June 1989. It was also an important emphasis in the testimony Donald Larsen brought to the House Subcommittee on Immigration, Refugees, and International Law in September on behalf of the voluntary agencies.

The focus in Geneva was on the bulging refugee holding centers in Southeast Asia and the danger that in desperation, these countries would compel the return of the refugees to their home countries to face imprisonment or even death. Voluntary agencies shared this concern, but they also reminded the United States government that its own first asylum policies needed to be reexamined. Larsen stated the case plainly, "The United States must carefully assess the impact of our policies against Haitians and Central Americans on the fragile international compact on refugee protection. . . We have very little moral weight in demanding a 'no repatriation' stance vis-a-vis Vietnamese from Hong Kong, while we summarily turn Haitians back at high seas and deport to an uncertain fate Salvadorans, Guatemalans, and Nicaraguans from our borders. We must get our own house in order at the same time as we insist that refugee populations be protected elsewhere around the world."[9]

Outrage over this blind spot in U.S. immigration policy had brought LIRS into an active program of advocacy for both Haitians and Salvadorans in 1981 and led to the launching of the Central American Concerns program. Six years later, the CAC program, broadened to include educational efforts and advocacy on behalf of any population that had fled to the United States seeking safe haven from life-threatening injustices in their home country, had become a major LIRS program.[10] Under the leadership of Sandra Edwards, who succeeded Lauren McMahon in 1987, the "small grants" program continued to support church-related and community projects serving persons seeking safe haven in the United States. At the time grant decisions were made in 1988, the First Asylum Concerns unit had a total of $225,000 to allocate, provided by the ELCA, the LWF, and the Ford Foundation. Fifty-two U.S. first asylum projects submitted applications, with requests adding up to $562,000.

Although the selection process was a very difficult one, Edwards was pleased to report that several Lutheran social service agencies were among the applicants, having undertaken service programs for asylum seekers or advocacy on asylum issues. She welcomed this an an indication that the partnership of LIRS with Lutheran social service agencies that had contributed to local Lutheran resettlement work with refugees was being extended to encompass undocumented persons seeking asylum in the United States.[11]

Lutheran congregations in the areas of greatest concentration of Haitian and Central American refugees also carried on ministries to asylum seekers, providing social services, counseling, and in some cases, sanctuary, to undocumented refugees. A special border ministries program, begun in 1987 in the U.S.-Mexican border area, was supported by the ELCA and the LCMS.[12]

In addition to broadening the scope of LIRS activities, concern over first asylum issues had the related effect of refocusing the agency's attention on one of its historic areas of service, namely, immigration. Since 1975, refugee and resettlement issues had dominated LIRS programs, and in 1985, for reasons of economy, the staff position in immigration had been dropped.

But with the growing need for legal advice and counsel for asylum seekers and the active involvement of LIRS in the legalization program, staff members frequently found themselves involved in procedures governed by immigration law. In many cases, close relatives of persons previously admitted as refugees were required by the INS to apply for immigrant visas, rather than be admitted as refugees.

Lutheran social service agencies and individual congregations that had taken part in the legalization program under LIRS' Qualified Designated Entity (QDE) umbrella, had developed interest and expertise in immigration work. It seemed likely that if the millions of undocumented people living in the United States were ever to be legalized, they would be treated as immigrants rather than refugees.

In September 1988, a proposal was prepared by John Griswold to reestablish a program unit for immigration, to be headed by an Associate for Immigration Concerns. In accepting the proposal, the LIRS Board of Directors reaffirmed a core component of the agency's original mission and ministry—indeed, of its name![13]

Celebrating the Mission of LIRS

At the same meeting the Board received the first report from a committee appointed to plan an anniversary observance for LIRS, commemorating 50 years of ministry to refugees and immigrants. On the basis of the committee report, the Board designated the year, beginning September 1989, and concluding in August 1990, as a special year of celebration. Under the theme: "Opening Doors— Yesterday, Today, and Tomorrow" the Board planned a year-long series of events designed to tell the story of the combined efforts of Lutherans in America in resettling 185,000 homeless people from virtually every part of the earth.[14]

Through working conferences, seminars, and observances in congregations and church conventions, LIRS proposed using the anniversary as an occasion for outreach. Opportunity would be provided to acknowledge the refugee ministry of congregations and individuals, to celebrate the contributions of immigrants and refugees to the building of this country and the church, and to foster a greater sensitivity among Americans to the political and sociological realities that continue to create refugees.[15]

The year opened with the Annual National Conference of LIRS in November 1989, in Washington, DC. A statement by the conference called for continued efforts "to create, develop, and strengthen open doorways that offer hope, acceptance, and support to refugees and immigrants." In accord with Donald Larsen's description of LIRS as "a marriage of service and advocacy," the official message of the conference summoned Lutherans and others of good will to "encourage governmental officials in the development of just and humane practices for refugees and immigrants," and to "ensure that those who must flee are protected against unjust deportation."[16]

The committee also commissioned a 50-year anniversary history and projected several film and video presentations during the year. Of special interest was the updated version of the award-winning film, "Answer for Anne," first shown in 1949 to promote sponsorships under the World War II Displaced Persons Program, the first major Lutheran resettlement effort. The updated version, produced by Robert E. A. Lee, still featured a young woman's search for an answer to the question, "Should our town take in refugees?"—a search as pertinent in 1989 as it had been in 1949.

Other observances included symposiums on refugees at all ten theological seminaries of the ELCA and the LCMS and an inter-agency-intergovernmental seminar at the United Nations in New York.

On May 17, 1990, in the midst of the year of celebration, the LIRS and the entire community of voluntary agencies were shocked and saddened by the sudden death of Donald Larsen, Executive Director of LIRS. Larsen had guided the transition of LIRS in 1988 from its position as a subordinate unit within LCUSA to its new status as an independent cooperative agency relating to the ELCA and the LCMS. August Bernthal, chairman of the LIRS Board of Directors, paid tribute to Larsen as "an advocate for the world's uprooted." His was no "ivory-tower ministry," said Bernthal, "but was in the blood and bone of human misery and human living. He took upon himself the needs of our neighbors and led others to do the same."[17]

The year of celebration concluded on a sober note of gratitude, both for Larsen's leadership and for the doors of opportunity that had been opened by LIRS for homeless people over the course of 50 years. There was no sense of triumphalism. Displacements of persons once thought to be local and temporary emergencies with tangible solutions were being acknowledged as chronic global phenomena in the nineties. In spite of reduced tensions between East and West, the world refugee population had risen to 16 million. Facing these realities, LIRS concluded its 50th year reaffirming its ministry to the world's displaced and homeless, remembering the Lord's commendation, "I was a stranger and you took me in."

Epilog

It would be difficult to say who have been the greatest beneficiaries of the 50-year Lutheran ministry to refugees: the thousands who have been given a new future, or the thousands who have had a part in providing it. Through seaports and airports, 185,000 refugees from every continent on earth have entered the United States by way of doors opened by LIRS. No one can calculate the value of restored dignity, renewed hope, and beckoning opportunity offered as America's gift to the new arrivals. Their diligent use of these gifts has enhanced their own lives and enriched the culture of communities throughout the United States.

But to those who have helped to open the doors, the refugees themselves have been a great gift. They have helped the Lutheran churches of America and their congregations view their ministry in a world context. From an early focus on members of their own household of faith, mostly in Europe, Lutheran congregations have learned to open their hearts to refugees from Uganda, Iraq, Hong Kong, Vietnam, Chile, El Salvador, and the Soviet Union, and have extended a helping hand to Buddhists, Moslems, and Hindus, as well as Christians.

Individuals in congregations who have sponsored refugee families have testified to the personal and spiritual growth they have experienced. One who had seen this happen described sponsorship as "a congregation's opportunity for love in action with people who have experienced indescribable tragedy. It is a ministry of love, faith, hope, and healing for the refugee and the refugee family—but for the sponsor, a life-changing experience."

Between the refugee and the sponsor there has been a company of caring people who have been the official doorkeepers, dealing with government regulation and procedures, providing the initial personal welcome, arranging travel, and meeting emergency needs. From a nerve center in New York, a network of Lutheran service agencies has extended across the entire country, offering counsel and encouragement and undergirding congregations in their ministry of outreach.

Their ministry to those who have fled oppression in other lands has given both incentive and opportunity to Lutherans to become advocates for justice, both at home and abroad. Not only has the LIRS urged the United States government to open its doors wider for both immigrants and political refugees; it has also spoken boldly against discrimination at our own borders.

With 16 million recognized refugees in the world in 1991, the future offers no promise of respite from the rigors of the refugee problem. It therefore seemed entirely fitting that in its quest for a new leader to carry its program into the troubled nineties, the LIRS should have selected someone already committed to the struggle for international justice.

Ralston H. Deffenbaugh, Jr., had just completed a year of special service as legal adviser to the Lutheran bishops and the Council of Churches in Namibia and assisted in shaping the Namibian constitution. From 1985 to 1990 Deffenbaugh directed the Lutheran Office for World Community at United Nations Headquarters in New York, representing both the Lutheran World Federation and the Evangelical Lutheran Church in America. In 1981, he had left his law practice in Denver, Colorado, to serve as assistant to the General Secretary of the LWF in Geneva, Switzerland.

As he assumed office on January 1, 1991, the new Executive Director of LIRS gave assurance that as they entered their second half-century, the LIRS and its supporting Lutheran churches would continue faithful to their mission on behalf of uprooted peoples of the world in the name of Christ. "We are still called," he said, "to open our doors with warm hearts, to welcome the stranger, and through such loving service to receive the many blessings which the stranger brings."

Notes

Chapter 1: They Heard a Cry (pp. 13–22)

1. Gordon Thomas and Max Morgan Witts, *Voyage of the Damned* (New York: Stein and Day, 1974).
2. Gary B. Nash and Julie Roy Jeffrey, eds., *The American People* (New York: Harper and Row, 1986), p. 768.
3. E. Theodore Bachmann, "The Way It Was in 1939", (unpublished address delivered at LECNA 50th Anniversary Convocation, Washington, D.C., November 5, 1989), p. 11.
4. The ACCGR sought to assist Christians of Jewish parentage, many of whom were members of families that had been Christian for several generations. The Nazi government based its anti-Semitic policies on race rather than religion.
5. "Working Agreement Between the Lutheran Churches of America and the ACCGR", July 15, 1938, Ralph H. Long Papers, ELCA Archives. Dallmann's early life in Germany, his conversion to the Christian faith, and his flight to the U.S. when Hitler dissolved the Evangelical Lutheran Central Association for Jewish Missions in Breslau are detailed in Carl K. Solberg, *A Brief History of the Zion Society for Israel* (Minneapolis, 1938), pp. 55–58.
6. Ralph H. Long to John S. Dallmann, April 5, 1938. Dallmann to Long, August 25, 1938, Long Papers, ELCA Archives.
7. Bachmann, "The Way It Was", p. 17.
8. Samuel M. Cavert to Clarence E. Krumbholz, June 1, 1939. Clarence E. Krumbholz Papers, ELCA Archives.
9. Report of the Executive Director, NLC, for 1938, p. 11.
10. Report of the Executive Director, NLC, for 1939, p. 16.
11. Bachmann, "The Way It Was", p. 19.
12. *The Lutheran,* March 1939.
13. *The Lutheran,* May 17, 1939.
14. *The Lutheran,* August 16, 1939.
15. Report of the Department of Welfare, NLC, 1939, pp. 42–43.
16. George Emodi to C.E. Krumbholz, November 20, 1940; Julia Richardson to Louis Sanjek, September 12, 1944; Frank Kingdon to Louis Sanjek, September 21, 1942; C.E. Krumbholz Papers, ELCA Archives.
17. C.E. Krumbholz Papers, ELCA Archives.
18. *National Lutheran,* December 1940, pp. 7–8.

19. Mimeographed Discussion Guide, "The Lutheran Church and the Refugee", March, 1941, C.E. Krumbholz Papers, ELCA Archives.
20. C.E. Krumbholz, in *National Lutheran,* Winter 1941, p. 32. A series of monthly reports from Karl Burger are in the Krumbholz Papers, ELCA Archives.
21. Richard W. Solberg, *As Between Brothers* (Minneapolis: Augsburg Publishing House, 1957), p. 145.

Chapter 2: Europe's Displaced Persons (pp. 23–33)

1. Stewart Herman, quoted in Solberg, *As Between Brothers,* p. 33.
2. Mark Wyman, *DPs: Europe's Displaced Persons, 1945–1951* (Philadelphia: The Balch Institute Press, 1989), pp. 61–85.
3. Gil Loescher and John A. Scanlan, *Calculated Kindness: Refugees and America's Half-Open Door, 1945 to the Present* (New York: The Free Press, 1986), pp. 1–16.
4. E. Clifford Nelson, *The Rise of World Lutheranism* (Philadelphia: Fortress Press, 1982), p. 353.
5. Solberg, *As Between Brothers,* p. 35.
6. Ibid., pp. 36–38.
7. *The Lutheran,* March 27, 1946.
8. Reuben C. Baetz, *Service to Refugees, 1947–1952* (Geneva: Lutheran World Federation, 1952), pp.9–20. Kenneth Senft, "The Lutheran World Federation and the Displaced Person", (unpublished B.D. thesis, Gettysburg Theological Seminary, 1952).
9. Quoted in Baetz, *Service to Refugees,* p.7.
10. Solberg, *As Between Brothers,* pp. 146–148.
11. Report of the Executive Secretary to the Committee of the Division of Welfare, NLC, September 17, 1946.
12. Minutes, Executive Committee, NLC, September 15, 1947.
13. Minutes, Division of Welfare, NLC, March 9, 1948.
14. Report of Executive Secretary to Division of Welfare, NLC, September 17, 1946.
15. Minutes, Executive Committee, NLC, September 15, 1947.
16. Minutes, Annual Meeting, NLC, January 30, 1948.
17. Loescher and Scanlan, *Calculated Kindness,* pp. 19–22.
18. Interview with Cordelia Cox by Robert Van Deusen, February 14, 1978, p. 2. Oral History Collection, Archives for Cooperative Lutheranism, LECNA. Hereafter referred to as OHC,ACL.

Chapter 3: Resettling the DPs (pp. 34–49)

1. Recorded video interview with Ross Hidy by Robert E. A. Lee, November 16, 1989. Transcript in LIRS Archives.

2. Mary Winston, "Lutheran Action in DP Resettlement," *National Lutheran,* May 1948, p. 44. Minutes, Division of Welfare, NLC, March 9, 1948.

3. *National Lutheran,* September 1948.

4. Interview with Cordelia Cox by Benjamin Bankson, August 25, 1989. Transcript in LIRS Archives.

5. Recorded video interview with Ross Hidy by Robert E. A. Lee, November 16, 1989. Transcript in LIRS Archives.

6. Interview with Cordelia Cox by Robert Van Deusen, February 14, 1978, pp. 33–37, OHC,ACL.

7. Minutes, Division of Welfare, NLC, October 29, 1948.

8. Minutes, First Meeting of Supervisory Committee, Lutheran Resettlement Service, April 18, 1949. Hereafter referred to as LRS.

9. Cordelia Cox, "DPs at Dockside," *National Lutheran,* March 1949, pp. 20–21.

10. Interview with Cordelia Cox by Benjamin Bankson, August 25, 1989, LIRS Archives.

11. *The Lutheran,* November 17, 1948.

12. *The Lutheran,* February 16, 1949.

13. *The Lutheran,* April 27, 1949.

14. Quoted by E. Theodore Bachmann, *Epic of Faith* (New York: NLC, 1952), pp. 42–43.

15. Interview with Cordelia Cox by Benjamin Bankson, August 25, 1989, LIRS Archives.

16. Interview with Cordelia Cox by Robert Van Deusen, February 14, 1978, OHC, ACL.

17. Interview with Paul Empie by Helen Knubel, 1977, pp. 120–121.

18. *National Lutheran*, January 1949, pp. 22–23.

19. Jessamine Fenner, "DP Professionals Need Jobs and Homes, Too," *National Lutheran,* March 1950, pp. 35–37.

20. Richard Bennett, "DP Students Arrive," *National Lutheran,* January 1950, pp. 39–41.

21. *National Lutheran,* January 1951.

22. Minutes, Supervisory Committee, LRS, September 24, 1949, April 30, 1951.

23. Minutes, Conference on Adjustment of DPs in the U.S., June 11, 1951.

24. Interview with Henriette Lund by Alice Kendrick, 1976, pp. 35–41, OHC, ACL. Alex Liepa, "Dossier Program for DPs," *National Lutheran,* May 1951, pp. 45–46.

25. Alex Liepa, "Remaining DPs Pin Hopes on Dossier Program," *National Lutheran,* November 1950, pp. 38–40.

26. Recorded video interview with Ross Hidy by Robert E. A. Lee, November 16, 1989, LIRS Archives.

27. *The Lutheran,* September 7, 1949.

28. Minutes, Annual Meeting, NLC, January 31, 1950.

29. *U.S. Statutes at Large,* Vol. 64, pp. 219–22.

30. Baetz, *Service to Refugees,* pp. 46–48, 55–56.

31. *Lutheran Herald,* April 15, 1952.

32. Cordelia Cox, "Progress Report to Lutheran Resettlement Committees #18," October 17, 1952.

Chapter 4: "Who Else Shall We Welcome?" (pp. 50–69)

1. Minutes, Annual Meeting, NLC, January 31, 1952.

2. "An Analysis of Some of the Provisions of the Immigration and Nationality Act of 1952," NLC, November 25, 1952.

3. Alex Liepa, "U.S. Immigration Policies", *National Lutheran,* November/December, 1952, pp. 8–12. Cordelia Cox, "Report to the President's Commission on Immigration and Naturalization," September 30, 1952.

4. Meeting of the New York Members of the Supervisory Committee, LRS, November 24, 1952. Cordelia Cox, "Progress Report to Lutheran Resettlement Committee #18," October 17, 1952.

5. Minutes, Supervisory Committee, LRS, March 24, 1953.

6. Minutes, NLC Annual Meeting, February 5, 1953.

7. Richard W. Solberg, "The Church and the Berlin Crisis," *Lutheran Standard,* September 16, 1961, pp. 8–9.

8. Solberg, *God and Caesar in East Germany* (New York: Macmillan, 1961), p. 156.

9. Solberg, Berlin Letter III, January l, 1956.

10. Loescher and Scanlan, *Calculated Kindness,* pp. 45–46.

11. Minutes, Executive Committee, NLC, October 2, 1953.

12. Minutes, Supervisory Committee, LRS, September 14, 1953.

13. Lutheran Refugee Papers: Correspondence, 1954. ELCA Archives.

14. Minutes, Lutheran Refugee Service Commission, August 27, 1954. Hereafter referred to as LRSC.

15. Interview with Cordelia Cox by Robert Van Deusen, February 14, 1978, OHC, ACL.

16. Minutes, LRSC, May 23, 1955.

17. Agenda, LRSC, Exhibit A, April 19, 1954.

18. "Functions and Structure of Lutheran Refugee Committee of LRS", Agenda, Exhibit C, LRSC, April 19, 1954.

19. Minutes, LRSC, August 27, 1954.

20. Minutes, LRSC, November 12, 1954.

21. Memorandum, Paul Empie to Presidents of NLC Church Bodies, November 24, 1954.

22. Lawrence Meyer to Oscar Benson, January 17, 1955. In Agenda, LRSC, Exhibit B, February 4, 1955. "Memorandum of Agreement between NLC and LCMS," Agenda, LRSC, Exhibit D, March 22, 1955.

23. Minutes, LRSC, February 4, 1955.

24. Minutes, LRSC, May 23, 1955.

25. Paul Empie, "Your Assurances Will Bring Refugees," *National Lutheran,* May 1955, pp. 5–10.
26. Minutes, Special Study Committee, LRS, March 2, 1956.
27. Quoted in Interview with Henriette Lund by Alice Kendrick, 1976, p. 39, OHC, ACL.
28. Letter of Paul Empie, reprinted in LRS Report to Area Committees, #12, February 8, 1956.
29. Report to LRS Area Committees, #12, February 8, 1956.
30. Report to LRS Area Committees, #13, March 10, 1956.
31. Report to LRS Area Committees, #11, January 20, 1956.
32. *National Lutheran,* March/April 1956, p. 14.
33. Report to LRS Area Committees, #19, October 10, 1956.
34. Report to LRS Area Committees, #21, December 12, 1956.
35. Anonymous letter from Budapest, included in information letter from Lutheran World Relief, November 21, 1956.
36. Quoted in James Michener, *The Bridge at Andau* (New York: Fawcett Crest, 1957), p. 89.
37. Loescher and Scanlan, *Calculated Kindness,* p. 52.
38. Memorandum, Cordelia Cox to all Area Committees, November 12, 1956. Summary Reports of LRS on Immigration of Hungarian Refugees, November 20, 29, December 28, 1956.
39. Interview with Cordelia Cox by Benjamin Bankson, August 25, 1989, pp. 7–8.
40. Minutes, Annual Meetings, NLC, January 31, 1957, February 7, 1958.
41. Minutes, LRSC, March 14, 1957. Interview with Cordelia Cox by Benjamin Bankson, August 25, 1989, p. 13.

Chapter 5: Lutherans in Transit (pp. 70–81)

1. Letter, Cordelia Cox to Carl Lund-Quist, April 23, 1957. In Appendix, Minutes LRSC, June 14, 1957.
2. "Brief Historical Summary: Service to Immigrants," *Lutheran Immigration Service Information Bulletin,* March 31, 1964. Hereafter referred to as LIS.
3. "Brief Historical Statement," *LIS Information Bulletin,* March 31, 1964.
4. Service to Immigrants, Annual Report, 1959.
5. Service to Immigrants, Annual Report, 1959.
6. Minutes, LRSC, June 14, December 17, 1957.
7. "Analysis of Public Law, 85–316," Agenda, LRSC, September 28, 1957.
8. Vernon E. Bergstrom, Memorandum #4, Refugee Resettlement Program, July 1, 1959.
9. Annual Report, LRS, 1959.
10. Minutes, NLC Annual Meeting, February 5, 1959. Agenda, LRSC, October 5–6, 1959.
11. Remarks by Vernon E. Bergstrom to NLC Annual Meeting, February 4, 1960.
12. Minutes, NLC Annual Meeting, February 4, 1960.
13. Agenda, LRSC, October 5–6, 1959. Frederick K. Wentz, *Lutherans in Concert* (Minneapolis: Augsburg Publishing House, 1968), p. 184.

14. Policy Statement of NLC, Annual Meeting, February 4, 1960.
15. Minutes, LRSC, September 28, 1958.
16. "Agreement by and between NLC and LCMS," Agenda, LIS Committee, March 10–11, 1960.
17. Minutes of first meeting of the LIS Committee, March 10–11, 1960.
18. Minutes, LIS Committee, September 18, 1961.
19. Minutes, LIS Committee, August 29–30, 1960.
20. Agenda, LIS Committee, March 12, 1965.
21. Minutes, LIS Committee, September 18, 1961.
22. *National Lutheran,* February 1962.

Chapter 6: From Hong Kong to Havana (pp. 82–93)

1. Agenda, LIS Committee, June 12, 1962.
2. Agenda, LIS Committee, February 12, 1963.
3. Letter, Donald Anderson to Kenneth Stumpf, July 6, 1962. Agenda, LIS Committee, Exhibit F, February 12, 1963.
4. *Lutheran World Action Bulletin,* December, 1962.
5. LIS Annual Report, 1963.
6. The country in which persons first take refuge when fleeing persecution in their homelands is called the "country of first asylum." If, subsequently, another country offers refugee status and admits such persons, it becomes a "country of second asylum."
7. David W. Haines, ed., *Refugees in the United States* (Westport, CT: Greenwood Press, 1985), pp. 4–5.
8. Minutes, LIS Committee, April 14–15, 1961, September 18, 1961.
9. Report of Eugene F. Gruell to Miami Lutheran Refugee Service Committee, January 8, 1963.
10. Agenda, LIS Committee, February 12, 1963.
11. Letter, Donald Anderson to Eugene Gruell, May 24, 1962, in Agenda, LIS Committee, June 2, 1962.
12. Minutes, Miami Lutheran Refugee Service Committee, January 8, 1963.
13. LIS Annual Report, 1963.
14. *National Lutheran,* March 1964.
15. Eugene F. Gruell, Director's Annual Report, 1964, Miami Lutheran Refugee Service, March 12, 1965.
16. *National Lutheran,* September, 1965.
17. Minutes, LIS Committee, March 12, 1965.
18. *LIS Information Bulletin,* March, 1966.
19. Agenda, LIS Executive Committee, Exhibit D, May 1, 1962.
20. Agenda, LIS Committee, June 12, 1962.
21. *LIS Information Bulletin,* March 31, 1964, LIS Annual Report, 1964.

22. *National Lutheran,* October, 1964.

23. Agenda, LIS Committee, March 12, 1965.

24. *National Lutheran,* May, 1965.

25. *LIS Information Bulletin,* October, 1965.

26. *LIS Annual Report,* 1965.

27. *LIS Information Bulletin,* March, 1966.

Chapter 7: Learning to Live in LCUSA (pp. 94–103)

1. W. Kent Gilbert, *Commitment to Unity* (Philadelphia: Fortress Press, 1988), p. 173.

2. Minutes, Department of Immigrant and Refugee Services, Division of Welfare, Lutheran Council in the USA, (DIRS), October 27–28, 1966.

3. Minutes, DIRS, February 10, 1967.

4. Agenda, DIRS, September 10, 1968; Minutes, DIRS, June 4, 1969.

5. DIRS Annual Report for 1971. In Appendix, Minutes of Standing Committee, DIRS, January 21, 1972.

6. Minutes, DIRS, August 17, 1967, September 10, 1968.

7. Minutes, DIRS, September 10, 1968.

8. *New York Times,* October 5, 1972.

9. Interview with Ingrid Walter by Cordelia Cox, December 28, 1982, OHC, ACL.

10. Memoranda, Donald Anderson to Harold Haas, Carl Mau, et al. October 4, 1972, November 20, 1972.

11. Statement of Donald Anderson to pastors of Washington, D.C., area, December 3, 1972.

12. Interview with Tatiana Trelin by Franklin Jensen, June 29, 1989, LIRS Archives.

13. Interview with Ingrid Walter by Cordelia Cox, December 28, 1982, OHC, ACL.

14. LCUSA *News Bureau,* November 3, 1972.

15. Interview with Betty Amstutz by Franklin Jensen, June 13, 1989, LIRS Archives.

16. *Des Moines Register,* December 23, 1973.

17. Story related by Marnie Dawson, LIRS New York staff, July 18, 1974.

18. John Lundquist, in *Minneapolis Star-Tribune,* December 25, 1972.

19. *Minneapolis Star-Tribune,* November 22, 1972.

20. Agenda, Standing Committee, DIRS, January 16, 1973.

21. Memorandum #6, DIRS, April 23, 1973.

22. Addendum to Minutes, Standing Committee, DIRS, January 16, 1973.

23. LCUSA *News Bureau,* March 5, 1973.

24. Draft of memorandum prepared by Donald Anderson for discussion by a sub-committee of DIRS on the relation of DIRS and LCUSA, April 2, 1973.

25. A working paper prepared by Donald Anderson for the DIRS Standing Committee, November 11, 1974.

26. Agenda, Exhibit D, Standing Committee, DIRS, October 21–22, 1974.

Chapter 8: Legacy of a Lost War (pp. 104–119)

1. "Last Chopper Out of Saigon," *Time,* May 12, 1975.
2. Loescher and Scanlan, *Calculated Kindness,* pp. 102–119.
3. Telephone conversation with Ingrid Walter by author, May 13, 1990.
4. Interview with Ingrid Walter by Cordelia Cox, December 28, 1982, OHC,ACL.
5. Minutes, Executive Committee, LCUSA, May 5–6, 1975.
6. Walter Interview by Cox, December 28, 1982, OHC,ACL.
7. Article by Maryann C. Lund, in *LIRS Bulletin,* December, 1975.
8. Telephone conversation with Neil Brenden by author, May 15, 1990.
9. Abner Batalden, "Final Report on Field Operations," Minutes, Standing Committee, DIRS, December 12, 1975. Interview with Tatiana Trelin by Franklin Jensen, June 29, 1989, LIRS Archives.
10. Batalden, "Final Report", December 12, 1975.
11. Interview with Neil Brenden by Bernard Confer, 1983, pp. 38–44, OHC,ACL.
12. List of LIRS Field Team Personnel, Agenda, Standing Committee, DIRS, June 5, 1975. Chart of Organization, Agenda, Standing Committee, LIRS, September 29–30, 1975. Interview with John Griswold by Franklin Jensen, August 16, 1989, LIRS Archives.
13. Donald Anderson, Report to LIRS Standing Committee, "LIRS/DIRS Staffing and Procedures", June 21, 1975. The designation "LIRS" was used interchangeably with "DIRS", with "LIRS" favored in external usages. Hereafter, "LIRS" will be used.
14. Report of the Director of LIRS to Standing Committee, LIRS, September 3, 1975. Tatiana Trelin, "Observations on the 45-day Reports," Agenda, Exhibit M, Standing Committee, LIRS, November 1, 1975.
15. Minutes, Exhibit H, Standing Committee, LIRS, January 8–9, 1976.
16. Agenda, Standing Committee, LIRS, March 29–30, 1976.
17. Ralph Baumbach, "A Sharing Report," in Agenda, Standing Committee, LIRS, May 25, 1975.
18. Loescher and Scanlan, *Calculated Kindness,* pp. 115–117.
19. Interview with James Smith by Franklin Jensen, June 12, 1989, LIRS Archives.
20. Minutes, Standing Committee, LIRS, September 2, 1975.
21. Anderson, "LIRS/DIRS Staffing," June 21, 1975.
22. Minutes, Standing Committee, LIRS, January 8–9, 1976.
23. Interview with August Bernthal by Franklin Jensen, October 19, 1989, LIRS Archives.
24. *LIRS Bulletin,* June 1982.
25. *LIRS Bulletin,* Fall 1975.
26. *Milwaukee Journal,* June 4, 1975.
27. Interview with James Smith by Franklin Jensen, June 12, 1989, LIRS Archives.
28. Interview with August Bernthal by Franklin Jensen, May 10, 1989, LIRS Archives.
29. Interview with Neil Brenden by Bernard Confer, 1983, pp. 38–44, OHC,ACL.

30. Standing Committee, LIRS, November 1, 1975.

31. Interview with Betty Amstutz by Franklin Jensen, June 13, 1989, LIRS Archives.

32. Interview with Merill Herder by Franklin Jensen, August 2, 1989, LIRS Archives.

33. Interview with Donald Larsen by Franklin Jensen, August 16, 1989, LIRS Archives.

34. Agenda, Standing Committee, LIRS, March 28–30, 1976.

35. Agenda, Standing Committee, LIRS, September 29–30, 1975

Chapter 9: Support for New Arrivals (pp. 136–143)

1. Report of the Director to the Standing Committee, LIRS, Exhibit B, September 3–4, 1975.

2. Agenda, Exhibit L, Standing Committee, LIRS, November 6–7, 1975.

3. Minutes, Exhibits B and C, Standing Committee, LIRS, January 8–9, 1976.

4. Minutes, Standing Committee, LIRS, December 22, 1975.

5. Minutes, Standing Committee, LIRS, January 8–9, 1976

6. Interview with Betty Amstutz by Franklin Jensen, September 28, 1989, LIRS Archives.

7. Anne Lomperis, "Report on English as a Second Language," Agenda, Appendix VIII–A, Standing Committee, LIRS, June 7–8, 1978.

8. Memorandum from Anne Lomperis, Agenda, Appendix VII, Standing Committee, LIRS, September 6–7, 1979.

9. Carol Smalley, Annual Report, 1982, Agenda, Appendix VIII–A, Standing Committee, LIRS, January 27–29, 1983.

10. Agenda, Appendix IX–D, Standing Committee, LIRS, February 4–5, 1981.

11. LIS Bulletin, 1981.

12. Minutes, Standing Committee, LIRS, October 11, 1975.

13. Agenda, Standing Committee, LIRS, November 6–7, 1975. Interview with Betty Amstutz by Franklin Jensen, June 13, 1989, LIRS Archives.

14. "Unaccompanied Refugee Minor Program," LIRS Board of Directors, May 4, 1988, September 20–21, 1988.

15. Minutes, Standing Committee, LIRS, January 27, 1983, May 8–9, 1985. Interview with Ingrid Walter by Cordelia Cox, December 28, 1982, OHC,ACL.

16. LIS Bulletin, Summer, 1988.

17. Marta Brenden, "Report on Youth Services," Agenda, Appendix VII, Board of Directors, LIRS, September 20–21, 1988.

18. Interview with Gno Pham by Franklin Jensen, May 24, 1989, LIRS Archives.

19. Minutes, Standing Committee, LIRS, May 13, 1987.

20. "Children Must Not Be Detained," Seeds for the Parish, October 1988, pp. 1–2. LIRS, Board of Directors, September 20–21, 1988.

NOTES

Chapter 10: Politics of Compassion (pp. 144–155)

1. Minutes, Standing Committee, LIRS, January 24–25, 1974. "Statement of the Resettlement Agencies of the American Council of Voluntary Agencies for Foreign Service, Inc. Concerning the Chilean Refugee Program," October 2, 1975, in Agenda, Standing Committee, LIRS, October 11, 1975.

2. Minutes, Standing Committee, LIRS, November 6–7, 1975. Agenda, Standing Committee, LIRS, January 8–9, 1976.

3. *LIRS Bulletin,* January, 1976.

4. Minutes, Standing Committee, LIRS, November 29, 1976.

5. Minutes, Standing Committee, LIRS, February 24–25, 1977.

6. Memorandum, Ingrid Walter to Standing Committee, LIRS, February 27, 1976. Minutes, Standing Committee, LIRS, March 4, 1976.

7. Minutes, Standing Committee, LIRS, March 29–30, 1976.

8. Minutes, Standing Committee, LIRS, September 6–7, 1977.

9. Loescher and Scanlan, *Calculated Kindness,* pp. 119, 122.

10. "Report of Meeting on Laotians with Men from Department of State," September 23, 1975. Minutes, Standing Committee, LIRS, October 11, 1975, January 8–9, 1976.

11. "Laos Resettlement Report," Agenda, Exhibit K, Standing Committee, LIRS, March 29–30, 1976.

12. Interoffice Memorandum, Minutes, Standing Committee, LIRS, January 8–9, 1976.

13. "Letter to Sponsors," Agenda, Standing Committee, LIRS, January 8–9, 1976.

14. Agenda, Standing Committee, LIRS, January 8–9, 1976.

15. Minutes, Standing Committee, LIRS, June 28–30, 1976.

16. Minutes, Standing Committee, LIRS, November 29, 1976.

17. Minutes, Standing Committee, LIRS, August 9, 1976.

18. Bruce Grant, *The Boat People* (New York: Penguin Books, 1979), pp. 28–30.

19. Loescher and Scanlan, *Calculated Kindness,* p. 127.

20. "Status Report on Sponsorship Promotion," Minutes, Appendix IX–A, Standing Committee, LIRS, January 24–25, 1978. Minutes, Standing Committee, LIRS, June 7–8, 1978.

21. Loescher and Scanlan, *Calculated Kindness,* pp. 129–136.

22. Movement totals, LIRS, May 22, 1978. In Minutes, Appendix VII–I, Standing Committee, LIRS, June 7–8, 1978.

23. Loescher and Scanlan, *Calculated Kindness,* pp. 137–146.

24. Interview with Donald Larsen by Franklin Jensen, August 16, 1987. LIRS Archives. Minutes, Standing Committee, LIRS, February 22, 1979, September 6–7, 1979.

Chapter 11: From Cambodia to Cuba (pp. 156–169)

1. William Shawcross, *Quality of Mercy* (New York: Simon and Schuster, 1984), p. 52. Shawcross provides a graphic account of the years of terror in Cambodia under Pol Pot in 1975–78, the subsequent mass exodus of refugees, and the international efforts to relieve the famine in 1979–80.

2. Loescher and Scanlan, *Calculated Kindness,* pp. 147–167.

3. LIRS Bulletin, August, 1980, Agenda, Standing Committee, LIRS, February 4–5, 1981. Interview with Donald Larsen by Franklin Jensen, August 16, 1989, LIRS Archives.

4. Minutes, Standing Committee, LIRS, Febrary 20–22, 1979, September 6–7, 1979.

5. Interview with Ellen Erickson by Franklin Jensen, May 22, 1989, LIRS Archives.

6. *LIRS Bulletin,* August 1979.

7. Agenda, Standing Committee, LIRS, February 4–5, 1981.

8. Interview with Adeline Marty by Franklin Jensen, October 19, 1989, LIRS Archives.

9. Minutes, Standing Committee, September 6–7, 1979.

10. *LIRS Bulletin,* February, 1981.

11. Agenda, Standing Committee, September 17–18, 1980.

12. *LIRS Bulletin,* January, 1980.

13. Interview with Ellen Erickson by Franklin Jensen, October 10, 1988, LIRS Archives.

14. *LIRS Bulletin,* May, 1979.

15. *LIRS Bulletin,* February, 1979.

16. *LIRS Bulletin,* Fall, 1989.

17. Minutes, Standing Committee, LIRS, February 20—22, 1979.

18. Agenda, Standing Committee, LIRS, December 1980.

19. Agenda, Standing Committee, LIRS, February 7, 1980.

20. *LIRS Bulletin,* August 1980.

21. Agenda, Standing Committee, LIRS, May 4, 1981, September 24–25, 1981.

22. *LIRS Bulletin Board,* February 1981.

23. *LIRS Bulletin,* March 1983, contains reprint of a *New York Times* report published May 17, 1983. See also David W. Haines, ed., *Refugees in the U.S.,* pp. 80–85.

24. *LIRS Bulletin,* August 1980.

25. Minutes, Standing Committee, LIRS, May 20, 1980. *LIRS Bulletin,* December 1981.

26. Minutes, Standing Committee, LIRS, May 20, 1980.

27. Minutes, Standing Committee, LIRS, May 20, 1980. Interview with Ingrid Walter by Cordelia Cox, December 28, 1982, OAC,ACL.

28. Minutes, Standing Committee, LIRS, May 20, 1980.

29. *LIRS Bulletin,* August 1980, Agenda, Standing Committee, LIRS, September 17–18, 1980.

30. Agenda, Standing Committee, LIRS, February 4, 1981. *LIRS Bulletin,* December 1981.

31. *LIRS Bulletin,* December 1981.

32. Livingston Chrichlow, "Cuban-Haitian Program," Minutes, Standing Committee, LIRS, September 28–29, 1982.

33. Agenda, Standing Committee, LIRS, May 4, 1981.

Chapter 12: The New Advocacy (pp. 170–181)

1. Interview with Betty Amstutz by Franklin Jensen, September 28, 1989, LIRS Archives.

2. Minutes, Standing Committee, LIRS, September 6–7, 1978; February 20–22, 1979.

3. Minutes, Standing Committee, LIRS, September 27, 1976. Interview with Ingrid Walter by Cordelia Cox, December 28, 1982, OHC,ACL. Interview with Ingrid Walter by Franklin Jensen, October 19, 1989, LIRS Archives.

4. Interview with August Bernthal by Franklin Jensen, October 19, 1989, LIRS Archives. Interview with Merill Herder by Franklin Jensen, September 28, 1989, LIRS Archives.

5. Minutes, Standing Committee, LIRS, February 24–25, 1977.

6. Agenda, Standing Committee, LIRS, April 17–20, 1977. NLC News Bureau, May 3, 1977.

7. Minutes of conference call, Standing Committee, LIRS, May 10, 1977.

8. *NLC News Bureau,* June 28, 1977.

9. Agenda, Standing Committee, LIRS, June 16–17, 1977.

10. Minutes of meeting of LIRS Regional Consultants in Dallas, TX, October 1977, quoted in Agenda, Standing Committee, LIRS, January 24–25, 1978. *NLC News Bureau,* October 19, 1977.

11. Agenda, Standing Committee, LIRS, June 6–7, 1978.

12. Minutes, Standing Committee, LIRS, September 6–7, 1978.

13. Minutes, Standing Committee, LIRS, November 29, 1976. Seminar on "Illegal Aliens: Patterns and Policies," conducted by LIRS in Los Angeles, June 28, 1976. Agenda, Standing Committee, LIRS, June 29–30, 1976.

14. Agenda, Standing Committee, LIRS, June 16–17, 1977.

15. Agenda, Standing committee, LIRS, February 6, 1980.

16. "Study Document of Principles on the Issue of Undocumented Aliens," adopted and published by LCUSA, February, 1981.

17. *LIRS Bulletin Board,* September 1982. Livingston Chrichlow, "The Cuban Haitian Scene: Resettlement and Advocacy," in Agenda, Appendix V, Standing Committee, LIRS, May 5–8, 1982.

18. Minutes, Standing Committee, LIRS, February 4–5, 1981.

19. "A Statement on Immigration Policies: Undocumented Persons," Agenda, Appendix X–C–3, Standing Committee, LIRS, April 1–2, 1981.

20. Mary Solberg, "A Report on the Salvadoran Situation," prepared for LIRS, September 15, 1981.
21. Minutes, "Advocacy Consultation" on November 9-10, 1982, in Agenda, Appendix VII–A, Standing Committee, LIRS, January 27–29, 1983.
22. Minutes, Standing Committee, LIRS, January 27–28, 1983.
23. Minutes, Standing Committee, LIRS, May 3–4, 1983.
24. Minutes, Advocacy Advisory Committee, LIRS, October 5–6, 1983.
25. Agenda, Board of Directors, LIRS, Appendix VII–h. September 20–21, 1988. *LIRS Bulletin,* Fall, 1989.

Chapter 13: Ministry to the Undocumented (pp. 182–193)

1. Agenda, Standing Committee, LIRS, May 10, 1982. Franklin Jensen, "Annual Report, 1982," Agenda, Appendix VIII A(2), Standing Committee, LIRS, January 27–29, 1983.
2. "Use of U.S. Government Reception and Placement Grants," January 25, 1982, in Agenda, Standing Committee, LIRS, May 10, 1982.
3. Interview with Walter Jensen by Franklin Jensen, August 16, 1989, LIRS Archives.
4. Minutes, Standing Committee, LIRS, September 24–25, 1981. Letter, Norman Runkles to Kenneth Stumpf, January 26, 1982.
5. Annual Report of Director, 1982, Agenda, Standing Committee, LIRS, January 28–29, 1983. Interview with Ingrid Walter by Cordelia Cox, December 28, 1982, OHC,ACL.
6. "Testimony of Dr. August Bernthal," April 22, 1982. Reprinted in Agenda, Standing Committee, LIRS, May 5–8, 1982.
7. *LIRS Bulletin,* March 1983.
8. Article in June 1985 issue. See also LIRS Bulletin Board, Summer 1985.
9. Minutes, Standing Committee, LIRS, April 12–13, 1982. Agenda, Standing Committee, LIRS, January 28–29, 1983.
10. Franklin Jensen, "Annual Report, Director for Policy and Program, 1982", Agenda, Appendix VIII–A(2), Standing Committee, LIRS, January 27–29, 1983.
11. Agenda, Appendix VI–(1), LIRS, Standing Committee January 27–29, 1983.
12. Agenda, Exhibit A, Standing Committee, LIRS, July 26, 1982.
13. Agenda, Standing Committee, LIRS, May 4, 1983.
14. Minutes. Standing Committee, LIRS, September 2, 25, 1981; *LIRS Bulletin Board,* December 1981.
15. Mary Solberg, "Central American Concerns," Agenda, Appendix XII–G, Standing Committee, LIRS, January 25–27, 1982.
16. "Program Update," Agenda, Appendix V–B, Standing Committee, LIRS, May 5–10, 1982.
17. Annual Report, Central American Concerns 1982, Agenda, Appendix VIII–A(8), Standing Committee, LIRS, January 27–29, 1983.
18. Mary Solberg, "A Report on the Salvadoran Situation," p. 19.

19. Annual Report, Central American Concerns 1982, Agenda, Appendix VIII–A(8), Standing Committee, LIRS, January 27–29, 1983.

20. "Central American Concerns," Agenda, Appendix XXI I, Standing Committee, LIRS, September 13–14, 1983.

21. "Giving Sanctuary—A Living Tradition," *LIRS Bulletin,* September 1983.

22. Agenda, Standing Committee, LIRS, May 3–4, 1983.

23. Daniel Cattau, "LCUSA Meeting Refers Sanctuary Issue," *LIRS Bulletin,* September 1983.

24. Lauren Pressman, "Annual Report, 1983." Agenda, Appendix XI–I, Standing Committee, LIRS, January 18–20, 1984.

25. "CAC Program," in "Program Developments in LCUSA Departments," 1985–86.

26. Minutes, Standing Committee, LIRS, September 27–28, 1984.

27. James Godemann, "LIRS on Simpson-Mazzoli," April 15, 1983.

28. Memorandum: Donald Larsen to Agency Executives, March 16, 1987.

29. Memorandum: John Griswold to LIRS Standing Committee, January 13, 1987. Agenda, Exhibit X, Standing Committee, LIRS, January 20–22, 1987.

30. Annual Report, LIRS, 1986–87.

Chapter 14: Strengthening Home Resources (pp. 194–201)

1. *LIRS Bulletin,* Winter, 1984. Interview with Donald Larsen, by Franklin Jensen, August 16, 1989, LIRS Archives.

2. Donald Larsen, "Annual Report, 1986–87," Agenda, Appendix A, Standing Committee, LIRS, May 13–14, 1987.

3. Statistics of U.S. State Department, in *New York Times,* January 22, 1989.

4. "Program Developments of Adjunct Agencies, LCUSA, 1983–84."

5. "Arrivals by LIRS Fiscal Year," May 1988, Agenda, Board of Directors, LIRS, September 20–22, 1988. LIRS arrivals in 1988 totaled 9,036; 1989, 6,840; 1990, 9,852, the largest number in a decade.

6. Annual Report, Orderly Departure Program, 1981, Agenda, Appendix XII–J, Standing Committee, LIRS, January 25–27, 1982. Program Progress Report, Agenda, Exhibit XI–A, Standing Committee, LIRS, January 20–22, 1987.

7. "The LIRS Standing Committee Statement on Sponsorship Policies and Procedures," Agenda, Exhibit VIII, Standing Committee, LIRS, January 25–27, 1982.

8. John Griswold, "Annual Report, Systems Resourcing Unit, 1983," Agenda, Appendix XI–D, Standing Committee, LIRS, January 18–20, 1984.

9. *LCUSA News Bureau,* August 22, 1986. John Griswold, "Annual Report, 1986–87, Associate Director, Planning and Development," Agenda, Appendix G, Standing Committee, LIRS, May 13–14, 1987.

10. Franklin Jensen, "Annual Report, 1983," Agenda, Appendix XI–A, Standing Committee, LIRS, January 18–20, 1984. John Griswold, "Report on On-Site Visits," August 31, 1983, in Agenda, Appendix XXI–J, Standing Committee, LIRS, September 13–14, 1983. "Regional Consultants Coordinating Committee, RC–3,"

Minutes, Standing Committee, LIRS, September 29, 1984. "Peer Group Analysis Team," Minutes, Standing Committee, LIRS, September 27–28, 1984.

11. Franklin Jensen, "Annual Report, 1983," Agenda, Standing Committee, LIRS, January 18–20, 1984.

12. Minutes, Standing Committee, LIRS, September 27–28, 1984. Agenda, Appendix XII, Standing Committee, LIRS, May 3, 1983.

13. "LIRS: Future Directions," Agenda, Exhibit VI, Standing Committee, LIRS, January 18–20, 1984.

14. "Report of CNLC/LCMS Committee on Cooperation," Draft #5, November 12, 1985, Agenda, Appendix XII, Standing Committee, LIRS, January 22–24, 1986.

15. Letter, Donald Larsen to Arnold Mickelson, January 2, 1986, in Agenda, Appendix XII, Standing Committee, LIRS, January 22–24, 1986.

16. "LIRS—A Financial Crisis: An Interim Plan," Agenda, Exhibit X–C(1), Standing Committee, LIRS, January 20–22, 1987.

17. Introduction to "Report: Recommendations Concerning LIRS Fiscal Crisis to Committee in Planning and Finance, LCUSA," January 23, 1987.

18. Letter, Eugene Linse to Donald Larsen, April 14, 1987, in Agenda, Appendix XIII–C, Standing Committee, LIRS, May 13–14, 1987. Minutes, Standing Committee, LIRS, May 13–14, 1987.

Chapter 15: The Fiftieth Year (pp. 202–211)

1. Agenda, Appendix VII–E, Annual Meeting, LCUSA, November 19, 1987.

2. Minutes, Initial Meeting of the Board of Directors, LIRS, February 10–11, 1988.

3. "Crisis of Success," March 16, 1988, in Agenda, Appendix IX, Board of Directors, LIRS, September 20–21, 1988.

4. Report of Executive Director, Agenda, Exhibit VI, Board of Directors, LIRS, September 20, 1988.

5. Statement of Donald Larsen before the Subcommittee on Immigration, Refugees and International Law, Committee on the Judiciary, U.S. House of Representatives, September 12, 1989.

6. Report of the Executive Director, Agenda, Board of Directors, LIRS, Exhibit VI, September 27, 1989.

7. Benjamin Bankson, "The New, and Old, Concern Afghans," LIRS Bulletin, Summer 1988.

8. LIRS Bulletin, Fall, 1989.

9. Testimony of Donald Larsen before Subcommittee on Immigration, Refugees and International Law, Committee on the Judiciary, U.S. House of Representatives, September 12, 1989, pp. 20–22.

10. Minutes, Standing Committee, LIRS, September 30, 1987.

11. "LIRS in 1988," Information paper prepared by LIRS Communications and Interpretation Unit, September 12, 1988.

12. Annual Report, LIRS, 1986—87.

13. John Griswold, "Proposal for Reinstatement of Full-time LIRS Immigration Service Staff," 1989.

14. Minutes, Board of Directors, LIRS, September 20–21, 1988.

15. "Case Statement," in Agenda, Appendix VIII, Board of Directors, LIRS, January 26–27, 1989.

16. "Opening Doors—Yesterday, Today and Tomorrow," Message adopted by National Conference of LIRS, Washington, DC, November 15, 1988.

17. *LIRS Bulletin,* Summer 1990, pp. 2–3.

Index

Richard W. Solberg is a recognized theologian, historian, and author. A graduate of St. Olaf College and Luther Theological Seminary, he also holds an M.A. in history from the University of Wisconsin and a Ph.D. in history from the University of Chicago. He holds honorary degrees from Augustana College, Rock Island, IL, and Bethany College, Lindsborg, KS.

Dr. Solberg served as pastor at Ingleside, IL, as professor at Augustana College in Sioux Falls, SD, as Vice President for Academic Affairs at Thiel College, Greenville, PA, and as Director for Higher Education for the Lutheran Church in America. Following his retirement from that position in 1982, he was commissioned by the Lutheran Education Conference in North America to write a history, *Lutheran Higher Education in North America*, which was published in 1985.

A highly qualified researcher and writer, Dr. Solberg has a vast background of experience that further commends him as the author of *Open Doors*. Between 1948 and 1956 he spent two periods in Germany. In 1949–50 he served as Religious Affairs Advisor for the U. S. Military Government in Germany and the U.S. High Commission in Berlin. From 1953–56, a time when church reconstruction and refugee resettlement were its major programs, he served as Senior Representative in Germany for the Lutheran World Federation's Department of World Service.

In recognition of his services, the Federal Republic of Germany awarded him the Grand Cross of the Order of Merit. The Inner Mission of the Evangelical Church in Germany recognized him with its Johann Hinrich Wichern Medal. In 1957, at the request of the Lutheran World Federation, Dr. Solberg wrote *As between Brothers*, a history of the Lutheran response to world need following World Wars I and II. In 1959 Dr. Solberg published *God and Caesar in East Germany*, the story of the church-state controversy in East Germany from 1945–1959.

Dr. Solberg is married to June Nelson, who has collaborated in the research and editing of all of his publications. The Solbergs have five adult children and reside currently in Thousand Oaks, CA.